International Citizens' Tribunals

International Citizens' Tribunals:

Mobilizing Public Opinion to Advance Human Rights

*Arthur Jay Klinghoffer and
Judith Apter Klinghoffer*

palgrave

INTERNATIONAL CITIZENS' TRIBUNALS

First published in 2002 by
PALGRAVE™
175 Fifth Avenue, New York, N.Y. 10010 and
Houndmills, Basingstoke, Hampshire, England RG21 6XS
Companies and representatives throughout the world.

PALGRAVE™ is the new global publishing imprint of St. Martin's Press LLC
Scholarly and Reference Division and Palgrave Publishers Ltd. (formerly
Macmillan Press Ltd.).

ISBN 0-312-29387-9

Library of Congress Cataloging-in-Publication Data
Klinghoffer, Arthur Jay, 1941- .
    International citizens' tribunals: moblizing public opinion to advance human
    rights / by Arthur Jay Klinghoffer and Judith Apter Klinghoffer.
    Includes bibliographical references and index.
    ISBN 0-312-293879
    1. Commissions of inquiry, International—History—20th century.
    2. Human rights. 3. Public opinion. I. Klinghoffer, Judith Apter. II. Title.

KZ6060 .K59 2002
341.4'81—dc21

2001036551

A catalogue record for this book is available from the British Library.

Design by Westchester Book Composition

First edition: March 2002
10 9 8 7 6 5 4 3 2 1

Printed in the United States of America

To Abraham Zeev Apter and Sidney Klinghoffer

Contents

Acknowledgments   ix

Abbreviation of Citations   xi

Chapter I: Citizens' Power   1

THE REICHSTAG FIRE CASE

Chapter II: The Berlin Cauldron   11

Chapter III: Rallying to the Defense   19

Chapter IV: Showdown in Leipzig   31

Chapter V: Aftermath   43

THE MOSCOW SHOW TRIALS CASE

Chapter VI: Deep Freeze   51

Chapter VII: A Tribunal Crystallizes   63

Chapter VIII: South of the Border   79

Chapter IX: Deliberations and Recriminations   91

THE VIETNAM WAR CRIMES CASE

Chapter X: The Activist Philosopher   103

Chapter XI: Plan of Action   111

Chapter XII: Behind the Scenes at Stockholm   123

Chapter XIII: The Swedish Context   139

Chapter XIV: Second Wind   149

CONTINUUM

Chapter XV: Proliferation   163

Chapter XVI: Agenda for Reform   187

Notes   195

Index   243

Acknowledgments

First and foremost we would like to thank the Danish-American Fulbright program and the Norwegian Nobel Institute for enabling us to spend a year in Scandinavia to research Trotsky's exile in Norway and the Russell Tribunal sessions in Sweden and Denmark. Later, a grant from the Rutgers Research Council was instrumental in facilitating research at the Bertrand Russell Archives at McMaster University in Hamilton, Ontario, and at the Morris Library of Southern Illinois University and the Center for Dewey Studies, both in Carbondale, Illinois. Special thanks must certainly go to Anne Kjelling, chief librarian at the Nobel Institute, and to Sissel Wahlin and Anna Larsson, who provided excellent translations from Danish, Swedish, and Norwegian sources. Similarly, Petra Garnett and Benno Inslicht were instrumental in translating Dutch and German materials. At Rutgers University, Dung Nguyen and Keemya Richardson were most helpful in assisting with Internet searches.

Several direct participants in the events covered in this study furnished accounts of their experiences via interviews, e-mail messages, and letters. Most noteworthy were the contributions of Dave Dellinger, Carl Oglesby, Ken Coates, Julius Lester, David Horowitz, Richard Falk, and Ebbe Reich. In terms of archival support, we benefited greatly from the efforts of John Wilson (Lyndon Baines Johnson Library), Carl Spadoni and Charlotte Stewart (Bertrand Russell Archives), David Koch and Shelley Cox (Special Collections, Morris Library, Southern Illinois University), and Larry Hickman, Harriet Simon, Barbara Levine, and Diane Meierkort (Center for Dewey Studies). Nicholas Griffin, chief researcher at the Bertrand Russell Archives, was especially generous with his time and insightful comments as was Princeton University historian Anson Rabinbach. At the Paul Robeson Library of Rutgers University, we tip our hats to the entire reference and circulation staffs that processed a huge number of requests for interlibrary loans with grace and alacrity. Also of great assistance were many helpful professionals at the Norwegian national library in Oslo; the university library in Aarhus, Denmark; and at our own local library in Cherry Hill.

Arthur and Judith Klinghoffer
Cherry Hill, New Jersey

Abbreviation of Citations

AGHP   Arthur Garfield Hays Papers, Seeley G. Mudd Manu-
            script Library, Princeton University, USA

BRA   Bertrand Russell Archives, Mills Memorial Library,
            McMaster University, Canada

CDS   Center for Dewey Studies, Carbondale, Illinois, USA

FBIS   Foreign Broadcast Information Service

H-DC   Hook-Dewey Correspondence, Special Collections,
            Morris Library, Southern Illinois University, USA

JDP   John Dewey Papers, Special Collections, Morris Library,
            Southern Illinois University, USA

LBJL   Lyndon Baines Johnson Library, Austin, Texas, USA

Archival sources are noted as box/file, such as 75/8.

Chapter I

CITIZENS' POWER

"'We'll be judge, We'll be jury,' said Bertrand with fury: And our verdict has just been released to the press.'"[1]

This sarcastic ode was sent to President Lyndon Johnson in January 1967 by his aide Joseph Califano. At the time, the British philosopher Bertrand Russell was busily preparing an international tribunal to charge the United States with war crimes, crimes against humanity, and genocide in Vietnam. Such a venue had no legal standing, but the U.S. government was gravely concerned about its public relations impact. Power ostensibly was being put into the hands of concerned citizens, and even the United States could not but recognize a serious threat to its sovereignty and international status. State authority was being challenged on the basis of human rights practices, and justice was being played out across national boundaries. Was such a process an instructive exercise in democratic assertion, a triumph of liberalism's standards of objectivity, or was it—as implied in the above ditty—a new form of kangaroo court? Could the populist remedy constitute a greater travesty of justice than the state's malfeasance?

Evolution

In the wake of World War I, there was a public reaction against Realpolitik and statesmen who were its practitioners. Law and ethics grew in importance, with Woodrow Wilson calling for a world community embodied in the League of Nations, which could settle disputes on the basis of international law. Public opinion was to be fundamental to the new Wilsonian order, since the American president did not envision the League of Nations as a prospective world government, but rather as a universal moral force.

Walter Lippmann quickly established his credentials as the most influential theorist on the role of public opinion. He was a Harvard-educated journalist and public intellectual who helped the Wilson administration prepare for the Versailles peace conference and disseminated his views widely via newspaper columns, books, and his role as associate editor of a leading liberal magazine, *The New Republic*. Lippmann realized that the intervention of world opinion was bound to be intermittent, and that those with expertise and "interested spectators" would inevitably take the lead. Still, an aroused international citizenry was an essential check on arbitrary power. The aim was to impact "the course of affairs," but, of course, the public could only back involved actors and not generate issues by itself. Lippmann explained: "Public opinion in its highest ideal will defend those who are prepared to act on their reason against the interrupting force of those who merely assert their will."[2]

Public pressure, especially in Britain, contributed to the charging of Kaiser Wilhelm II of Germany with war crimes and Turkish leaders with crimes against humanity for atrocities committed during the expulsion of the Armenians.[3] Diplomatic concerns and issues of domestic jurisdiction, however, quickly sidetracked the course of justice, and there were no meaningful prosecutions of the perpetrators.

Human rights advocates thus developed international commissions of inquiry during the interwar period as the antidote to an ineffective legal order. These panels of intellectuals scrutinized the legal institutions of Nazi Germany and the Soviet Union by organizing hearings on the Reichstag fire of 1933 and the Moscow show trial of 1936. Such commissions were attuned to Lippmann's belief that those with special knowledge and education would be at the forefront of public opinion in areas of their particular competence. Uninformed sectors of the public would be of little value in influencing the affairs of state, as there was a need for "an independent, expert organization for making the unseen facts intelligible to those who have to make the decisions."[4]

This elitist approach was exactly that adopted by the commissions. Their members were not average citizens, such as those who served on juries, but prominent personalities with legal skills and considerable social and political standing. They were well aware of the official limitations of their endeavors but had a strong faith that the public would compensate by exerting an influence on the course of justice.

The Russell Tribunal continued the tradition of the two earlier tribunals in the sense of harnessing public opinion to the wagon of human rights. It differed, however, in accentuating state-to-state relations under international law—thereby setting the stage for later hearings that transformed such law in the direction of leftist radicalism. Under the guidance of legal theorists emerging from the New Left, the term "international people's tribunals" has become standardized since the late 1970s. This usage of the term "people's," with its ideological connotations of totalitarian and terroristic concepts of justice, unfortunately undermines the democratic image that proponents are trying to foster. Indeed, the Nazis had "people's courts" that could pass death sentences on those who were deemed anti-Hitler in any way, and the Red Brigades in Italy staged "people's tribunals" to determine the fate of kidnapped state officials. This study, in order to accentuate participatory but nonextremist norms, will therefore refer to the quasi-judicial bodies under examination as "international citizens' tribunals."

Tribunals are now increasing in frequency, and their scope is broadening to include women's rights, indigenous people's rights, and workers' rights. A dynamic metamorphosis of the international legal system is now being attempted, but scant attention has been paid to this phenomenon. Redress is surely in order, for international citizens' tribunals deserve to be recognized—as well as critically evaluated.

The Humanitarian Upsurge

Prior to the twentieth century, individuals were mainly objects in a system of international law focused on states. Now they have become subjects as the decline of state sovereignty has ushered in a new order. The inadequacies of international law in regulating the behavior of states has been evident since the Hague System failed to prevent or terminate World War I, and the League of Nations was unable to head off World War II.

Conflicts between states had, of course, been endemic for millennia. More critical for the development of international law was rising concern about how states, through the perversion of domestic laws, were mistreating their citizens. Nazi Germany and the Communist-ruled Soviet Union were using their instruments of power for internal repression as the concept of totalitarianism entered the political lexicon. Under such circumstances, the legitimacy of courts came to be questioned by liberal intellectuals who emphasized means rather than ends, and objective truth rather than ideological dogma. It is thus only natural that the first two international citizens' tribunals, pertaining to Germany and the Soviet Union, were established to investigate legal proceedings in the context of burgeoning totalitarianism. Intervening while injustices were still being committed could possibly influence the judicial process or, at least, expose the shams perpetrated by totalitarian legal systems.

The relatively successful International Military Tribunals organized at Nuremberg and Tokyo after World War II marked a crucial turning point in state-citizen relations. New legal principles were applied regarding global jurisdiction over internal matters and individual responsibility for acts of state—including prosecution of government officials for those acts carried out in accordance with domestic law. The establishment of the United Nations Commission on Human Rights (1946), the Genocide Convention (1948), and the International Covenants on Economic and Social Rights and on Civil and Political Rights (1966) soon followed.[5]

The Russell Tribunal on Vietnam (1967) tried to build on the Nuremberg tradition. "Crimes against humanity" and the legal accountability of government officials were duly recognized. So, too, was the importance of establishing new juridical structures, such as tribunals, where none existed. The U.N. did not include any institutional body authorized to examine an issue such as alleged American war crimes in Vietnam. Predictably, the United States had no intention of submitting to an evaluation by a self-appointed supranational panel, even on the basis of Nuremberg legal standards. It feared, realistically, that documentation and facts introduced as evidence could undermine the ethical basis of its policies.[6]

To proponents of the Russell Tribunal, that was the key point. Nuremberg was ex post facto, but their tribunal could potentially alter American actions and stop the war.[7] Nuremberg was deemed to be "victors' justice" applied by Allied judges, whereas the Russell Tribunal included American panelists—albeit not representatives of the government.[8] Most significantly, citizens rather than states were to be the vehicle. Russell, echoing Lippmann, proudly exclaimed: "Our tribunal, it must be noted, commands no State power. It rests on no victorious army. It claims no other than a moral authority."[9]

Since the end of the Cold War, the international community has been attempting to assert authority for the furtherance of human rights. U.N. military interventions on the basis of Chapter VII provisions of the U.N. Charter are now interpreted in such a way that internal actions within states may be considered threats to international peace and security due to their generation of cross-border refugees. The United Nations also has set up tribunals to deal with human rights abuses (including genocide) in the former Yugoslavia and Rwanda, and a new International Criminal Court is being established. Nevertheless, such efforts have a common defect: States that hold a veto power in the Security Council can avoid being targeted. International citizens' tribunals can therefore serve as a corrective mechanism through which public intellectuals mobilize world public opinion against powerful countries shielded from sanctions under international law. If the absence of effective and permanent legal structures is the problem, then tribunals may offer an appropriate solution.

The Radical Challenge

Tribunals dealing with the Reichstag fire, the first Moscow show trial, and the Vietnam War were based on somewhat traditional legal concepts. Now most tribunal proponents (despite their own evident intellectual elitism) advance a more radical and populist vision grounded in "transnational democracy" and "globalization from below," and portray such panels as integral to an "emerging global civil society." They reject globalization directed from what is perceived as above, an order pejoratively termed "global capitalism." The prime aim is to transform international law so that justice will be based on giving voice to those considered weak and oppressed. Unfortunately, this may be at the expense of due process.

The Princeton international law specialist Richard Falk argues that "law belongs to all of us" and "we must reclaim it from the destructive forces that are crystallized in imperial power politics at this time."[10] The Italian socialist lawyer and politician Lelio Basso, now deceased, described tribunals as "an emanation of the popular will" and maintained that the people themselves, not states, should be the locus of power in the international community. He saw tribunal legitimacy deriving from an interpretation of moral conscience.[11] Harvey Cox, the noted Harvard divinity professor, similarly postulates that natural law has to be carried out even if states do not codify its principles into positive law. Governments that fail to protect their citizens are deemed violators of natural law.[12]

In accordance with this interpretation, citizens have the secondary responsibility to act against injustice if states and international organizations neglect to carry out their primary responsibility. The Nobel Peace Prize laureate Jose Ramos Horta of East Timor declares that if governments do not defend the people's rights, "we will have to find new forms of action that will."[13] The Martens clause in the 1907 Hague Conventions is cited as an important precedent. It indicates that states are bound by usages deriving from "the laws of humanity and the dictates of the public conscience." Also presented as substantiation for this evolving radical approach are Articles 1 and 55 of the U.N. Charter and General Assembly Resolution 1514 (1960), which state that all peoples are entitled to self-determination. The

Universal Declaration of the Rights of Peoples, formulated in Algiers in 1976, serves as the ideological underpinning of the radical movement within international law.[14]

Richard Falk states that "the peoples of the world enjoy ultimate sovereignty, including the right to appropriate legal forms, and to establish legitimate institutions and procedures as needed." He views sovereignty in the theoretical context of the French Revolution, in which the will of the people was emphasized and that of the state discredited. In his countertraditional interpretation of what constitutes international law, sovereignty of the people was gradually expanded to collective group rights in reference to the sovereignty of "peoples." Falk depicts law as a "progressive" weapon, a "political tool" used to facilitate change and he juxtaposes his interpretation to that of "bourgeois" analysts whose stress on procedure is at risk of deteriorating into "empty legalism." For Falk, law must be a means of empowerment and it includes undertones of class warfare.[15] The fact that "bourgeois" law in democratic societies is derived from the deliberations of elected representatives is not mentioned.

Problems, such as those dealing with the environment, are increasingly acquiring an international dimension and corporate business practices are patently becoming transnational. State laws, according to the legal theorist Sally Engle Merry, should therefore be replaced by "plural law," which also includes "indigenous law" and "global human rights law." International citizens' tribunals thus challenge the primacy of state law and demonstrate recognition of a "global notion of justice." In reference to a tribunal on indigenous rights in Hawaii, Merry clearly relates this concept of law to political activism when she refers to the appropriation of "legal forms and symbols in an effort to harness the power and legitimacy of law in a movement of resistance."[16]

International citizens' tribunals cannot impose their decisions on transgressing states, but this apparent weakness may be turned into an advantage—at least theoretically. Such tribunals are not indebted to states, nor are they influenced by them. Powerlessness may thus prove to be a positive attribute, and contribute to legitimacy. After all, the militarily victorious Allies conducted the Nuremberg and Tokyo trials—and their legitimacy is still being questioned today. Tribunals must be carefully differentiated from truth commissions, even though both operate separately from the court system, since the latter are state sanctioned and funded and are organized as official investigations.[17]

Drawing Parallels

When comparing international citizens' tribunals, the issues of public relations, timing, and effect on the country providing the venue are critical. Since these tribunals lack legal standing and may not apply punishment, the public relations impact through media attention is the key to furthering their legal and moral cases. As Lelio Basso observed: "The mass media represent the main channel between us and the international community, which is at once our matrix and our executive arm."[18] As will be demonstrated, tribunals have tried to maximize coverage by emphasizing the roles of celebrities such as Albert Einstein, John Dewey, Jean-Paul Sartre, and Simone de Beauvoir, and by recognizing that a country's media attention is enhanced when one of its citizens with considerable credibility serves as a tribunal member.

In regard to timing, it is important to consider whether a tribunal is established in order to influence the verdict of an ongoing trial. If so, a state's behavior could be modified and the tribunal could have a deterrent effect on future actions through a process similar to sanctions.[19] By contrast, ex post facto tribunals dealing with the Armenian genocide of 1915 through 1916 and the treatment of Native Americans in past centuries have less of a contemporary policy impact. They nevertheless perform the crucial function of public acknowledgment, or even apology.

Also to be considered are the repercussions on host states. What foreign policy ends are served when a country permits an international citizens' tribunal to operate on its territory, and how does the tribunal session interact with that country's internal political cleavages? Furthermore, what efforts are being made by accused states to undermine the organization of tribunals?

Tribunals, thus far, have had deficiencies that have hindered efficacy, but most of these problems are rectifiable. They are assembled in a somewhat elitist, rather than democratic, manner, by self-appointed committees that may try to stack the deck with partisans. There consequently may be some unenunciated political cause other than justice, and panelists may be selected for their ideological predilections rather than their legal probity. Bertrand Russell tried to deal with this issue of preconceived opinions prior to his Vietnam tribunal, admitting that those invited to serve had strong convictions. He maintained, however, that these panelists were of solid character and could still be just. You don't have to be indifferent, argued Russell, to be impartial, nor have an empty mind in order to assure an open mind.[20] This may be so, but the appearance of partiality undermined the tribunal's credibility in the eyes of the media—especially when the rather extreme verdict including a finding of genocide, was announced. It is evident that tribunal panelists often approach their duty with a clear conviction that an injustice has been committed. Rather than question the premises of cases they consider, they are more concerned with gathering evidence that may be used to effect a remedy.[21]

Also arguable is the general rejection by tribunal advocates of moral equivalence. Just as Allied crimes were not considered at Nuremberg or Tokyo, later international citizens' tribunals similarly do not want to give equal status to the crimes of those identified as victims. Those who are weak, argue tribunal proponents, represent the will of the people and may therefore resort to violent acts of "resistance." Any war crimes committed in resistance are not deemed morally equivalent to the acts of those with superior force who violate international norms systematically.[22] Still, the failure to acknowledge dual responsibility provides critics with their strongest ammunition.

Although international citizens' tribunals are not formal judicial bodies, they stress adherence to legal procedures in order to enhance their legitimacy. When evaluating their fairness, it is therefore germane to raise questions such as: Did any members of the tribunal comment prior to the hearings on the matter of guilt? Was cross-examination of witnesses permitted? Were panelists absent from the proceedings during the presentation of evidence? Did charges of legal violations take into account a distinction between premeditation and unintended consequences? Problematic in a legal context is the participation of the defendants. They are often invited but rarely agree to appear before what they consider to be a biased forum. Sometimes, the tribunal appoints an expert to present testimony on behalf of the defense—but surely the prosecution side of the issue predominates. In absentia defendants thus tend to be the norm rather than the exception.

Tribunals sometimes arrive at judgments without due deliberation. This is especially true in regard to sessions that last only one or two days—including the testimony of witnesses. This leads to the suspicion that judgments may be predetermined, or even written in advance. While not germane in reference to the Reichstag fire, Moscow show trial, and Vietnam tribunals, it is unfortunately the case in other instances. For example, a tribunal investigating the perils of globalization admitted that an indictment was approved quickly, but defended such action on the ground that the panelists had considerable previous knowledge of the issues and were "not starting from zero." Going further, there was also a strong inference regarding prior preparation of the text as indicated by the comment that "the panel will sign the indictment if they agree with its general tenor."[23]

Applying legalistic terminology is often confounding. Commissions of inquiry accentuate a search for the truth as they gather evidence and come up with "findings;" they do not assume a juridical function, but do try to influence an ongoing legal process. Since the 1967 Russell hearings, the term "tribunal"—with its overtones of a court trial—has become standard. There is no claim of actual authority or jurisdiction, but this quasi-legal format has produced confusion regarding the role of tribunal members. As there is no formal adversarial structure, they may seem to act like prosecutors. After all, there wouldn't be a tribunal unless there was evidence of a crime.

The image of tribunal members as judges or jurors is at odds with a prosecutorial role.[24] Judges are likely to reflect legal training and the issuing of dissenting opinions. Jurors are laymen who reach verdicts on the basis of consensus. In reference to the Russell Tribunal, Sartre commented that members would not wear robes, since jurors do not wear such attire. Russell had a somewhat different interpretation, viewing the tribunal members as "witnesses."[25] This observation is in line with the radical populist argument that tribunal members should not appropriate the responsibility of being judges, because everyone is entitled to judge, especially those directly affected by the issue being considered.[26] Looking at the tribunal as a grand jury may be most instructive. It can sift through the evidence in order to determine whether an indictment should be drawn up, a more suitable function than preparing verdicts, as the defense rarely has an opportunity to present its testimony.

Reflections

The Reichstag fire and Moscow show trial tribunals accentuated the right of defendants to have a fair and impartial hearing, with the chairman of the latter panel, John Dewey, stressing that democracy is a process rather than an end.[27] Starting with the Russell Tribunal, pragmatic procedural standards have given way to an interpretation based more on the application of international law (with the Mumia Abu-Jamal case being a notable exception).[28] This is because of the influence of Nuremberg, as well as efforts to universalize tribunal guidelines. It is important to recognize, however, that legal framework since the Russell Tribunal has been based on the newly developing radical interpretation of international law that is rejected by many traditionalists.

Tribunals are shifting away from examinations of miscarriages of justice against specific individuals toward broader indictments of "the system." Anticapitalist, deconstructionist attitudes are clearly present in the following description of tribunals: "They help move to deeper knowledge, weaving together the objective analysis with the subjective testimony, the personal with the political, challenging the logic of the dominant discourse of human rights, of development, of globalization, of all that is hegemonic and powerful."[29] In essence, tribunals have become a weapon of the radical left in its battle with "global capitalism"; if states can band together to create a G-7 framework, then anticapitalists can counter with tribunals.[30] Until the very recent example of hearings on Lithuanian communism, no tribunals have had a rightist political agenda and the infrastructure for tribunals has been provided by the radicals through the Russell II tribunals, the Italian-based Lelio Basso International Foundation, and the Permanent People's Tribunal.

Tribunal proponents endorsing the new approach to international law identify institutional causes of problems, and are critical of liberals who are accused of failing to do so, even though they are aware of the effects.[31] The conflict between those accentuating ideological ends and liberals concentrating on objective means, now features the former in the ascendancy. Little heed is paid to Arthur Garfield Hays and John Dewey, liberal stalwarts of the Reichstag fire and Moscow show trial hearings, respectively. This evolving linkage between international citizens' tribunals and radical populist platforms has had a negative impact on public relations, with the media devoting decreasing attention to recent cases.

International citizens' tribunals fill a need in the current system of justice, and it is not surprising that their number is proliferating. Through an examination of the three pathbreaking twentieth-century examples, plus many hearings in recent years, this survey attempts to explore why tribunals are constituted, by whom, what procedures they adopt, and what results they produce. The aim is to identify defects, and then to propose remedies that can strengthen the process. Tribunals can indeed contribute to the public good, and are conducive toward furthering civil society, but first they must undergo reforms that go back to the basics of promoting democratic values and the ideological blindness of justice.

The Reichstag Fire Case

Chapter II

THE BERLIN CAULDRON

S talin's ascendancy in the Soviet Union, efforts by the Communist International (Comintern) to foment revolution in capitalist states, the growing appeal of Mussolini's Italian fascism, and depressed economies all put Western democracy under siege. Then, on January 30, 1933, Adolf Hitler was appointed as Germany's chancellor. In quick succession, right-wing forces gained control in Greece and Finland, Austria's democracy disintegrated, and the military assumed power in Bulgaria.[1] While a calamitous ideological clash was developing in Europe amidst a growing threat of war, Germany became the focal point of left-right passions—as well as a testing ground for democracy's ability to withstand the onslaught of totalitarianism. Hitler pledged to save Europe from Bolshevism, but could he do it without simultaneously undercutting the Weimar Republic's rule of law? The Communists surely had their own expansionist and totalitarian agenda, with the spotlight on Germany. The Comintern combatively declared: "Still more than hitherto the question of Germany is becoming the central question of the revolutionary movement of Europe and of the whole world. Now more than ever the tempo of the maturing revolutionary crisis in the whole of Europe will depend upon the development of events in Germany."[2]

Within this historical context, the Reichstag fire case emerged as a prime symbol of a deepening ideological struggle. It is therefore not surprising that it led to the establishment of the first and most successful international citizens' tribunal.

The Red Specter

Late in the evening on February 27, 1933, a fire in Berlin seriously damaged the building housing the Reichstag, Germany's parliament. A twenty-four-year-old Dutchman named Marinus van der Lubbe was apprehended on the spot and was immediately denounced by Nazi officials as a communist arsonist. Hitler personally went to the scene of the blaze and vowed to have all communist deputies hanged that very night. This did not actually happen, but at least four thousand communists were immediately arrested.[3]

Ideological battle lines were being drawn as the March 5 parliamentary election approached. The Nazis had just come to power on the strength of their November 1932 garnering of 196 Reichstag seats. Although the largest party, they still commanded only a minority of the 583 available. The Communist Party held 100, and the Social Democratic Party 121, but the left was riven by in-fighting. Stalin, who dictated a radical line, ordered Communists not to work jointly with Socialists, in part because he expected that a triumph of Nazism would represent the final stage of capitalism and produce a proletarian revolution. The German Communists were also angry at the failure of the Social Democrats to support the presidential candidacy in March 1932 of the Communist leader Ernst Thaelmann, backing instead the successful reelection of Field Marshall Paul von Hindenburg—the man who ended up appointing Hitler as chancellor.[4]

While the Nazis were proclaiming that the Reichstag fire was a signal for a Communist uprising, the Communists were charging that the Nazis had set the fire themselves in order to scapegoat the Communists and sway the public against them in the forthcoming Reichstag election. Indeed, on February 23, the leader of the Communist delegation in the Reichstag, Ernst Torgler, had warned the Prussian State Council that "a staged attack is planned on Hitler's life, to be followed by the suppression of the Socialists and Communists in the manner done in 1878." Torgler was referring to Chancellor Otto von Bismarck's dissolution of the Reichstag and outlawing of the Socialists, after accusing them of involvement in an unsuccessful assassination attempt against Kaiser Wilhelm II.[5] The Central Committee of the German Communist Party called for the exposure of the real perpetrators of the Reichstag arson, while Communist parliamentarians proclaimed: "The Communist Reichstag fraction declares that it is ready at any time to prove before any regular court, which grants them the possibilities of defense, that Minister Goering and Chancellor Hitler are guilty of the act of incendiarism in the Reichstag."[6]

Marinus van der Lubbe had set the fire; it is also likely that he had engaged in arson at three locations in Berlin just two days earlier.[7] The issue was whether he was acting alone or as part of a Communist or Nazi conspiracy. Although it is true that van der Lubbe had past associations with Dutch communists and had been a youth league member until 1931, he had turned against the party afterward.

The defendants, in addition to van der Lubbe, were Ernst Torgler and three Bulgarian Communists who were in Germany illegally. Torgler, accompanied by fellow Communist parliamentarian Wilhelm Koenen, was the last person to leave the Reichstag that night. He was an important public face for the Communists but was not especially influential within the party and was not a member of its Central Committee. He turned himself in for questioning on February 28 on hearing that the Communists had been accused of the arson, apparently trying to clear his party in order to avoid a repetition of the 1878 incident.

Closing the circle were the three Bulgarians who were arrested on March 9. Vassily Tanev and Blagoj Popov were Comintern agents in contact with the German Communists. Georgi Dimitrov was a longtime Communist activist sentenced in absentia to death by Bulgaria in April 1925 for his role in blowing up the Sofia Cathedral. The mayor and more than fifty government officials were killed.[8] He headed the Balkan secretariat of the Comintern and became director of the Western European Bureau of the Comintern in March 1929. He also was one of three aides assisting Stalin in running the Comintern. Dimitrov spent most of his time in Berlin, where he lived under a pseudonym, carried a false passport, and failed to register with the police as a resident. Like other agents in the Comintern's international relations section, he distributed funds and set up courier routes; however, he kept away from the German Communist Party headquarters and maintained separate files.[9] When arrested, the Nazis did not seem to be aware of his prominence and it is unclear when they learned about it. In any case, they preferred to remain silent for fear of aggravating relations with the Soviet Union.

The Communist threat to Germany could possibly have been real, for there had been at least four efforts to subvert the Weimar Republic by force. The Reichstag fire was not connected to any fifth attempt. Only van der Lubbe, among those arrested, was indeed a perpetrator; the three Bulgarians and Torgler all had airtight alibis and had no relationship to van der Lubbe. The Dutchman proudly claimed that he had acted alone, and that his aim was to protest Nazi injustices in the face of what he saw as laxity on the part of the German working class. If so, his effort backfired, since the

Nazis were strengthened and leftists rounded up. Basically, van der Lubbe was an idiosyncratic social activist akin, as a Dutch journalist keenly observed, to a contemporary punk band singer. He hoped to emerge as a hero of the anti-Nazi struggle, so he submitted to arrest without any resistance, but was then psychologically crushed when he was not given credit for sole responsibility. Van der Lubbe may well have been expressing the truth when he claimed that he had no intent to hurt anyone and had therefore flamed the Reichstag, a public building symbolic of state power, at night.[10]

The Nazis had used the fire as a pretext for a purge of leftists, while the Communists tried to counter Nazi contentions of their complicity with appeals to world public opinion. They did so brilliantly, and were not beneath the use of forgery to further their cause. The famous "Oberfohren memorandum," purportedly written by the German former leader of the Nationalists and published in a liberal British newspaper, alleged Nazi involvement and created a sensation.[11] It also placed the Nazis in the unenviable position of having to prove a negative.

The Totalitarian Impulse

The February 27 Reichstag fire occurred during a Nazi campaign against the Communists, which reflected an effort to suppress them in the run-up to the March 5 Reichstag elections. They had been scheduled by President Hindenburg, at the request of Hitler, just one day after the latter was appointed chancellor. On February 24, the Communist headquarters in Berlin was raided and many documents were seized. On February 28, the day after the arson, the Nazis announced that the documents found in the Karl Liebknecht House proved that the Communists had planned a terrorist insurrection. This accusation was probably spurious, as the documents were never publicly released nor were they introduced as evidence in the case of the fire trial defendants. Nevertheless, this pretext was used to suspend civil liberties. On February 28, President Hindenburg invoked Article 48 of the constitution, effectively ending juridical controls over the police and eliminating the rights to counsel and appeal. In Prussia, repression was carried out under the direction of that state's Minister of the Interior, Hermann Goering.[12]

The Nazi assault on civil liberties was at first directed primarily against the Communists. Their Reichstag deputies were arrested, and the party's remaining leadership was forced underground or into exile, notably in Paris. Party chairman Ernst Thaelmann was apprehended on March 3, but he was never indicted for the fire. Assets belonging to Communists were confiscated on the ground that they were being used to fund subversion. Thousands of Communists were sent to detention camps under an 1849 law that permitted such a procedure for up to three months, and granted the right of appeal. These stipulations were disregarded, as the government claimed the need to protect the detainees from the vengeance of the people.[13] Under such circumstances, files of the Comintern's Western European Bureau were secreted to safe haven in Paris and Copenhagen. The anticommunist campaign particularly affected the Jews, as Nazi ideology had long maintained that Bolshevism was linked to a Jewish conspiracy. In protest, Albert Einstein proclaimed that he was relinquishing his citizenship.[14]

The Nazi crackdown established favorable conditions for the March 5 elections, so they went ahead as scheduled. Benefiting from the anticommunist hysteria generated in conjunction with the fire, the Nazis won 288 seats. The Social Democrats held steady at 120, and the Communists dropped to 81. Perhaps the Communists had been permitted to run so that their supporters would not flock to the Social Democrats.[15] In any case, the matter soon became moot. On March 23, Hitler pressured the Reichstag into giving his government absolute power to make laws for four years. The Communist Party was then banned on April 1, and the Nazis were proclaimed the sole legal party on July 14.

While Germany was rounding up Communists, its relations with the Soviet Union remained largely unaffected. On March 1, Foreign Minister Konstantin von Neurath met in Berlin with his Soviet counterpart, Maxim Litvinov. Neurath said that there would be no change in ties to the Soviet Union, and Litvinov did not raise the issue of Communists being accused of setting the Reichstag fire.[16] On March 23, Hitler set forth his basic guidelines in an address to the Reichstag: "The fight against Communism in Germany is our internal affair in which we will never permit interference from outside. Our political relations with other Powers to whom we are bound by common interests will not be affected thereby." Litvinov thanked the German ambassador in Moscow for the chancellor's remarks.[17]

The Soviet Union and Germany had strategic stakes in their relationship that they did not want undermined. Moscow looked warily at Japanese advances into China, and hoped to shore up the Western front in preparation for a possible showdown in Asia. Germany had been training its troops in the Soviet Union since 1922 as a means of circumventing restrictive provisions of the Treaty of Versailles. The German military establishment, which was vehemently anticommunist domestically, favored strong bonds with the Soviet Union.[18] Note that Germany did not publicize the Comintern connections of the three Bulgarians arrested in the Reichstag fire case, even though Dimitrov's May 30 written statement to the Supreme Court acknowledged contacts in Germany with other Comintern agents.[19] Basically, the Soviet Union and Germany tacitly agreed that each country could restrict acts by its own citizens, but that public attacks on each other's ideologies were permissible. Moscow would continue to speak up on behalf of antifascist forces, and Berlin would do likewise as a bastion of anticommunism.

On April 28, Soviet ambassador Lev Khinchuk complained to Hitler and Neurath about the persecution of communists, but the Fuehrer finessed the matter by saying that Germany wanted normal relations, including trade, with the Soviet Union.[20] At the beginning of May, Germany ratified an extension of the April 1926 Treaty of Berlin, which required each state to remain neutral if the other was subjected to attack. At the same time, however, Hitler was not prepared to exonerate the Reichstag defendants for the sake of German-Soviet cordiality. He had too much invested in proving their guilt, and needed to demonstrate that his assumption of extraordinary powers and purge of the Communists were justified by the existence of a revolutionary threat. It was an argument that Stalin understood only too well.[21]

On the Docket

The arson directed at the Reichstag was not a capital crime under German law, but on March 29 Hitler took care of that problem by signing a retroactive death penalty law, which included the crime of "revolutionary arson." The Dutch government protested that van der Lubbe could therefore be executed under a law not in place at the time of the infraction.[22] On April 22, the examining magistrate of the Supreme Court, Paul Vogt, indicated that the fire trial would be heard as part of a broader Communist treason trial; in fact, Thaelmann and other party leaders were already in custody. On May 25, this idea was discarded, and a separate trial related to the Reichstag fire was affirmed. Based on a specific criminal act, it was to precede a broader trial dealing with political activities. There was some tenuous evidence linking Torgler to the fire, since he had been in the Reichstag building that night. He had parliamentary immunity as a member of the Reichstag, but the April 1 banning of the Communist Party effectively removed that immunity, even though the arson had taken place earlier. Connecting Thaelmann to any crime would have been a much more difficult task.[23] On May 30, Leipzig was announced as the site of the fire trial, but no date was set.

Meanwhile, Dimitrov and his fellow defendants were in jail awaiting their fate. His hands had been shackled on April 4, freed only for dressing and meals. Torgler was suffering the same treatment. A trial was looming but, so far, there had been no indictment. It was finally issued on July 24, but not made public. Dimitrov received a copy on August 3. When he tried in an August 24 letter to the French author Romain Rolland to reveal some of its contents, German authorities refused to forward the communication.[24]

Both the Soviet Union and Germany recognized that bilateral state ties had their limits. The Kremlin was not about to cede an advantage to the Nazis in the battle between rival ideological camps, nor was it prepared to stand by while the German Communist Party was decimated. Acting behind the scenes through the Comintern, it therefore orchestrated a campaign to prove the innocence of the four Communists accused along with van der Lubbe of setting the fire.

Chapter III

RALLYING TO THE DEFENSE

illi Muenzenberg, a German Communist, was the point man for the Comintern's effort to counter the Reichstag arson accusations. This master at public relations organized an anti-Nazi coalition to influence European public opinion and in April 1933, initiated the creation of a Commission of Inquiry, which he expected to convene just prior to an official German trial.[1] Muenzenberg and other Communists adapted to democratic sensibilities by intentionally staying in the background, but the process soon gained its own momentum as liberal intellectuals (such as the American civil libertarian attorney Arthur Garfield Hays) came to emphasize an objective rule of law and the fate of individual defendants rather than ideological confrontation. Thus, the first international citizens' tribunal was established, setting forth the guidelines for future similar endeavors.

Red Alert

Muenzenberg was the West European propaganda chief of the Comintern, as well as a Communist deputy in the Reichstag.[2] He was a vital agent of the Comintern's international liaison department, reporting in Moscow to the Orgburo director Ossip Piatnitsky. As described by a German researcher of his activities, Muenzenberg "the activist and organizer, had no time or taste for literary or philosophical sophistication. Ideas were levers for social action, not material for debate and individual spiritual enrichment."[3] In October 1920, he put together the Communist Youth International, which campaigned against Hungary's "white terror." In September 1921, he established International Workers' Aid to help Russia during its famine. In August 1932, he orchestrated an antifascist rally in Amsterdam; the next month, he formed the League Against War and Fascism.[4] Most significantly, Muenzenberg succeeded in attracting noncommunists who were unaware that a Comintern operative was pulling the strings. The public image of these movements did not include recognition of Communist sponsorship, a perception enhanced by securing the support of prominent noncommunists such as Albert Einstein. The prestigious German-Jewish physicist was a member of International Workers' Aid and served on the steering committee of the League Against War and Fascism.

Muenzenberg was in Berlin when the Reichstag fire broke out. While thousands of Communists were being arrested that night, he managed to make his way to the Saar and later crossed into France. Since a Popular Front was being assembled there against Nazi Germany, Muenzenberg was granted political asylum. Headquartered in Paris, he played a major role in planning the March 23 protest against the arrest of the fire trial defendants; Andre Gide and Andre Malraux were in attendance. With Comintern financial backing, he purchased the respectable publishing house Editions du Carrefour and used it as an arm of his anti-Nazi activities.[5] It was his office that prepared the forged "Oberfohren memorandum" accusing the Nazis of the Reichstag arson.[6] Muenzenberg also formed the World Committee for the Victims of German Fascism and recruited the British Labour peer Lord Dudley Marley to be its chairman. Einstein was a member.[7] During the period of June through August 1933, Muenzenberg spent most of his time in Moscow consulting with Comintern officials and he secured approval from Piatnitsky and executive committee member Bela Kun for a countertrial sponsored by the Commission of Inquiry.[8]

Muenzenberg's most famous accomplishment was preparation of the "Brown Book," which sought to shift the blame for the Reichstag fire from the Communists to the Nazis. This polemical work was written by Muenzenberg's associates, especially Otto Katz (also known as Andre Simone).[9] Officially, the World Committee for the Victims of German Fascism was cited as the sponsor of the "Brown Book." Lord Marley, then serving as Deputy Speaker of the House of Lords, contributed the introduction and the English and French editions made it appear that Einstein was the actual author. He was referred to as the organization's "president" in other editions. Einstein was admittedly a member, but he was furious about references to his supposed authorship and implied presidency. He acknowledged his agreement with the spirit of the "Brown Book" but denied writing even one word of it. The World Committee was prepared to let him resign and to remove his name from its letterhead, but the renowned scientist rebuffed this offer and indicated that he would not permit himself to be forced out. He praised the organization for the good work it had already done, but stayed true to his democratic convictions and refused to be manipulated by the Communists.[10]

The Brown Book of the Hitler Terror was first published on August 1, 1933 by Muenzenberg's Editions du Carrefour. It was translated into seventeen languages, with the English edition being issued in London on September 1 by Victor Gollancz. The "Brown Book" was directed at European public opinion, and copies were successfully smuggled into Germany to exert an influence there as well. It sought to counter the German indictment and challenge the legitimacy of the upcoming Leipzig trial by maintaining the innocence of the four Communists, while admitting the guilt of van der Lubbe. The Dutchman was presented as a mentally defective, degenerate homosexual who had intimate liaisons with Nazi officials and collaborated with them in setting the fire. It also was alleged that van der Lubbe was chosen to incinerate the Reichstag because he was a former Communist, the Nazi plan being to charge an international communist conspiracy. The "Brown Book" accused the Nazis of the fire plot, specifically naming Reichstag president Goering and propaganda chief Goebbels, but refrained from implicating Hitler, whom the German Communists had earlier accused of "incendiarism."[11]

Countertrial

The Commission of Inquiry into the Origins of the Reichstag Fire (sometimes called the International Juridical Investigatory Commission on the Reichstag Fire) was the brainchild of Willi Muenzenberg, although he eschewed a public role in order to hide Comintern connections. The German media were aware of his activities, and alleged that he was involved in a Bolshevik-Jewish conspiracy, but the media elsewhere did not similarly cite Muenzenberg's participation.[12]

Working through the International Lawyers' Defense Committee, the German Communist masterminded the first international citizens' tribunal. He pulled the strings from behind the stage, letting his associate Otto Katz play the major public role. To get the Commission of Inquiry underway, Katz arrived in London on July 7 despite being on British intelligence's blacklist. Lobbying efforts by prominent Labourites paid off. Although the "Brown Book" had not yet been published, Katz discussed its contents with journalists and revealed that he was one of its editors. Katz also indicated that he would furnish the Commission of Inquiry with evidence establishing Nazi responsibility for the Reichstag fire, and would assist in the provision of witnesses. The dashing young operative (later purported to be the model for the character Victor Laszlo in the movie "Casablanca") asserted: "We feel sure that the evidence we produce will have a great effect on public opinion, and that when our trial is going on the Hitler government will not be able to condemn the guiltless."[13] Afterward, Muenzenberg's frequent colleague Romain Rolland tried to serve the anti-Nazi cause by preparing a letter to the German ambassador to France. The Nobel laureate in literature professed the innocence of the Bulgarians and offered to provide exculpatory evidence.[14]

On August 24, the German government announced that the fire trial would begin on September 21 in Leipzig. Acting quickly, countertrial organizers scheduled a September 2 meeting in Paris, chaired by the renowned French trial lawyer Vincent de Moro-Giafferi. London was selected as the venue for the hearings, since considerable support was available there from Labourites, and September 14 was chosen as the opening date because it was crucial to make a public relations impact prior to the official Leipzig trial. In the meantime, a subcommission was appointed to gather evidence from witnesses in van der Lubbe's homeland of the Netherlands. On September 6 and 7, sixteen witnesses were deposed by Commission members Betsy Bakker-Nort (Dutch liberal democratic feminist parliamentarian), Pierre Vermeylen (Belgian ex-minister of justice), and George Branting (prominent Swedish social democratic lawyer).[15]

The countertrial, clearly lacking in legal standing, sought justification on various grounds. After all, it was going to question Germany's judicial process even before that country held its own trial of the defendants. The main argument advanced was that refugee witnesses were not assured of their safety and probably wouldn't be able to testify at Leipzig. Another was that the defendants were not being allowed to prepare a proper defense, as they were denied a copy of the indictment as well as the services of foreign lawyers.[16] Commission member Arthur Garfield Hays, an American lawyer who became instrumental in asserting the tribunal's independence, presciently argued that if the tribunal was to establish Dimitrov's innocence, then world public opinion might be able to prevent his murder by the Nazis, following an acquittal.[17] Hays's perspective was rather novel, since most antifascists assumed that Dimitrov would be found guilty in a German show trial. Hays publicly distinguished between the German judicial system and the Nazi regime, trusting only in the integrity of the former.

The Commission of Inquiry, an international citizens' tribunal, held hearings in London from September 14 to 18. Its members were Moro-Giafferi, Bakker-Nort, Vermeylen, Branting, and Hays, plus Valdemar Hvidt (Danish centrist and founder of the National Association Against Unemployment), Gaston Bergery (French newspaper editor), and Denis Nowell (D. N.) Pritt (British). None was a Communist, and none had any connection to the "Brown Book." Tellingly, all were lawyers.[18] Pritt served as chairman of the sessions. He was a Labour parliamentarian and a King's Counsel, a prestigious category of barrister. Pritt had not been an anti-Nazi activist, but he did visit the Soviet Union in 1932 and came away with a favorable impression of its legal system. He then wrote and lectured on Soviet courts, and criticized those in Britain for their class bias.[19]

The opening address was made by Labourite Stafford Cripps, a former Solicitor General who was later to serve as ambassador to the Soviet Union and as Chancellor of the Exchequer. He was a strong critic of Nazism and an advocate of assistance to German refugees. Cripps contended that the upcoming Leipzig trial would be politically influenced and that lawyers would be intimidated and witnesses not assured of their safety.[20]

Countertrial members followed court protocol and acted dignified in the manner of judges. An audience of two hundred raptly followed the testimony in an overcrowded room provided by the Law Society. Former Communist Reichstag deputy Wilhelm Koenen affirmed that he had been in a restaurant with Torgler at the time of the fire. Paul Herz, who had been a Social Democratic member of the Reichstag for thirteen years, discussed security arrangements at the German parliament and surmised that attendants would have intercepted the large quantity of flammable material needed to set the blaze had it passed through either of the two entrances. He concluded that it had been secreted into the Reichstag via the engine room or the underground passageway connecting parliament to Reichstag President Goering's residence. George Bernhard, a former newspaper editor, maintained that only the Nazis would have stood to gain from the fire, while Rudolf Breitscheid, former Social Democratic leader, stated that it was "very improbable" that the Communists had been responsible. Albert Grzesinski, who had served as chief of police in Berlin, pointed out that no fire alarm had sounded, so someone in authority must have given the orders to prevent any alarm. Ernst Torgler's son Kurt, aged fifteen, reported that his father's wrists were chained and that he had become thin and depressed. He also testified that his father had slept at the home of fellow Communist Otto Kuehne the night of the fire, so he was not in his own house at 5:00 A.M. when two policemen came to search it.[21] Note that considerable attention at the countertrial was paid to the activities of Torgler and little to those of Dimitrov, even though his sister Elena did appear as a witness. Conclusive evidence was presented, indicating that Dimitrov was on a train en route from Munich to Berlin on the fateful night of February 27.

Some witnesses spoke in closed sessions and had their names kept secret because they feared Nazi intimidation. There had been a death threat issued by British Nazis, featuring the posting of photos of German exiles with an exhortation to kill them. A Nazi agent operating in Britain is alleged to have been in attendance at the countertrial. One potential witness was suspected as a "plant," so he was not allowed to testify.[22] There was no subpoena power, Nazis implicated in the fire plot were not present to offer rebuttals, and witnesses were not cross-examined. Nevertheless, the rule of law started to be applied as the Communist organizers began to lose control of the tribunal to its liberal members. Assertions in the "Brown Book" were not used to castigate the Nazis, and members of the panel were skeptical that van der Lubbe had been introduced to Storm Trooper commander Ernst Roehm and other Nazis for homosexual trysts.[23]

Pritt, as the chair, dealt strongly with prior bias demonstrated by Commission member Vincent de Moro-Giafferi at a September 11 rally in Paris, where he had proclaimed the four Communists innocent and Goering guilty. Moro-Giafferi also charged the Germans with a "parody of justice," with the guilty acting as judges. About six thousand people attended this event, which was organized by the French League Against Anti-Semitism. One speaker, in reference to Einstein's anti-Nazi proclamations, threatened the taking of German hostages in Paris if the scientist was harmed.[24] The Paris rally took place three days before the opening countertrial session, and was meant to drum up support. Pritt, however, felt that Moro-Giafferi had compromised himself in Paris and again by repeating his allegations at a preliminary discussion among Commission members. In his memoirs, Pritt writes that he would have preferred that Moro-Giafferi not serve as a Commission member at the countertrial, but he had permitted him to remain since he was an invited participant. Still Pritt continued to irritate the Frenchman by emphasizing that evidence should precede a decision—and that evidence had not yet been presented. Moro-Giafferi attended the first day of the hearings, and then left.[25]

On the night of September 20, the "final conclusions" were announced. Emanating from a commission of inquiry, "conclusions" were the natural outcome. There was no "verdict" because there had been no trial. The conclusions, prepared by Bergery with the assistance of Branting and Hays, were based solely on evidence presented at the hearings—not on the "Brown Book" or the "Oberfohren memorandum." The German indictment was not cited, since no copy of it was publicly available.

The conclusions were more temperate than polemical: The four Communists were deemed innocent; van der Lubbe was found not to have been a Communist at the time of the fire; it was considered probable that the passageway connecting Goering's home to the Reichstag building was used as a means of entry by the arsonists; and it was strongly suggested that the Nazis started the fire. Specific Nazis were not charged with the crime; however, and van der Lubbe was not definitively linked to the Nazis.[26] There was, therefore, some caution in placing the blame on the Nazis, but aspersions as to guilt were obvious. Copies of the conclusions were quickly flown to Germany for distribution to the judges and prosecutor. Chief prosecutor Karl Werner said that "we have no reason to dodge the charges that have been made abroad against high functionaries of the German government."[27] The defendants were not allowed to receive copies.

Foreign media attention was generally positive, with *The New Statesman and Nation* asserting that the countertrial had to be taken seriously. It pointed out that newspapers that had treated it as a "joke" had changed their attitude once the hearings had produced pertinent testimony. The conservative *Spectator* did not expect the Leipzig trial to be a farce, and considered it unfair to have a countertrial prior to the actual trial. The German judiciary had to be given a chance. Nevertheless, the British publication greeted the opening of the countertrial positively, since its evidence could provide a standard of comparison with the later official trial. Once the hearings were completed, *The Spectator* still referred to the high reputation of Germany's Supreme Court but indicated agreement with the countertrial's conclusion that the four Communists were innocent and that the arson was most likely the responsibility of the Nazis. Any evidence presented at Leipzig would have to be "overwhelming in volume and impregnable against skilled examination to justify a verdict of guilty." *The New York Times* adopted a cautious approach, maintaining that the countertrial's actions were unofficial and ex parte, but that its conclusion would have to be considered by the German court.[28]

The Comintern's newsletter *Inprecorr* of course endorsed the countertrial, which used the "greatest objectivity and reserve" and attracted extensive coverage by the world's media. From its class-oriented perspective, *Inprecorr* emphasized that the Commission members were "bourgeois jurists," and that growing international support was coming from the bourgeoisie. If even the bourgeoisie could react in such a manner, it was surely incumbent on the proletariat to organize demonstrations to help save the defendants.[29]

The Nazis reacted to the international publicity with a combination of image enhancement and rebuttal. On September 9, Rudolf Hess (head of the political section of the Nazi Party) had ordered that foreigners in Germany should not be harassed; on September 11, there were no Nazi provocations when a trainload of Jewish refugees left Berlin. The Nazis also appear to have been behind the publication on September 14 of "Armed Insurrection—Revelations on the Attempt at Communist Revolution on the Eve of the National Revolution," an effort to counter the "Brown Book" and the London tribunal opening that day. It was issued by the All-German Union of Anti-Communist Associations and was filled with gruesome pictures of Nazis killed by Communists.[30]

The British Venue

International citizens' tribunals inevitably interact with the politics of the host country. In the British case, a rather unusual arrangement existed at the time, as the Conservatives controlled the House of Commons and were participating in a national unity government with some Labourites. Thirteen Labour members of Parliament backed the government, and the prime minister was Labour leader Ramsay MacDonald. Labourites, such as Pritt and Cripps, were anti-Nazi and challenged the German government's account of the Reichstag fire. The Conservatives, who were anti-Soviet and often critical of the Versailles restrictions imposed on Germany, began turning against Hitler's redirection of Germany's policies and did not prevent the tribunal from taking place. The Foreign Office, too, was beginning to look askance at Germany, especially in the persons of Foreign Secretary John Simon and Permanent Undersecretary Robert Vansittart.[31]

The Nazi crackdown on Communists, Jews, and political dissidents alarmed much of the British public. Labourites saw forces of reaction assaulting the working class; Liberals discerned the undermining of democratic values by a tyrannical regime. Conservatives reevaluated their traditional amity with Germany, with Winston Churchill and former Foreign Secretary Austen Chamberlain speaking out against the Nazis in the House of Commons. This act generated a protest to the British government by the German ambassador.[32] In May 1933 Hitler dispatched Alfred Rosenberg to Britain to promote Germany's image. He headed the foreign policy office of the Nazi party and was an influential theoretician of Nazi ideology. Rosenberg was poorly received by all sectors of public opinion. Emblematic of his negative reception was his meeting with Lady Margaret Asquith, widow of the former Liberal Prime Minister Herbert Asquith. She had been a long-time friend of Germany, but she told Rosenberg that he and Hitler didn't understand "how much the British detest all suppression of freedom and how little we are impressed by a one-man show."[33]

The Labourites championed the cause of these suppressed Germans, and staged rallies throughout Britain. Cripps, who did not support the national unity government, was particularly active, but ideology rather than abstract justice seems to have provided motivation. In March 1933, six British engineers were among those charged with economic sabotage in the Soviet Union's Metro-Vickers case. Applying a double standard, Cripps proposed that the guilt or innocence of the defendants should not be pre-judged and that no British action should be taken until after a verdict was rendered by the Soviet court. Cripps warned about jeopardizing relations with Moscow, expressed concern about the well-being of the defendants if pressure was applied, and opposed any British economic sanctions.[34]

The Commission of Inquiry's countertrial took place in London due to the efforts of Labourites. The government took a middle-of-the-road position by not banning the gathering, but also by obstructing it. While German protests were parried with the claim that the government could not prevent a private meeting, some witnesses were barred from entering Britain and the foreign ministry tried, unsuccessfully, to get the Law Society to deny use of its hall for the hearings.[35] Basically, the British government had become firmly anti-Nazi, but many members feared that countering Hitler's regime too forcefully could abet the rise to power of the German Communists and that permitting a countertrial could undermine the authority of national courts.

Legal Counsel

Germany acted harshly toward legal efforts by the defense. The fire trial defendants were confronted with many obstacles in securing lawyers, in part because of the unpopularity of their cause, and also as a result of the Supreme Court's rejection of their own choices. Torgler's attorney, Kurt Rosenfeld (a Jew, and the former Minister of Justice in Prussia), was harassed into leaving Germany. Dimitrov complained that eight lawyers he requested were turned down by the court, and another lawyer he retained dropped out of the case.[36] When the Supreme Court assigned Paul

Teichert to defend Dimitrov, the latter pointed out that he had hired Stepan Detchev, a Bulgarian, and that his sister had retained the services of three French lawyers, one of them being Moro-Giafferi.[37] German authorities were willing to let Detchev assist Teichert, but Teichert did not approve of this arrangement and wouldn't let Detchev see the evidence. As Dimitrov headed toward trial, he had a poor working relationship with Teichert and tried to get him to accept another Bulgarian, Petr Grigorev, as an assistant. Dimitrov also wanted to mount a political defense, a strategy opposed by Teichert. Dimitrov angrily declared that he would conduct his own defense if Teichert didn't cooperate with him.[38]

The idea of foreign lawyers serving as primary counsel was blocked by the Supreme Court. The French could not represent Dimitrov; two Dutchmen were rejected as van der Lubbe's lawyers; and Torgler's effort to retain British counsel was turned down. Two Czechs were also rebuffed. The main reason cited was inadequacy in German. If the aim was only to serve as assistants to German lawyers, it was maintained that foreigners had to be requested by them.[39] Of course, Nazi leaders knew that a Commission of Inquiry was being formed and they were leery of any external involvement in their judicial process. David Levinson, a Philadelphia attorney, was very persistent in trying to become part of the defense team at Leipzig. He asked U.S. ambassador to Germany William Dodd to write a letter to Nazi authorities on his behalf, but Dodd demurred. Teichert said that if foreign lawyers could participate as assistants, he would prefer having a Bulgarian to Levinson. The Supreme Court quashed Levinson's plans but, indirectly, he played a critical role through the recruitment of Arthur Garfield Hays.[40]

Hays, a prominent American civil rights attorney, was a liberal who favored U.S. diplomatic relations with the Soviet Union—but he was not a Communist. In June 1933, he received a cable (similar to those addressed to Felix Frankfurter, Clarence Darrow, and Paul Cravath) from Levinson, who was in Moscow. Levinson, identified by Hays as a Communist, claimed that Dimitrov's mother wanted Hays to assist in the defense. Hays replied positively, but made it clear that he was Jewish and that the German government would possibly try to keep him out of the case. In fact, Germany was in the process of removing all Jewish judges, prosecutors, and lawyers from the courts.

Hays went to Paris to meet with Detchev and Rosenfeld, who were trying to represent Dimitrov and Torgler, respectively. He then convened in Leipzig with Teichert, who had by then been appointed by Germany's Supreme Court to defend all three Bulgarians. Hays unsuccessfully sought an appointment with Chief Justice Wilhelm Buenger, and then sent him a letter asking if evidence from witnesses in exile could be accepted at the Leipzig trial. Such was not to be the case. Hays additionally tried to be assigned as cocounsel for the three Bulgarians, but was told that he did not know German and could only serve as an assistant, at Teichert's request. Hays was agreeable, but Teichert was reluctant because Hays had not told him about his possible participation in the countertrial. Including Hays on his team could thus undermine Teichert's credibility as a loyal officer of the court, should the countertrial point toward Nazi instigation of the fire (as indeed it did). Teichert was probably concerned about possible retribution by his government, so he loudly asserted that both he and the defense were "free and independent."[41] For his part, Hays would have had a potential conflict of interest had he become part of the Leipzig defense team, since he was supposed to be an unbiased member of the Commission of Inquiry. Had he been permitted to play a major role in Leipzig, Hays could presumably have helped solve this problem by dissociating from the Commission's countertrial.

Commission member George Branting also had interaction with the Leipzig legal process. On August 10, chief prosecutor Werner wrote to Branting and Romain Rolland asking if the Commission of Inquiry could supply evidence to the German court. This opening lent crucial legitimacy to Commission involvement. Branting responded that he would turn over evidence to the defense rather than the court, pending approval by his Commission. He also made ten requests regarding the rights of defendants and witnesses. Werner sidestepped most of Branting's concerns, but did make a conditional commitment to provide safe conduct to witnesses based on their person and deeds. The Comintern organ *Inprecorr* interpreted Werner's actions as indicative of the inadequacy of the German evidence, undermining the credibility of the indictment.[42] In the end, Branting did not furnish evidence to either the defense or the court. The real point, however, was that Werner demonstrated an awareness of outside public opinion embodied in the tribunal process; German courts could not just go it alone in such a politically charged case. When the countertrial assembled in London, Torgler's court-appointed lawyer, Alfons Sack, attended the first day's session and invited Branting to come to the Leipzig trial. He refused, in contrast with Hays's strong desire to take part.[43] Hays was prepared to take on the Nazis even though, as a Jew, he was exposing himself to great danger. He was encouraged to participate by members of the Commission of Inquiry, since he could serve as their eyes and ears in Leipzig.

The Commission of Inquiry had not yet completed its mission. The countertrial had focused media attention on Leipzig, and had made Germany's judicial system take cognizance, but this international citizens' tribunal was determined to continue its operation as a shadow legal forum.

Chapter IV

SHOWDOWN IN LEIPZIG

The Nazis had been placed on the defensive in their own court because of the countertrial, so the emphasis was more on exonerating themselves than convicting the Communists. The fairness of their judicial process was being scrutinized by the world's media due to the countertrial's publicity: Could a German court consider the fate of the alleged insurrectionists impartially, or would political considerations turn the defendants into prejudged scapegoats?[1] A right-wing Leipzig newspaper declared: "Only a person with historical perspective can understand the court's plan. The issue is to deal world communism an annihilating blow." Ominously, eleven Communists had been sentenced to death on September 7 in two separate cases of alleged attacks on Nazis.[2]

A protest by about one hundred supporters of the accused demonstrated outside the courthouse as the trial got underway, and it was evident inside that the prosecution was forced to deal with the "Brown Book" and Commission of Inquiry transcript as "invisible defendants."[3] Viewing this spectacle was a multitude of reporters; eighty-two seats were reserved for the foreign press, and forty-one for the German. Propaganda minister Joseph Goebbels complained about such extensive coverage, but Hitler sought political advantage through this Nazi-Bolshevik verbal confrontation and recognized the importance of public opinion in liberal democracies.[4] He also wanted to demonstrate the integrity of German courts.

Days in Court

On September 18, 1933, the defendants were transferred to Leipzig. Three days later, the trial opened in the Fourth Penal Chamber of the Supreme

Court. Presiding over four other judges was Wilhelm Buenger. None was a Nazi, and this was not a special court set up to handle political crimes. The regular German judicial system was at work, and the world watched carefully. In accordance with legal procedures, defense attorneys did not play a prominent role, but defendants did. Hearsay evidence was permitted, and there was little cross-examination. President of the Court Buenger was allowed to consult the pretrial investigatory file, and he also had considerable leeway in questioning witnesses. More than one hundred were called to testify.[5]

The trial had three basic phases. From September 21 through October 7, sessions were held in Leipzig on the events leading up to the Reichstag fire. Testimony by the defendants was featured. From October 10 through November 18, proceedings shifted to Berlin to examine what happened at the time of the fire. It was at this stage that most witnesses were called. From November 23 through December 23, there were again hearings in Leipzig, in which the political aspects of the case were considered, such as the connection between the arson and the alleged uprising planned by the Communists.[6]

Tactical differences led defense attorneys to concentrate on the personal guilt of their clients, not ideology, while the Communist defendants sought a political forum for their viewpoints. Torgler expressed irritation that Alfons Sack was defending him as a person, while he wanted to exonerate the German Communist Party. Sack was a Nazi supporter, thus strengthening his credibility with the court, if not with the rest of the world, but he was not about to take the Communist side in the ideological struggle.[7] Torgler acted submissive and distressed during the trial, and Sack missed fifteen days of the hearings. German Communists, generally, were not pleased with Torgler's performance, which *The New York Times* described as "respectful" and "unprovocative," but Buenger treated Torgler graciously and even bestowed honor by calling him "Herr Torgler."[8]

Van der Lubbe was obviously guilty. He didn't try to present a defense and refused to cooperate with a Dutch lawyer sent by his family to assist him. Van der Lubbe usually appeared disoriented, and perhaps even crazy. He didn't help his lawyer, Philip Seuffert, with the case. Psychiatrists who examined him in March through April 1933 found him to be normal, so one theory regarding his strange behavior is that the unwillingness of German authorities to accept his claim of sole responsibility destabilized him, or, alternatively, led him to dramatize this rebuff by acting as if he was mentally ill.[9]

Nevertheless, a commission of twelve scholars under the leadership of

Swiss historian Walther Hofer has concluded that van der Lubbe was probably an unwitting dupe of the Nazis and was set up to carry out the act without knowing that his instigators were Nazis with links to Goering. Fritz Tobias, a German socialist with no sympathy for the Nazis, had maintained earlier that there was no evidence of Nazi responsibility. He asked, if such was the case, why didn't van der Lubbe implicate his Communist codefendants, or why didn't the Nazis kill him immediately after the fire, in order to render him silent? These questions indeed would have been pertinent, had van der Lubbe known that he was part of a Nazi plot, but Hofer's naive dupe theory undercuts their salience.[10] If van der Lubbe acted alone, as claimed by Tobias, then perhaps he was a competent anti-Nazi activist. British historian H. R. Trevor-Roper described him as "an independent Dutch radical who resolved to show, by a flaming gesture, that not all the European Left would go down in silence before Hitler." Some Dutch scholars similarly question the image of van der Lubbe as a mentally unbalanced man of limited intelligence, instead arguing that he was a hero of the anti-Nazi resistance. The complete truth about van der Lubbe most likely will never be known, since the Nazis "cleansed" the files on the case, and the East German Communists later did likewise.[11]

Popov and Tanev were minor players, mere appendages of the main Bulgarian defendant Dimitrov. The latter's fiery rhetoric mesmerized the audience throughout the trial as he, in effect, made the Nazis the defendants. Dimitrov, not Torgler, was surely the Communist star of the proceedings. Referring to his alleged role in the Sofia cathedral bombing nearly a decade earlier, Dimitrov proclaimed that he was innocent then, just as he was innocent in the fire case. His lawyer Paul Teichert said little before the court, since Dimitrov preferred to act as his own counsel. Dimitrov asserted that his choices for attorneys had been turned down by the court and that he did not have the "necessary confidence" in Teichert.[12] When he asked Teichert to secure a copy of the "Brown Book" for him, Teichert refused. Dimitrov then made the same request to the court, with similar results. Dimitrov pointed out that the prosecution and Sack had referred to the "Brown Book" during the hearings, but was told that he couldn't see it, since it contained "Communist propaganda."[13]

Another of Dimitrov's problems was that he was frequently banished from the courtroom for his aggressive tactics, and then not permitted to read the transcripts of sessions he had missed. He was clearly trying to dramatize what he portrayed as the persecution of the Communists by the Nazis, but in a letter to Buenger, he claimed that his manner in court was a consequence of not knowing the rules of German jurisprudence.[14] Dimitrov also was restricted in questioning Communist witnesses. He had to submit a list of potential questions to the court daily, and some were rejected.[15]

Martha Dodd, the daughter of the American ambassador to Germany, attended the trial and sharply contrasted the behavior and appearance of Dimitrov and Torgler. She described Dimitrov as "a brilliant, attractive dark man emanating the most amazing vitality and courage I have yet seen in a person under stress," and she referred to his "magnificent voice and face." Torgler was "tense, scared, and nerve-racked," and had "a greenish-gray prison pallor on his face." Dimitrov was "burning," whereas Torgler had "a cold, reserved intellectualism."[16]

The prosecution provided an account of the case to journalists just prior to the trial. It was supposedly based on documents seized in the February raid on Karl Liebknecht House, but such items were never introduced in court.[17] The countertrial transcript was also not placed into evidence, despite the efforts of Hays and other supporters of the defense. Werner said he would do so, but after reading it "conscientiously," he changed his mind (perhaps due to Nazi pressure?). This was surely a somewhat unanticipated blow to the defense. Dimitrov later wrote to Pritt: "What a pity that I was unable to know of this material during the trial, and use it in my fight before the Court."[18] Also problematic was that chief prosecutor Werner was not particularly helpful in securing safe conduct guarantees for potential witnesses who were outside Germany. Sack pressed on this issue in order to introduce evidence clearing Torgler, but Werner said that it depended on the specific offenses charged against these individuals and that he could not fully ensure their safety from Nazi "protective arrest."[19] Introducing countertrial testimony by these witnesses would have been an effective backdoor procedure in reference to the Leipzig trial, but Werner successfully blocked that effort as well.

Witnesses included three prominent Nazis who were called to refute charges of their own regime's culpability, and to stress the role played by Nazis in saving Europe from Bolshevism. Buenger said that the testimony of these Nazis was needed to counter "foreign slanders."[20] Goering, the minister of the interior (he had been president of the Reichstag at the time of the fire); Goebbels, the minister of propaganda; and Count Wolf von Helldorf, the Berlin police chief, all testified. Helldorf, as head of the Brown Shirt stormtroopers, had led the roundup of Communists the night of the Reichstag blaze. Mounting the ideological barricades, he declared: "In our view, all criminals against the State are Marxists. The Reichstag fire was a crime against the State. Therefore we arrested all Marxists."[21]

Goering sarcastically observed: "If communism had won, you gentlemen would not be sitting here. The revolutionary tribunal of Herr Dimitrov would have used a shorter procedure."[22]

The charged ideological atmosphere produced a flap right at the outset when two Soviet journalists working for Tass and *Izvestiia,* respectively, were taken from their beds to police headquarters. They were held for eight hours, and released after a protest from the Soviet embassy. The Leipzig police chief apologized, blaming subordinates for "mistakes." Hitler used the occasion to suggest that relations with Moscow were not strong, but he didn't want to provide any pretext for breaking them.[23] Dimitrov's important Comintern role was not revealed in court until the very end of the trial, and Goering explained while testifying: "What happens in Russia is of no interest to me. I have only to deal with the German Communist Party, and with the foreign crooks who come here to fire the Reichstag."[24]

The Leipzig trial demonstrated that accusations by the Commission of Inquiry had to be parried in order to assure world public opinion, which was generally skeptical about Nazi justice. Not only did Nazi leaders rally to protect their government's image, but the Supreme Court did not resort to any in camera sessions that were legally permissible. The court also did not interfere with the defense's right to present its own witnesses available in Germany, nor with the ability of defense witnesses to assist their clients, and it organized an inspection of the tunnel from Goering's residence to the Reichstag as an obvious response to allegations raised at the counter-trial and in the "Brown Book," regarding Nazi complicity. When chief investigatory magistrate Paul Vogt testified, he felt as if he was under assault when questioned about misleading van der Lubbe by telling him that Torgler had confessed. He self-righteously declared: "I am a German judge. I am a member of the Supreme Court and, besides, my name is Vogt. I have never done anything contrary to the honor of a German judge."[25]

The Course of Justice

The Nazis' party program of 1920 called for the replacing of Roman law with German common law. Once in power, they effected this change, with crimes against the state being punished more severely. The concept of a "living constitution" stressed civic duties rather than individual rights for, as Prussian Minister of Justice Hans Kerrl advocated, there should be no objective law—only what serves the German nation and people.[26]

Within this context, the retroactive law on "revolutionary arson" was used against the fire trial defendants. Legal precedent had already been set in the case of Oswald Maly, who was accused of inciting a minor to commit arson. The prosecution had requested the death penalty, but a Berlin court sentenced him to fifteen years in prison.[27] Surely van der Lubbe had torched the Reichstag, so the issue was whether he had accomplices who were part of a treasonous conspiracy. Both the Nazis and the Communists claimed that he did, but van der Lubbe insisted that he had acted alone. This stance made it difficult for the Communists on trial and the Dutchman to present a common defense.[28]

The prosecution recognized that Dimitrov had an airtight alibi, so any connection to the fire would have to be based on "advice or psychological influence." A link had to be established between him and van der Lubbe, acting as part of a Communist conspiracy, so Werner maintained that the latter "felt and behaved as a Communist," even though he had not been a party member since 1931.[29] Evidence tying Communists to the fire was weak, but it was important to demonstrate that they were morally responsible. Also, to prove treason under the "revolutionary arson" law, collusion had to be shown in order to validate the treason charge.[30]

Goering testified that van der Lubbe had not been hanged immediately because he was needed as a witness against the other conspirators. The Dutchman refused to play this role, and appeared to be in despair during the trial since his anti-Nazi act of arson had unintentionally involved innocent Communists. His lawyer, Seuffert, argued that van der Lubbe should not be subjected to a death sentence since he was merely a petty criminal, not a conspirator.[31] On November 23, a frustrated van der Lubbe said that the trial was too long; he wanted a rapid verdict, even if it meant capital punishment for him. President of the Court Buenger replied that the length was because of van der Lubbe's unwillingness to name accomplices, but van der Lubbe countered that there weren't any. He explained: "The whole trial has gone wrong because of all this symbolism and I an sick of it." Werner asked, what symbolism? Seuffert then cited the prosecution argument that the fire had been a signal for a Communist uprising. Van der Lubbe then remarked: "It was a matter of ten minutes or, at most, a quarter of an hour. I did it all by myself."[32] Van der Lubbe may have been broken physically and psychologically, but not ethically.

In defending the three Bulgarians and Torgler, Teichert and Sack relied on the conclusions drawn at the countertrial. Teichert had a problem because the Bulgarians had lied about their activities in Germany. He acknowledged their dishonesty, but argued that this did not connect them in any way to the Reichstag blaze.[33] Dimitrov defiantly asked for financial compensation for the four Communists, and criminal liability for his accusers, on the ground of filing false charges. He proclaimed that a future proletarian dictatorship would ascertain the true perpetrators of the fire.[34] He knew that the whole Leipzig process was an ideological exercise, and he concurred with Kerrl that there was no objective law—even high treason was a relative concept "dependent on time and circumstances." Dimitrov wrote in his notes: "I can no more believe in the blind Goddess of Justice, Themis, than I can believe in the existence of a God."[35] Nazis and Communists basically agreed on the importance of ideology in their confrontation; it was the lawyers who tried to concentrate on individual responsibility.

In his closing statement, chief prosecutor Werner denied Nazi guilt for the fire and rebutted the claims of the "Brown Book." He also reversed course and called for the acquittal of the three Bulgarians because of a lack of evidence. Werner recommended death sentences for van der Lubbe and Torgler. Van der Lubbe wept when Werner advocated Torgler's execution, but was complacent in regard to his own possible fate.[36] The case against Torgler was actually weakened when Werner asked for the acquittal of the Bulgarians, since many of the witnesses testifying against Dimitrov and his fellow comrades were also prominent in presenting evidence against Torgler. For his part, Dimitrov resented Werner's remark that there was a lack of evidence against the three Bulgarians; he wanted a definitive statement declaring that they had played no role in the entire affair.[37]

Werner's remarks on acquittal were attuned to an attitude that the trial had been unsuccessful for the Nazis. Goering said it "had disappointed the entire German people," and that it was necessary to go beyond the law on criminal cases of a political nature. The right wing newspaper *Boersen Zeitung* predicted the acquittal of Torgler and the virulently pro-Nazi *Volkische Beobachter* expressed concern that a negative finding in regard to arson would produce an acquittal on the charge of treason. Even before a verdict was announced, German newspapers were pressing for a new trial for the Bulgarians and Torgler.[38] The implication was that van der Lubbe would be found guilty, and Torgler innocent. Actually, Goering himself had undermined the prosecution's case during his own turn on the stand. He had threatened Dimitrov's death after the trial, no matter what its outcome, thereby acknowledging the possibility that he would be adjudged not guilty. At the same time, Goering shattered any illusions about the Nazi system of justice and galvanized world opinion against the Leipzig proceedings.[39]

Keeping Watch

As the Leipzig trial convened in September, an editorial in *The New York Times* greeted it with the observation that it would have to respond to the countertrial's conclusions and evidence, which had affected world opinion and the conscience of the German people.[40] This turned out to be the case as the prosecution and Nazi witnesses did their best to refute its findings. Of course, there was an element of resentment for, as Goering queried, would the American, British, and French members of the Commission of Inquiry defend the interference of a countertrial in the judicial affairs of their own countries?[41] An editorial in *The Times* backed the German perspective and Austen Chamberlain (a critic of Nazism) told the House of Commons that decisions of a foreign court should not be prejudged. He also expressed concern about British-German relations in such circumstances. Even George Bernard Shaw, a stalwart of the left, feared that outside pressure could be counterproductive and lead to the execution of the defendants.[42]

Nevertheless, the countertrial lawyers continued the battle of public opinion against the Leipzig trial. Many of them (including Hays and Moro-Giafferi, but not Pritt) met in Paris on October 4 and 5, where they heard witnesses, including Dimitrov's sister, Elena. The session concluded that all defendants other than van der Lubbe were innocent and, in order to link the Dutchman to the Nazis, that he was actually an anticommunist.[43] On November 17 Elena Dimitrova was greeted with verses from the Communist anthem "The Internationale" when she appeared at a rally in London. In a performance that must have caused consternation among the more moderate supporters of the Commission of Inquiry, she referred to the four Communist defendants as sons of the working class, portrayed events in the framework of a capitalist-proletarian struggle, and predicted that the workers would soon rule the world.[44]

From December 18 through 20, just prior to the Leipzig verdict, members of the Commission of Inquiry met again in London. They already knew that Werner had called for the acquittal of the Bulgarians, so the focus was on Torgler. He was proclaimed innocent and the German court was warned not to execute him as this would constitute "judicial murder" and engender "universal protest." This international citizens' tribunal asserted that documents citing a Communist plot in conjunction with the Reichstag fire probably didn't exist and that the arson was carried out by the Nazis. Van der Lubbe did not act alone.[45]

Supporters of the countertrial tried to rally public opinion, especially in the United States and Britain. On November 11 Hays cited a telegram from the Commission of Inquiry predicting that Germany would end the trial quickly and execute the defendants. Immediate action was needed. That same day David Levinson participated in a protest outside the German consulate in New York and hyperbolically claimed that death sentences would be issued in three days. German consul Johannes Borchers responded that protest should not precede the court's verdict. The American Civil Liberties Union and the American Committee Against Fascist Oppression in Germany, sent letters to German ambassador Hans Luther—with Hays among the signatories of the latter group's communication.[46] Later, coinciding with the countertrial's London session, there were Communist demonstrations at the German embassy in London and at the consulate in New York.[47]

Germany did not sit idly by. A British journalist, Noel Panter, was arrested for publishing an unflattering account of Nazism that was deemed treasonous and based on espionage. Probably not so fortuitous was the announcement that he was to be tried in Leipzig. British Foreign Secretary John Simon protested to the German ambassador and Panter was released five days afterward for lack of evidence.[48] Neither Germany nor Britain openly related the Panter case to London's hosting of the countertrial, but such a connection appears likely.

The Commission of Inquiry encouraged Arthur Garfield Hays to be their main link to the fire trial. He then provided legal advice, almost served as a witness, and acted as an invited observer of the court process. *The New York Times* referred to him as a "mediator" between the countertrial and the German court. Teichert had not wanted Hays on the defense team for the Bulgarians, but Buenger suggested that he work with Torgler's lawyer, Alfons Sack, who had developed a good relationship with Hays at the London countertrial. Sack was offended and offered to withdraw from the case. Torgler didn't want Hays's participation. It was then agreed that Hays would only assist Sack, and the American announced that he wouldn't be so presumptuous as to defend a client in a German court.[49] He was not German-speaking, and not knowledgeable about German law. Hays's concern about being Jewish never developed as an issue, with Hays believing that the Nazis did not malign him because they thought that he was an official representative of the U.S. Bar Association. He also had a protective cover, as the Encyclopedia Britannica had asked him to write an article on the trial.[50]

Hays gave Sack some evidence furnished by Communists who feared involvement with German defense lawyers and he convinced Sack to introduce sections of the countertrial testimony that he felt supportive of Torgler's innocence. Sack would not use countertrial and "Brown Book" charges of Nazi complicity in the fire.[51] He was, however, willing to present Hays as a witness to introduce evidence from the countertrial transcript. Hays, preferring that Sack take the lead on this, reluctantly agreed. Prosecutor Karl Werner then short-circuited the matter by objecting. When Hays was called to the stand, the court did not permit him to testify.[52]

Five foreign lawyers, including Hays, acted as trial observers. The others were Leo Gallagher (American), Marcel Villard (French), and the aforementioned Stepan Detchev and Petr Grigorev (Bulgarian). Hays and Gallagher had been invited by Sack; the others were there independently. In accordance with a new Prussian law that foreign lawyers had to be "nationally dependable," these gentlemen were deemed observers rather than participants—but they surely did not prove "dependable."[53] A confrontation with the court quickly developed, as four observers (excluding Hays) protested the treatment of Dimitrov and challenged evidence that contradicted testimony given to Commission of Inquiry investigators by a Dutch police commander. Going further, they wrote to a judge that the trial was a frame-up and that Teichert was a Nazi stooge. They were expelled from the courtroom and ordered to leave Germany. Gallagher, a former law professor, was then given permission to remain in the country because he was there at the invitation of Sack.[54] Hays distanced himself from the other legal observers, preferring tact to confrontation.

Hays left Germany on October 28, while the trial was still in its second stage. In his appearances on returning to the United States, he stressed the importance of the Commission of Inquiry and public opinion and predicted that all except van der Lubbe would be found not guilty. He indicated, perhaps tactically rather than analytically, that the German court process appeared to be fair and that defense lawyers were performing effectively. Before going to Leipzig, he had expected that the trial would be a farce, with defense lawyers only making "a pretense" of defending their clients. Hays declared: "It is a test of whether the courts and the old type of Germans, who are Nazis only because of expediency, are controlled by the Hitler government."[55] Maintaining consistency in his civil libertarian viewpoint, Hays supported free speech and the right of public assembly for American Nazis, arguing that the United States had to retain its democratic principles and not resort to fascist behavior.[56]

The Verdict

Hays wrote to the Leipzig court just before the verdict was issued: "If these men are acquitted, the world will realize that at least one court in Germany is objective and independent and that even in the midst of terror instituted by the Nazis, you judges have shown the courage of your convictions."[57] His expressed degree of faith in the court proved to be well-founded. On December 23 it acquitted the three Bulgarians and Torgler for lack of evidence. Van der Lubbe was found guilty of "high treason, insurrectionary arson, and attempted common arson," and was sentenced to death.[58] The court was prepared to spurn the prosecution on the issue of Torgler's guilt, but it also deferred to Nazi sensibilities and did not want it to appear that they had started the Reichstag fire. After all, who had carried out the act in collusion with van der Lubbe, if all of the defendants had been acquitted? The court therefore affirmed the prosecution's argument that there had been a Communist conspiracy. Communists purportedly planned an insurrection and they were responsible for the arson.[59] The Nazis, it was claimed, had no reason to set the fire, since they were going to win the Reichstag election anyway. The court affirmed: "The party's ethical principles of restraint preclude the very possibility of such crimes and actions as are ascribed to them by unprincipled agitators."[60]

The Communists won the case, as they were acquitted and had successfully used the court as a revolutionary forum. They had also forced the prosecution into a defensive posture, attempting to refute "Brown Book" and countertrial charges of Nazi complicity. The court also won, demonstrating its independence by allowing Communist defendants to present their case and even accuse Nazis of crimes. The prosecution did go overboard in its conspiracy charges, but recognized by the end of the trial that the three Bulgarians were not guilty. The defense attorneys served their clients well, but were careful not to attribute the arson to the Nazis. Sack, a pro-Nazi, said it would be beneath the level of a German lawyer to introduce the charges made in the "Brown Book."[61]

Controversy surrounds a possible Nazi-Soviet deal regarding the trial, for if true, it renders moot the triumph of justice in a German court and the impact of the countertrial supporters and world public opinion. The argument advanced is that Stalin and Hitler had their own interests in undermining Ernst Roehm's stormtroopers, which would be weakened by the acquittal of the Reichstag defendants. That is why the prosecution downplayed Dimitrov's Comintern and Soviet connections and why Dimitrov acted so boldly at the trial—he knew he would be found not guilty.[62]

Evidence for this theory is thin, since fairly cordial Soviet-German relations in the face of the trial does not necessarily lead to the conclusion that the verdict was based on a deal.[63]

Circumstantial evidence points to a division within the Soviet camp. Litvinov, the foreign minister (and a Jew), rejected close ties to Germany, but was opposed by Prime Minister Vyacheslav Molotov and the Comintern specialist on Germany (and also a Jew), Karl Radek. Without Litvinov's knowledge, Molotov met with German ambassador Herbert von Dirksen while the trial was in session–and allegedly treated him lavishly. When Dirksen was soon replaced by Rudolf Nadolny, the new ambassador arrived in Moscow with instructions to develop good relations (but he also warned about interference in internal affairs).[64] In addition, the November 28 meeting of the Comintern's executive committee did not emphasize the fire trial, nor mention it in the final resolution.[65]

There probably wasn't any deal. The two countries just had a vested interest in continued military collaboration and a common strategic perspective regarding a potentially resurgent Poland. If there was a deal, Goering could not have known about it when he threatened Dimitrov's life and proclaimed the trial a "disappointment." The acquittal of four defendants most likely was due to the lack of evidence and the judges' integrity, plus the influence of the countertrial and world public opinion. These latter factors may not have been enough to sway the verdict on their own, but they surely focused media attention on Hitler's regime and forced him to accept that even in Nazi Germany, justice could be allowed to take its course. The first international citizens' tribunal had temporarily achieved its goal of getting innocent defendants acquitted by pressuring the German court to adhere to the rule of law—but the battle was not yet over. The Nazis soon came up with a countermeasure more suited to the advancement of the ideological needs of a totalitarian state, which then undercut the verdict and produced a new confrontation over the fire trial defendants.

Chapter V

AFTERMATH

The Leipzig verdict was assailed by the German media, and the Nazi party's press bureau proclaimed that true justice "has its roots in the feelings of the people." It decried "alien liberalistic reasoning," which prevented the court from removing the "communist menace" from Germany. Judicial reform was therefore essential to establish "true law."[1] For most outside observers, the opposite interpretation predominated—namely, that the German court had acted fairly and the innocent had been exonerated. In Britain, home of the countertrial, there was little disagreement over the end result, but the issue of foreign pressure on the court remained controversial. Leftists credited the Commission of Inquiry and public opinion with being major influences on the verdict, and were critical of the court's attachment to the Communist conspiracy thesis. The Commission of Inquiry gladly took the credit, and claimed that it had forced the defendants to be tried in the "court of world opinion." Conservatives stressed the court's objectivity and condemned "busybodies" who affronted the German legal system by having called for the acquittal of defendants before the trial had taken place.[2] Quickly, however, the need for external leverage again became apparent as Germany shocked the world's sensibilities. Acquittal did not turn out to mean freedom for the defendants! What countertrial chairman D. N. Pritt termed the "second stage" of public opinion was thus set in motion.[3]

Measured Justice

In his fire trial testimony, Hermann Goering had ominously placed German justice under suspicion when he fumed at Dimitrov: "You have reason to be afraid when you leave the custody of this court!" The minister of the interior asserted that the guilty would be punished, irrespective of the court's verdict.[4] Anticipating acquittals as the trial neared completion, pro-Nazi newspapers advocated new trials for Torgler and the Bulgarians on the ground of treason. This charge would be decoupled from the arson accusation made in Leipzig.[5] Such subversive foreshadowing turned into reality after the verdict when the four acquitted defendants were placed in "protective custody." Those who had been fighting to prove their innocence had reason to fear the worst as four German Communists under detention (including Central Committee member John Scheer) were mysteriously killed.[6]

Efforts to free the acquitted defendants were made along several tracks. A committee, including a secretary to Lord Marley, attempted to negotiate with the German government about an armed guard that could escort the four men across the Czechoslovak border—from where they could possibly proceed to the Soviet Union or France.[7] At the same time, members of the Commission of Inquiry asked French supporters Andre Gide and Andre Malraux to go on a mission to Berlin. It proved useless, since Nazi leaders were then attending a conference in Munich. The Frenchmen only managed to leave a letter of concern.[8] Leo Gallagher, who had remained in Germany after being removed from the Leipzig courtroom, was also active, even as he was in the process of being deported. Backed financially by Dimitrov's sister, he lobbied for the release of the Bulgarians and addressed an appeal to Goering.[9] Dimitrov wrote to the Leipzig police chief inquiring as to why he was still detained, on whose authority, and when he would be released. His mother visited the interior ministry on his behalf and she and Tanev's wife brought a Bulgarian lawyer to Germany to assist them. Bulgarian relatives of the defendants were threatened with expulsion if they continued to talk to reporters and a Bulgarian who had acted as an interpreter for the defendants during the trial was deported.[10] For its part, Germany tried to assure the outside world that the prisoners were not in danger. On January 23, photos appeared in both the German and world press showing the three Bulgarians reading newspapers and playing chess.[11]

British attitudes toward Germany, which had become more cordial as a result of the Leipzig verdict, rapidly shifted. *The Times*, which had treated the Nazi regime rather gently, began to hammer away at the continued imprisonment of the acquitted defendants and warned that Germany was unintentionally improving the Communist image at the expense of its own. Committees, one secretly backed by Muenzenberg, were formed to free the prisoners and there were demonstrations against Germany.[12] Britain's Defense Requirements Committee (comprising military, foreign service, and treasury representatives) reported to the Cabinet on February 28 that Germany had become the country's greatest strategic threat, despite Japanese expansionism.[13] Stafford Cripps, who had greeted the London countertrial, was so alarmed by Nazism that he called for the organization of a private army of British socialists and communists to counter the internal fascist threat. His Labour Party decried such an undemocratic proposal and rejected a common front with the Communists, but it was indicative of the prevailing fearful mood. The German media ridiculed what it saw as British alarmism, claiming that it was because of a lack of experience with Communist terrorism.[14]

Dimitrov and his fellow Bulgarians had worried since their arrests that Germany would extradite them to Bulgaria to face old criminal charges. Now the situation had changed, as their lives were endangered in a German prison—they wanted to get out at any cost. Emboldened by his success at Leipzig, Dimitrov subsequently telegrammed the Bulgarian prime minister, seeking safe conduct to return to challenge the Sofia cathedral conviction. The reaction, as his mother learned from the Bulgarian embassy in Berlin, was that he, Popov, and Tanev had been deprived of their Bulgarian citizenship.[15] The Soviet connection then became crucial.

Wilhelm Pieck, a prominent German Communist, served as a liaison between Berlin and Moscow. Apparently, with German government encouragement, he met on December 28 with the Comintern's Orgburo chairman, Ossip Piatnitsky, and asked him to sound out Stalin on whether the Soviet Union would consider giving political asylum to the three Bulgarians. Torgler was not included in the request because he was a German citizen and the Nazis wanted to keep him in prison as part of their campaign against internal Communists.[16] While considering some deal with Germany, the Soviet Union was careful not to be antagonistic, and so the Leipzig trial wasn't even mentioned at the January through February 1934 Soviet party congress and the Comintern attributed the favorable verdict to Hitler rather than the judiciary.[17]

The Soviets had difficulty communicating with the imprisoned Bulgarians, but moved with alacrity, once learning that they had been stripped of their Bulgarian citizenship. On February 15, the Soviet Union granted them citizenship. The next day, via the Berlin embassy, a request was made for their repatriation. Hitler acceded and the German foreign ministry announced on February 17 that they would be released.[18] Goering then obstructed matters. In a February 20 interview with a German newspaper, he said that even if Dimitrov did not set the Reichstag fire, he still deserved to die for his prior activities. Goering opined: "If his side had won they would have hung us up without mercy. I see no reason why we should be more considerate." He declared that Dimitrov would remain in prison as "such a man is too dangerous to be let loose on society." Goering admitted that "perhaps Dimitrov did not set the Reichstag on fire" but that he "did his best to inflame the German people."[19] Hitler assured a British journalist that all three Bulgarians would be freed and expelled, stating "surely they will." A letter to *The Times* then tartly commented: "If the prisoners are not released within a few days the world will know that the Fuehrer is as frightened of General Goering as General Goering is of Dimitrov."[20]

Goering retreated after his chancellor's remarks, maintaining that he did not have any disagreement with Hitler. He explained that the release of the prisoners had been delayed as a reaction to pressure from the foreign press. Goering also put forth the claim that he had favored their release but had unintentionally discoursed on Dimitrov to mislead the press so it wouldn't find out details about their departure.[21]

On February 27, the anniversary of the Reichstag fire, the Bulgarians left Berlin as deportees en route to Koenigsberg. Carrying Soviet passports, they passed through Polish territory and then flew to Moscow from the East Prussian city. Three passengers were bumped and the release of the Bulgarians was not revealed until they were airborne. Almost one hundred journalists interviewed them on arrival in the Soviet capital, since the Kremlin wanted publicity for what it viewed as Dimitrov's victory over the Nazis. Dimitrov thanked "the great mass of honest intelligentsia in all countries who struggled for our liberation," and defiantly declared: "I hope to return as the guest of the German Soviet Republic." Meanwhile, the Soviet embassy in Berlin indicated that it would not offer citizenship to Torgler and the German government stated that the delay in releasing the acquitted defendants had been because of Bulgaria's slow response in clarifying their citizenship status.[22]

Dimitrov was lionized in Moscow because in Leipzig he had defended the Communist cause and effectively assailed the Nazis. On April 7 he attended a Politburo session where he was warmly greeted by Stalin. He was also made the de facto head of the Comintern, and officially assumed this post in August 1935. Once the Communists assumed control in East Germany, the area adjacent to the Leipzig courthouse was renamed Dimitrov Square.[23] Tanev died in combat in World War II, while Popov became a Bulgarian diplomat once the Communists gained power in that country at the end of the war.

Standoff

After Leipzig, the focus was on the Bulgarians, with the acquitted Torgler lost in the shuffle. The Soviet Union did not press for his release, perhaps due to his submissive performance at the trial and his January 1934 promise to the Nazis that he would not engage in political activities. The Germans claimed that he was no longer being held for his own protection, but for investigation of his role in a Communist conspiracy. A new trial was being considered, but it never took place. Torgler accommodated himself to the Nazis, was freed in June 1935, and continued to live in Germany. He was expelled from the German Communist Party.[24] Van der Lubbe, who was sentenced to death, was clearly guilty and was never a cause celebre among leftists, who had tried to link him to the Nazis. The Dutch government protested on his behalf, emphasizing his conviction under an ex post facto law, and requested clemency. Appeals were rejected on January 9, 1934 and he was guillotined the following day. Germany refused to return his body to the Netherlands, perhaps fearing a martyr's shrine, and he was buried in Leipzig. There is now a movement in van der Lubbe's home town, Leiden, to have his remains repatriated.[25]

For the Communists and most anti-Nazis, the major concern was the release of Communist Party Chairman Ernst Thaelmann. He had been arrested on March 3, 1933, but had never been charged with participating in the Reichstag arson, nor brought to trial. A German lawyer who tried to represent him was disbarred and then imprisoned for two years.[26] After the Leipzig verdict a Thaelmann trial on the ground of high treason was scheduled. World opinion then forced Germany to prevaricate and there were nine postponements. The Nazis wanted to make sure that acquittals such as those at Leipzig could not happen again and they were particularly distressed by the not guilty verdict on Torgler, a German citizen. In April 1934 the government therefore decided to establish people's courts, comprised of two judges and five Nazi party (or military) lay judges. The aim was to secure convictions for treason and sedition, and all anti-Nazi or procommunist acts were considered to be treasonous. Defendants would not be allowed to choose counsel. There would be no legal representation during the preliminary proceedings, and the court would appoint lawyers for the trial.[27] The Comintern pertinently referred to the "Thaelmann law" on people's courts and predicted that "this law means the death sentence against Thaelmann."[28]

At an October 3, 1934 Berlin conclave on the Thaelmann case, attended by fire trial prosecutor Karl Werner, it was decided that the

Leipzig format had to be scrapped in favor of a people's court. In an effort to head off foreign protests, there would be only short notice on the trial date and a quick judicial procedure. There would be no attempt to connect Thaelmann to the fire (the linkage strategy had backfired when used against Torgler and the Bulgarians), just to a planned Communist insurrection.[29]

Outside pressure was already building up on the prosecution. In March, an appeal for Thaelmann's release had been sent to Hitler by British citizens; in October, there was a rally in London at which a telegram from two bishops to Hitler was read. It objected to a trial in people's court and requested a regular public trial and the right to appoint counsel. Pritt remarked that such protests had saved Dimitrov's life.[30]

Communists were highly active in support of their comrade, Thaelmann. The Comintern's press service produced a barrage of articles on the Thaelmann case. The main theme was that public opinion had worked at Leipzig; Dimitrov had been acquitted and freed. Dimitrov had additionally been able to use the trial to promote communist ideology. Thaelmann should similarly be given his day in court. Thaelmann, it asserted, as "the leader of the coming Soviet Germany . . . will defeat the fascist murderers before the court, as Dimitrov defeated them in the Reichstag trial."[31] Dimitrov, at a press conference and in a pamphlet, prophetically declared that securing Thaelmann's release would be more difficult than it had been to attain his own freedom. Nazi justice could not resolve the situation; only public relations could induce Hitler to act. Dimitrov observed that the Nazis had to be shown that it was in their political interest not to execute Thaelmann.[32]

World opinion remained the key. The countertrial had altered the legal course of Nazi Germany, so continued pressure was to be used to save Thaelmann. Indirectly, the first international citizens' tribunal had kept him alive, as he was never brought to trial. Thaelmann then continued to stay in prison while the clash between foreign opinion and Nazi justice produced a standoff. In 1944, Thaelmann was killed—probably while interned at Buchenwald. Germany announced that he had died in an American air raid. Other evidence suggests that he was murdered by the SS.[33]

Hays *Redux*

After the Bulgarians found refuge in Moscow, American opponents of Nazism continued their public relations battle against the Hitler regime. On March 7, 1934, a mock trial of the German chancellor was staged in

Madison Square Garden in New York. Organized by the American Federation of Labor and the American Jewish Congress, it heard witnesses for four hours and then the twenty thousand "jurors" unanimously found Hitler guilty of "crimes against civilization." Arthur Garfield Hays was among the participants.[34] There also was an American Committee Against Fascist Oppression in Germany, which had a legal focus and was particularly concerned about the new people's courts. It had hoped to include Pritt, Cripps, and Moro-Giafferi in its sessions.[35]

Arthur Garfield Hays had been the link between the Commission of Inquiry and the Leipzig trial. The Commission's secretariat then remained in operation as the chief coordinator of the anti-Nazi effort, and Hays extended its activities into the United States. He formed an American Commission of Inquiry, and attracted Clarence Darrow as its chair. Hays was so anxious to include the prominent trial lawyer that he wrote: "If when the time comes you cannot be there much of the time, no harm will be done." He also iterated that if Darrow missed sessions, he could count on Hays's reports to be representative of Darrow's viewpoint.[36]

Hays invited German ambassador Hans Luther to attend hearings, either as an observer or as a lawyer entitled to engage in the cross-examination of witnesses. Luther demurred, since Germany did not want to be involved officially in what would surely be a strongly anti-Nazi forum. However, a German-American attorney named Alphonse Koelble then proposed that he do the cross-examining. This would have amounted to an indirect German role, as Koelble was clearly pro-Nazi. His letter to Hays, a Jew, pulled no punches: "I have a high regard for the sincerity and integrity of those members of your proposed Board whom I know but having in mind the power of the Jews, their racial solidarity and loyalty, and the 'London Investigation' of the burning of the Reichstag building and the so-called 'trial' of the Hitler Government at Madison Square Garden, I am justified in feeling that the Board may be planned, or at least be turned into a vehicle for Jewish propaganda." Koelble's attempt to participate was rejected unless he could secure official authorization from the German embassy or consulate, or from the Friends of New Germany. The organizers assumed that the German government was actually behind his effort, so it should own up to it. Koelble ended up not serving at the Commission's hearings.[37]

The American Commission of Inquiry met in New York on July 2 and 3, 1934. The focus was on people's courts and the need to rally opinion against Germany so that they could not be used to convict Thaelmann and Torgler. The Commission's aim was clearly to help keep these men alive.

At another session in October, the alleged Nazi role in the Reichstag fire was investigated.[38] An interesting aspect of the anti-Nazi campaign was the appearance in the United States of Willi Muenzenberg, the Comintern's chief publicist against Hitlerism. Seeking to raise funds, Muenzenberg spoke in six major cities and was the guest of honor at a reception in New York.[39]

Hays was a leading proponent of international citizens' tribunals, as well as a prominent anti-Nazi activist. Cooperating with Communists in a common struggle was deemed necessary, but Hays was never attracted to the Marxist-Leninist cause and always tried to keep legal tribunals free from Communist influence. The countertrial in London and the Commission in New York, were independent bodies attempting to serve justice— although Communists such as Dimitrov and Thaelmann were beneficiaries of their endeavors. World public opinion was the vehicle transporting some degree of the rule of law into Nazi Germany, but it was only temporarily and partially successful. This was ruefully acknowledged by Hays when commemorating the three-year anniversary of the fire trial verdict, as he decried the development of German people's courts and observed: "On the theory that the German government was anxious to appear civilized, it was assumed that the victory in the Reichstag case might affect governmental policy. Yet the tyranny of the Nazi regime has become increasingly more brutal."[40]

After the Reichstag fire case, Hays remained committed to the concept of international citizens' tribunals. Whereas he had worked in conjunction with pro-Soviet Communists against the Nazis, his new target was the Soviet Union and its Moscow show trials of "enemies of the people."

Chapter VI

DEEP FREEZE

On December 1, 1934, a mentally unbalanced thirty-year-old Soviet Communist named Leonid Nikolaev fatally shot Leningrad Communist Party leader Sergei Kirov, thereby ushering in a series of events eerily reminiscent of those surrounding the Reichstag fire. Nikolaev was a social misfit who often changed jobs and who had been expelled from the party in March of that year. In May he had been reinstated, with the explanation that his strange behavior had been due to nervous fatigue as a consequence of his previous work in the Arctic city of Murmansk. Nikolaev had difficulty finding a new job and he felt that the influential Kirov should have responded to his written entreaties for assistance. He saw Kirov's lack of involvement as symptomatic of the bureaucratic inadequacies of the Communist Party and he came to believe that the Party was betraying the 1917 revolution. Perhaps an act of martyrdom could attract attention to this historic tragedy?

The Kirov assassination case was like the Reichstag fire revisited, with Nikolaev as the new van der Lubbe. Again there was a question about sole responsibility for a crime. Nikolaev's diary provided no indication that others may have participated in the plot; he maintained during interrogation that the killing had been committed by him alone and that there were no accomplices. Stalin ominously had a different interpretation.[1]

Parallels

On the day of the assassination, Stalin labeled Nikolaev a "Zinovievite." This was a clear indication that he was going to use the event as a pretext to round up his perceived political opponents, just as Hitler had done after blaming the Reichstag blaze on the Communists. Stalin had been wary about Grigory Zinoviev and his ally Lev Kamenev, who had been part of the so-called Left Opposition that Stalin deemed to be sympathetic to his arch enemy, Leon Trotsky, during the post-Lenin power struggle. Trotsky was already in exile, but Zinoviev and Kamenev could conceivably, in Stalin's rather paranoiac mind, rally internal opposition forces against him. They were prominent revolutionaries and original members of the Polit-buro. They had been party chiefs in Leningrad and Moscow, respectively, and Zinoviev had served as the president of the Comintern.

Also, on that same day, Stalin moved quickly on the legal front in an effort to avoid a repetition of what had gone awry for Hitler in the Reich-stag fire case. Stalin could not countenance any international campaign or countertrial, so he issued a directive on the handling of terrorist crimes that permitted trials without resort to appeals or requests for clemency. The decree became law that night when it was signed by Abel Yenukidze, Sec-retary of the Presidium of the Central Executive Committee (parliament). As Nikita Khrushchev later explained in his 1956 "secret speech," this decree "became the basis for mass acts of abuse against socialist legality."[2]

Stalin at once took personal control over the investigation and went to Leningrad to interrogate Nikolaev. The psychologically fragile perpetrator did not deny his own guilt, but Stalin was unable to coerce him into any meaningful confession regarding accomplices that could stand up in court. Thirteen "Zinovievites" were arrested and charged with complicity, but only two could be forced to confess. Stalin therefore realized that a trial of the accused would have to be carried out in secret. He contacted judge Vassily Ulrikh and told him to apply the death penalty. The fourteen defendants then appeared in court on December 28 and 29. After the tes-timony but prior to sentencing, Ulrikh asked Stalin for more time, which he said was needed for additional investigation. He tried to entice Stalin with the argument that more terrorists could possibly be linked to the case, but the Soviet general-secretary would have none of it and ordered "finish it."[3] All were found guilty and executed. Ulrikh seemed to have had mis-givings about the strength of the case, but his acquiescence to Stalin was hidden because of the closed judicial process. In the fire trial Buenger was able to adhere to the law as he saw fit, and not submit to political pressure, because the trial was public and his fairness was being evaluated by the media.

Zinoviev and Kamenev were arrested in December 1934 for their sup-posed conspiratorial roles in conjunction with Nikolaev. On January 15, 1935, most likely because of the absence of confessions, they were put on trial secretly, along with five others. The charge was not any direct role in Kirov's assassination but, rather, having had counterrevolutionary ideas that contributed to his murder. Zinoviev and Kamenev were portrayed as bearing moral responsibility and possessing a terroristic frame of mind. Ironically, Communists had challenged Germany on the very same issue in regard to four of the fire trial defendants. Stalin seems to have learned from the German experience that including a charge of actual involvement in a plot was not really necessary, and could only complicate matters. On January 16 Zinoviev and Kamenev were convicted and sentenced to ten and five years, respectively.[4]

Confrontation

The Reichstag fire trial had not yet produced a verdict when Goering issued a statement bemoaning the inability of the legal system "to judge" the defendants appropriately, in a manner commensurate with Nazi wishes, or "to expiate" German society by rooting out Communists (purportedly) responsible for political crimes against the state.[5] Goering realized that the Leipzig trial had turned Dimitrov from being an accused criminal into a defiant hero. So did Stalin and his accomplices when they began to prepare the Moscow show trials. The prosecution charged prominent Communists with counterrevolutionary acts aimed at undermining the Soviet system in collusion with Leon Trotsky. Stalin was determined to prevent the charismatic and eloquent Trotsky from becoming another Dimitrov, either by permitting him to testify in Moscow or by appearing before any external commission of inquiry. Trotsky avidly sought to move toward center stage, where he could condemn Stalinism. A contest of wills thus developed, as Stalin tried to disparage Trotsky while keeping him on ice. Trotsky sought to come in out of the coldness of exile and isolation by capturing the media spotlight, as had Dimitrov at Leipzig.

Leon Trotsky played a pivotal role in Russia's October Revolution of 1917 and served as Commissar of Foreign Affairs and then Commissar of War in the new Bolshevik government. After Lenin's death in January 1924, he lost the succession struggle with Joseph Stalin and his political career went into eclipse. Trotsky then became a vocal critic of Stalin and the Soviet system, condemning entrenched bureaucracy, a decline in revolutionary fervor, "state capitalism," and reversion to tsarist practices. A committed Communist, more radical than Stalin, Trotsky advocated "permanent revolution" and accused Stalin of abandoning the Marxist path embarked on by Lenin. Stalin came to portray Trotsky as the impetus behind any antigovernment dissent or action—real or imaginary. He became the scapegoat for the regime's failures, a Jewish anti-Christ representing the dark forces of reaction.

Exile

In January 1928 Stalin banished Trotsky to Alma-Ata, Kazakhstan. In January 1929 Trotsky was ordered to leave the Soviet Union and he arrived in Istanbul, Turkey, the next month. He then lived on the island of Prinkipo for more than four years and his Soviet citizenship was revoked in February 1932. Turkey was not his first choice of residence. While still in Kazakhstan, he had asked the Politburo to arrange his exile in Germany, but he was told that Germany would not accept him. He then applied on his own after settling in Turkey, promising to refrain from political activity, but Germany rejected him again.[6] Trotsky also tried to secure a visa for Norway, but he was turned down. He was, however, given permission to address Norwegian students, but family problems prevented him from making the journey.[7] In the fall of 1932, while lecturing in Denmark, Trotsky requested a visa to stay there, but Soviet pressure on the Danish government contributed to nonapproval. He also used the occasion to try to secure a Swedish visa, but the Soviet ambassador in Stockholm, Alexandra Kollontai, blocked his effort.[8]

Finally, France agreed to accept the famous exile. He arrived there in July 1933 and proceeded to get involved in communist politics. In August, Trotsky called for a new revolutionary organization—the Fourth International—to challenge the pro-Stalinist Third International (Comintern). Within a year, France was already considering his expulsion, as its ties to the Soviet Union were strengthening.[9] The mutual defense treaty of May 1935 settled the matter, and Trotsky was ordered to leave.

Using his son Lev ("Lyova") Sedov as an intermediary, as well as contacts with Norwegian non-Trotskyist editor Olav Scheflo, Trotsky learned that Norway would permit him entry for six months, provided that he avoid political activity within Norway "or against any friendly state." He applied for a visa on June 7, received approval two days later, sold his house, and secured a Belgian transit visa. On June 12, France demanded his departure within twenty-four hours, so he left for Antwerp the following day, sailed for Oslo on June 15, and arrived in the Norwegian capital on June 18. On July 30, Minister of Justice Trygve Lie told Trotsky that there had not been any Soviet pressure to deny him entry. Trotsky believed that the Soviets didn't even know he had headed for Norway.[10] It appeared that the peripatetic revolutionary had found a new home.

A leftist Labour government had come to power in March 1935 and it extended a six-month residency permit that later was renewed twice. Konrad Knudsen, a socialist, put up Trotsky and his entourage at his own home in Wexhall, and the dissident Communist exile promised the government that he would not engage in politics. His presence in Norway was strongly opposed by both extremes of the ideological spectrum. Pro-Soviet Communists claimed that he was operating a terrorist base against the Soviet Union. The fascist National Union, led by Vidkun Quisling, charged a "Jewish-Marxist plot" against Norway.[11] In the early morning hours of August 5, 1936, members of the National Union broke into Trotsky's residence while he was away and stole some of his papers. Intentional leaks of some of these materials were aimed at demonstrating a technical violation of his no politics pledge and were accompanied by calls for his expulsion. It had already been evident that Trotsky was receiving foreign visitors and the papers then confirmed that he was engaged in communist politics via his correspondence. Trotsky's Norwegian supporters accused the fascists of abetting Stalin's wish to see Trotsky's residence permit terminated.[12]

Trotsky's engagement in politics also came into question with regard to comments he made in a June 9 newspaper article on France, in which he had called for the establishment of workers' councils (known as soviets) in preparation for revolutionary "victory." He declared that "it is time to pass from words to action." French authorities had promptly initiated a crackdown on the Trotskyists.[13] The Norwegians investigated Trotsky's pronouncements on France, as well as his other activities, and the Ministry of Justice then announced on August 8, 1936, that he had been cleared of violating any residency provisions. It was also revealed that he had been under constant surveillance since entering the country. Six days later, Oslo's police chief met with Trotsky for three hours and then affirmed that he was satisfied that he had observed the conditions of his stay in Norway.[14]

In the Line of Fire

On August 15, 1936 Trotsky heard that Kamenev, Zinoviev, and others were to be tried again for fomenting terrorism against Soviet leaders, including Stalin and the deceased Kirov. This time, Trotsky was to be portrayed as a conspirator linked to Germany and Japan who sent couriers from Oslo to direct a terrorist campaign in the Soviet Union. The first show trial in the "Great Purge" was about to begin, as an exercise not only in consolidating Stalin's power, but also as an antifascist forum at the time of the Spanish Civil War and the remilitarization of the Rhineland. Sixteen defendants appeared in a Moscow court from August 19 to 24, in which Prosecutor-General Andrei Vyshinsky was the dominant force. Trotsky was not charged in absentia lest he demand to testify and thereby challenge the Kremlin with a Dimitrov-like performance.[15] Trotsky was certainly presented as the eminence grise, but he was attacked obliquely by defendants and witnesses rather than by the prosecutor. It was also announced that he would be arrested if he tried to enter Soviet territory.[16]

Fifteen of the show trial defendants publicly confessed their crimes and world journalistic reaction was more accepting of the veracity of the charges than it had been in reference to the fire trial. Pritt, who had presided at the Reichstag countertrial, attended the Moscow proceeding and declared that the trial was fair and the accused were indeed guilty. All were executed at once, even though they had a legal right to appeal within seventy-two hours and had also planned to seek clemency.[17] Stalin was sure to leave no opening for any international effort to save their lives.

The timing of the trial may have been related to Trotsky's completion earlier that month of his book manuscript *The Revolution Betrayed,* a searing indictment of Stalin's perceived perversion of Leninism. It was sent to a Paris publisher, but Mark Zborowsky, a Soviet agent in Trotsky's inner circle, forwarded sections to Moscow, where Stalin personally looked them over. The trial, in part, was therefore part of a campaign to undercut Trotsky and his book, which was not actually published until the following May.[18]

Trotsky saw the trial, which "put the Dreyfus scandal and the Reichstag fire in the shadow," as political vengeance. He insisted that his records would effectively undercut the validity of charges against him and vowed (hoping to imitate Dimitrov) to "make the accusers the accused." Trotsky additionally saw antisemitic implications, since ten of the sixteen defendants were Jews. Efforts to link Jewish defendants and himself, to the Nazis were seen by him as ludicrous.[19] The wandering Jew also feared that one of the aims of the Moscow trial was to get him expelled from Norway so that Soviet agents could seize him.[20]

Trotsky called for an international commission of inquiry to investigate the Moscow trial and clear his name. On August 20 he met with members of the press and condemned the show trial as a fraud. He queried: "With what conviction can the democratic countries develop a common front with Soviet Russia against reaction if she descends to the methods of barbarism of the Fascist world?"[21]

In October Trotsky declared an intent to present his case before the League of Nations Commission on Political Terrorism. On the Soviet Union's advent to the League in 1934, Stalin had championed the establishment of such a commission. His effort succeeded and at the end of the show trial, the Soviet government had averred that League states should cooperate against terrorists. Ironically, Trotsky then upset Stalin's apple cart with his own request—dampening the latter's enthusiasm.[22] In the end, Trotsky was unable to arrange a hearing.

Prior to the show trial, the Soviet government did not pressure Norway about terminating Trotsky's residence there. On returning from Moscow on August 15, Foreign Minister Halvdan Koht said that Soviet officials did not raise the matter.[23] There was then an abrupt reversal once Trotsky went public on August 20 against the upcoming trial, and the defendants were soon found guilty of conspiring with him. The Soviet media put Norway on the defensive with allegations that the Labor government had not prevented Trotsky from engaging in anti-Soviet activities. Norway then countered with two investigations, one by the foreign ministry and the other by the Immigration Office, even though the Ministry of Justice had already given Trotsky a "clean bill of health" on August 8. Norway was obviously trying to clear itself, but to do so, it produced evidence refuting show trial testimony and exonerating Trotsky. In particular, the police could find no substantiation for the charge that someone named Julian Berman had come to Norway to consult with Trotsky on plans to assassinate Stalin. In response, the Soviet government newspaper *Izvestiia* accused Norway of emitting "the lethal gases of hypocritical lies to cover up the trails of Trotsky and his helpers in Norway." Norway's protection of Trotsky was partly self-serving, but Oslo was willing to stand up to Moscow on matters of historical truth.[24]

On August 29, Soviet ambassador I. S. Yakubovich, citing the Moscow trial verdict, presented a letter to Koht that asked for Trotsky's expulsion. His extradition was not demanded, as this would have required a court hearing at which Trotsky could again attack the show trial. The Soviet note threatened a setback in bilateral relations, should Norway fail to comply.[25] The Norwegians interpreted this as a reference to economic sanctions, particularly a possible Soviet boycott of Norwegian herring. Shipowners involved in trade between the countries were especially concerned.[26]

Officially, Norway rejected the Soviet demand. Foreign Minister Koht affirmed: "The principle of asylum will be maintained by the present government of Norway. We will not let ourselves be subdued in such matters by anyone." He additionally commented that "Norway does not intend to dance to another government's pipe." Minister of Justice Lie wrote to the Soviets that Trotsky had been isolated prior to the Soviet protest and could not harm relations. He also pointed out that the prominent exile could not have plotted against Kirov from Norway, as he was not living there as of December 1934. Lie additionally questioned the Soviet Union's legal right to request Trotsky's expulsion, since he had been stripped of Soviet citizenship.[27] Behind the scenes, however, the Norwegian government did take cognizance of the Soviet threat and started to see Trotsky as a nuisance and liability.

Persona Non Grata

When the August 1936 Moscow trial ended, Trotsky called for a Norwegian judicial inquiry so that he could refute Soviet charges. The Norwegian Immigration Office had different ideas. On August 26 Trotsky was told that he had violated conditions of his stay because of his June comments on France. The Ministry of Justice had ruled just the opposite less than three weeks earlier. Trotsky countered rather tenuously with the argument that restrictions on political activity applied only to secret and illegal actions against friendly states. The immigration director asked him to sign a document promising not to get involved in foreign politics. Trotsky insisted on his right to respond to the show trial and refused to sign.[28] He at once wrote to Minister of Justice Lie, complaining that the Immigration Office was not in a position to determine the difference between political commentary and his ostensible technique of social science analysis. The exiled Communist then indicated that if he had in fact violated terms of his stay, he should be arrested and permitted to comment on the Soviet Union at a trial. Otherwise, he should be free to speak. Pointedly, Trotsky reminded Lie that the latter had approved his August 20 press conference and had been present.[29] That same day, apparently before receiving the letter, Lie had decided to post a guard outside of Trotsky's home. This was done on August 27, two days before the official Soviet protest.[30]

Also on August 27, Trotsky told a Norwegian newspaper that he had adhered to the country's residence guidelines. He proclaimed himself a revolutionary, but insisted that he was not a terrorist active against European governments. Trotsky remarked: "If Moscow's allegations were true, I would no doubt be guilty of having violated the right of asylum. But I will prove publicly that the charges are untrue."[31] The next day, under police questioning about the fascist break-in at his home, Trotsky acknowledged that he had called for an uprising in France. Papers stolen by Quisling's men clearly showed that Trotsky had sent letters to French revolutionaries. Following this interrogation, Trotsky met with Lie. The Minister of Justice asked him to sign a statement about refraining from political activity and accepting censorship of his communications. He was polite but also maintained that political asylum was a privilege rather than a right. Lie accepted Trotsky's claim not to be a terrorist but said that he surely was involved in politics. Trotsky retorted that he had pledged only to stay out of Norwegian politics. Privately, Lie asked him to leave Norway, but Trotsky asserted that it would be difficult to secure a visa for another country—especially since Norway had accused him of a visa violation.[32] The statement presented by Lie was not signed.

Lie, backed by King Haakon VII, decided to isolate Trotsky. He was forbidden to make phone calls, give interviews, or meet with others without prior approval. His two aides, Erwin Wolff and Jean van Heijenoort, were pressured into signing agreements to depart from Norway—and they did so on August 29. They were told that failure to leave on their own would mean deportation to Germany. Two days later, the Ministry of Justice imposed a temporary regulation, according to which a foreigner could be interned if he acted against state interests and could not or would not depart from Norway. Certainly, Trotsky was in mind.[33]

After hearing of the Soviet threat, Norwegian Prime Minister Johann Nygaardsvold had exclaimed: "We shall have to find a Norwegian Siberia for Trotsky." Indeed, on September 2 Trotsky was moved to a farm in Hurum patrolled by thirteen policemen, where he was placed under house arrest and could be visited only by his attorneys.[34] Trotsky later quipped sardonically in reference to the Soviet secret police: "Yakubovich was the man who succeeded in obtaining my and my wife's internment, but who didn't succeed in obtaining my deliverance into the hands of the GPU." Norway denied that it had bowed to the Soviets. The foreign ministry's September 3 response to the August 29 Soviet letter reiterated that restrictions had been placed on Trotsky prior to the latter date. This is true, but the house arrest had come afterward.[35]

From the Soviet perspective, Trotsky had still not been silenced politically. After all, his son Lev Sedov was busy in his Paris archives gathering materials in support of his father. In fact, he was working on a "Red Book" (obviously modeled after the "Brown Book") that would refute the show trial charges, and had successfully published part of it in the October issue of the *Bulletin of the Opposition*. His efforts were thwarted by Mark Zborowsky, however, who acted as a spy within his office and arranged with Soviet intelligence for the theft of some of Trotsky's papers. Ironically, it took place on the anniversary of the Bolshevik revolution—November 7. The perpetrators missed many important documents, but those purloined included identifications of Trotsky's French supporters.[36] Later, Trotsky was incapable of producing certain documents requested by an international citizens' tribunal.

Trotsky continued to challenge the Moscow trial's charges, accusing both rightist and communist newspapers of defamation for linking him to the Kirov murder plot. When he asked a Norwegian court on October 26 to permit him to refute terrorism charges, he was rejected as there was fear that he was trying to establish a countertrial. Oslo certainly did not want to play London while Moscow was staging another Leipzig, and it was trying to live up to a promise to the Soviets to keep Trotsky under wraps politically. On October 29, the Ministry of Justice ruled that an interned alien could not be a plaintiff without the permission of the ministry, and such permission was of course not granted. Trotsky also tried to sue periodicals in France, Belgium, Switzerland, and Czechoslovakia, but he was denied the right to do so from Norway and was forbidden to communicate with lawyers abroad.[37]

The Norwegian government decided in early November that it would be best if Trotsky left the country, but finding an alternative exile for him was not an easy matter. Lie told Trotsky that he couldn't stay at Hurum because it was too expensive to guard him there. If he remained in Norway, Lie pressured, he would have to move even further north. Lie visited Hurum several times, and Trotsky indicated an interest in relocating to Mexico. This was apparently due to its proximity to the United States, where Trotsky could attract extensive publicity. Foreign Secretary Eduardo Hay had indicated on December 7 that Mexico would accept him if a request was made. This was the same day that Prime Minister Nygaardsvold mentioned that Trotsky's residence visa would expire on December 18, and that he would be ousted if he did not leave voluntarily. Complicating the situation was that Norway and Mexico did not have diplomatic relations, and that Norway had recently spurned a Mexican attempt to establish them. Contacts between the two countries over the Trotsky affair were therefore handled by emissaries in Paris.[38]

Meanwhile, on December 11, Trotsky got to testify in court in the break-in case. At the hearing, which was closed to the public, Trotsky attacked Lie as an accomplice of Stalin. All four fascist defendants were found guilty, but three were given suspended sentences. The fourth was sentenced to ninety days, because of an added charge of forgery.[39] Two days later, Lie informed Trotsky that it was time for him to go. An angry Trotsky complained about his treatment in Norway and, in the manner of a biblical prophet, warned that Lie and Nygaardsvold would themselves become refugees within three years.[40]

Trotsky was willing to go to Mexico, but he first wanted to visit his son in Paris. Perhaps he hoped to use the opportunity to generate court action there. Lie refused, saying that he had to proceed to Mexico directly. On December 15, Mexican diplomats in Stockholm provided a travel document for Trotsky, but he refused to sign it. He even considered asking Mexico to withdraw its invitation. He was worried about his safety, since his lawyer had said the previous week that he was looking into the possibility of "foul play" by Trotsky's enemies in luring him to Mexico.[41]

Lie provided a ship to take Trotsky to Mexico and assured him that no one else but the ship owner knew about the voyage. Lie certainly did not want to have Trotsky's blood on his hands. Stalin, conversely, would have loved to get his adversary killed before he could appear before a commission of inquiry. Trotsky and his wife Natalya boarded on December 19, and were the only passengers other than police assigned for his protection. The apprehensive exile remarked that a Soviet submarine could torpedo the vessel. He doubted the ship's ability to defend itself, and was perturbed that he was not permitted to use the onboard radio to respond to questions from American reporters. Only on entering the Mexican port of Tampico did Trotsky sign his travel document.[42]

After his arrival in Mexico, Trotsky wrote in his notes that the Soviet Union had been surprised by Mexico's willingness to accept him.[43] He was to prove a troublesome guest, since he soon became embroiled in Mexican politics, caused a split within the American left, and achieved his goal of undermining the veracity of the Moscow trials with his testimony as the key witness at the second international citizens' tribunal.

Chapter VII

A TRIBUNAL CRYSTALLIZES

J ust after the exiled revolutionary had departed from Norway, *The New York Times* printed an editorial entitled "Trotsky in Retreat?" that stated: "Trotsky in Mexico is not as formidable as Trotsky a short train ride from the Russian border. Even with modern facilities an ocean is a strategic handicap."[1] This surely did not turn out to be the case, as Trotsky reversed his Norwegian failure and successfully used Mexico as a base of operations to challenge the Moscow show trials and seek personal vindication.

When Trotsky arrived at the Mexican port of Tampico, American supporters George Novack and Max Shachtman were there to greet him. Contacts in the United States were critical for Trotsky because of the limited public relations opportunities available in his new home country. In Mexico City, Communists loyal to Stalin were already holding a rally calling for his expulsion. President Lazaro Cardenas nevertheless received Trotsky warmly, providing a special railway car to transport him to Mexico City and assuring him that he was a guest of the government—not just a recipient of political asylum.[2] Trotsky moved into a home in the suburb of Coyoacan, owned by Frida Kahlo, where he and Natalya lived with Kahlo and her fellow artist husband, Diego Rivera.

From January 23 through 30, 1937, there was another Moscow show trial featuring Karl Radek and Grigory Piatakov as defendants. Radek had been a Comintern expert on Germany, while Piatakov had served as a leading economic planner. The charges were industrial "wrecking," efforts to restore capitalism, espionage, and collusion with Germany and Japan to dismember the Soviet Union. Trotsky was again implicated, as was his son Lev. Eight of the seventeen defendants were Jews.[3] Eleven received death sentences; Radek got ten years. Radek had given testimony damaging to other defendants, leading Trotsky to conclude that he had made a deal with Stalin. Once again, all of the defendants confessed to their alleged crimes, with Trotsky remarking that they could not stand up strongly like Dimitrov at Leipzig because they lacked world press support. A trial observer from Great Britain drew the same conclusion regarding the Dimitrov parallel, explaining that there was no sympathy "inside or outside the court" for the defendants. He discerned widespread backing for Stalin and for the credibility of the confessions. After all, why didn't the defendants stand up for themselves, as Dimitrov had? Pritt took that position, too, prompting Trotsky to label him a "paid prostitute" of Moscow and to call a juridical defense of the trial "Prittism." *The New York Times* had a different slant that stressed manufactured evidence and false confessions and maintained that the "burden of proof" lay not on Trotsky but on Stalin.[4]

Trotsky assured Mexico that he would stay out of its politics and would practice "absolute abstention from actions that might hamper Mexico's relations with other countries." Mexico and the Soviet Union did not have diplomatic relations, however, so he felt free to lambaste the Moscow trial and to request a commission of inquiry before which he could prove his own innocence. Communists had organized the fire trial hearings, he mused, so they would find it difficult to attack the creation of another commission to examine the Moscow show trials. He perceptively reasoned: "If the first trial had convinced the world, the second would not be necessary." Trotsky did not anticipate that commission hearings would be held in Mexico, expecting them to take place in New York, Paris, or somewhere in Switzerland. Alternatively, Trotsky asked the Soviet Union to extradite him so he could face charges against him there. He maintained that he would accept execution if found guilty, but this was basically an exercise in bravado, since Moscow did not try to extradite him when he was in Norway for fear that he would prove to be another Dimitrov. There was no extradition agreement between Mexico and the Soviet Union.[5]

Hot Climate

In November 1936, New York activists seeking a haven for Trotsky had contacted Mexican muralist and former Communist Party member Diego Rivera. It was apparent that Trotsky's days in Norway were numbered, so Rivera was asked if he would contact President Cardenas and encourage him to admit Trotsky to Mexico. Rivera had broken with the Mexican Communist Party in 1927 over Stalin's crackdown on the "Left Opposition" and he continued to be at odds with the artist David Alfaro Siqueiros and other Mexican Communists who maintained their unwavering support for the Soviet leader. Rivera was an independent, anti-Stalinist communist who admired Trotsky's courage in attacking both Stalin and the defects of the Soviet system and he had announced in September 1936 that he backed Trotsky's planned Fourth International.[6]

Communist Party General-Secretary Hernan Laborde opposed Trotsky's entry into Mexico and advocated the resumption of diplomatic ties to Moscow. Cardenas's decision to welcome Trotsky was therefore a slap at the Communists and an act bound to divide the Mexican left.[7] Meanwhile, in the United States, Norman Thomas and his Socialist Party were prominent in pressing for Trotsky's political asylum in Mexico. Motivated by their anti-Stalinism and disenchantment with the Soviet Union, they helped orchestrate a petition calling on Cardenas to act favorably on the Trotsky case. Once the Mexican president responded positively, Thomas and other Socialists praised him at a New York rally.[8]

Cardenas had enjoyed good relations with the Mexican Communists. Their party functioned legally and membership reached its high point under the Cardenas administration (1934–40). In February 1936, one of the "Fourteen Points" in his labor program asserted: "Small groups of communists do exist within the country—as they do in Europe and the United States—but their activities in Mexico do not endanger the stability of our institutions nor do they alarm the government, and they need not alarm the industrialists."[9] In November the president signed legislation permitting expropriation as a means of distributing wealth more equitably—a measure endorsed by the Communists. Cardenas also joined them in a Popular Front against fascism, funneled arms to Republican forces in Spain, and admitted Spanish refugees.[10]

Because Cardenas was furthering the Popular Front and carrying out policies amenable to the Communists, Moscow was rather low-key in attacking Mexico's granting of asylum to Trotsky. Also, the Soviet Union could exert little pressure over Mexico, since relations had been broken in 1930 by a previous Mexican government as a reaction to Communist Party provocations. Still, Trotsky's presence did exacerbate tensions between Cardenas and the Communists—endangering the Popular Front. Cardenas was moving away from alignment with the Communists, a transition made more apparent in January 1937 when the president neutralized somewhat the impact of the November reform by indemnifying seized assets through the issuance of bonds.[11] The Comintern organ *Inprecorr,* which had generally commented favorably on Cardenas, became more critical once Trotsky took up residence in Mexico. According to *Inprecorr*, "The arrival of Trotsky, the agent of international fascism, has sharpened the struggle for the Popular Front because of the strength it gives to its enemies and because of the keen understanding of the workers who have already sensed the danger."[12]

Possibly intentionally, Cardenas kept the left divided. This pleased the army, which protested the Popular Front collaboration with the Communists and the Catholic press, which gladly had been reprinting Trotsky's attacks on the Soviet Union.[13] Trotsky opposed the Popular Front, ostensibly because he preferred a purely proletarian revolution with a narrower base. More likely, this attitude was a consequence of his persistent anti-Comintern posture. The Communists and the main labor movement, the Confederation de Trabajadores de Mexico (CTM), were pro-Popular Front and anti-Trotsky, but a faction of the CTM broke with Secretary-General Vicente Lombardo Toledano and began to back Trotsky.[14] Then there was the case of Francisco Mugica, a radical leftist who had left his imprint on the 1917 constitution and was known as the "Lenin of Mexico." Mugica had considerable influence over Cardenas, served as his Minister for Communications and Infrastructure, and strongly encouraged the president to extend asylum to Trotsky.[15] Clearly the very presence of Trotsky had stirred up the Mexican pot.

Getting Organized

Once Trotsky was portrayed as a terrorist conspirator at the August 1936 show trial, a group of leftists in New York started to organize a defense committee. Some participants, such as Suzanne La Follette, Ben Stolberg, and Sidney Hook, were anti-Stalinists sympathetic to Trotsky's plight, but were not committed Trotskyists. Instead, they sought to use Trotsky to discredit the Moscow trials. Herb Solow had earlier been a member of the Trotskyist party. George Novack and Felix Morrow were active Trotskyists who wanted to influence public opinion on his behalf.[16] The original impetus behind the project was largely ideological, as it had been when Muenzenberg gathered support for the arrested Communists in the Reichstag fire case, but the difference was that Trotskyist involvement was not carefully kept hidden: Novack and Morrow served as the committee's secretary and assistant secretary.

On October 22, 1936, plans were announced for establishing the Provisional American Committee for the Defense of Leon Trotsky—and it became operational by December. The committee's immediate concern was that Trotsky was being held under house arrest in Norway and was unable to respond appropriately to Moscow's charges. Its members argued that he deserved a right to a hearing before a commission of inquiry—and Norway would not permit such a hearing within its borders. It was therefore mandatory to find asylum in a country that would. The committee claimed to be "indifferent" to Trotsky's political views, and didn't necessarily affirm his innocence. The issue was his ability to seek justice through public testimony.[17] Such a stance was aimed at broadening the committee's appeal to liberals, thus following the example of the effective Reichstag fire countertrial. Stating that it would not function as an anti-Soviet forum, the Committee called for an investigation of the Moscow trial and then made an unsuccessful request that the Soviet authorities act as Germany had, in allowing committee observers to attend the January 1937 show trial.[18]

Stalin may have blocked another Leipzig, but he couldn't prevent the liberal philosopher John Dewey's involvement in the matter. The writer Louis Adamic commented in reference to fellow committee member Dewey, a non-Trotskyist, that "the idea to clear Trotsky as a matter of principle of justice was probably clear and paramount only in John Dewey's mind; I admired him for it."[19] Dewey complained that the committee was promoting Trotsky's political agenda and was not focusing on securing a hearing. For Dewey, adhering to democratic procedures was the key. Regarding a committee press release, Dewey regretfully observed: "I was willing to sign the statement about Trotsky's right to a public hearing, although I have no sympathy with what seems to me to be his abstract ideological fanaticism." He explained, however, that the statement was then released as part of an attack on the Moscow trial, and he would not have signed had he known this could happen.[20]

Dewey, the pragmatist philosopher, was but one of the eminent intellectuals attracted to the defense committee, others being Norman Thomas, the leader of the Socialist Party; Franz Boas, the noted anthropologist; Edmund Wilson and Dwight Macdonald, literary critics; and James Farrell, the author of *Studs Lonigan*.[21] Several members were perturbed, however, by use of the term "defense" in the organization's name. It implied a pro-Trotsky bias, not just a civil rights concern. Dewey maintained that the term caused "misunderstanding," and philosopher Sidney Hook called it a "mistake." The basic explanation, as proffered by both Dewey and Ben Stolberg, was that it originally was used to support Trotsky's right to asylum at a time when he was still in Norway. According to Stolberg, the Committee had not intended to defend Trotsky, just to enable him to defend himself.[22]

Another problem was that Trotsky discerned antisemitic scapegoatism underlying Soviet charges against himself and the show trial defendants. This made many Jews uncomfortable because they had been accentuating the Soviet Union's important role in combating Nazism. Reform Rabbi Stephen Wise, a liberal anticommunist, called Trotsky "disingenuous" in raising the Jewish issue and refused to join the defense committee. He labeled Trotsky's complaint as "unsubstantiated."[23] Of course, many Jews did serve on the defense committee, but the antisemitic angle was downplayed.

The experiences of the committee member Louis Adamic are noteworthy. He favored asylum for Trotsky and went along with advocacy of a hearing, but opposed challenging the veracity of the Moscow show trials. Adamic also did not agree with Stolberg, who told him that there was a need to keep Stalinism on the defensive and that Trotsky was another Dreyfus. For him, Dreyfus had been a prisoner isolated on Devil's Island, whereas Trotsky was still a major revolutionary leader. Troubled by the term "defense," Adamic considered quitting the committee. Simultaneously, he was being pressured by Stalinists threatening to deny him future Soviet visas and to curtail publication of his books in Russian if he would not resign. Resenting this undue influence, Adamic decided to remain on the committee.[24]

Adamic was just one of the committee members subjected to Soviet intimidation in 1936–37. Several bowed to Soviet demands and withdrew; others did so on their own once Trotsky was given refuge in Mexico. The Soviets offered bribes and free trips to sway committee members and issued warnings and smears. Soviet agents also infiltrated the Trotskyist movement in the United States and acted as provocateurs. Prominent among them were Dr. Gregor Rabinovich, who was affiliated with the Red Cross in New York, and his subordinate, Louis Budenz.[25]

Note that there were Trotsky defense committees in Great Britain, France, and Czechoslovakia. Bertrand Russell, who was later to organize an international citizens' tribunal on the Vietnam War, supported the British committee but was not active. Russell had criticized the Soviet Union in 1933 during the Metro-Vickers trial, maintaining that "it should be an absolute rule of criminal procedure that confessions should never be admitted." Sidney Hook later encouraged him by letter to come to the aid of Trotsky. George Bernard Shaw condemned the first Moscow trial, but wouldn't join the committee. He asserted that Trotsky's attacks on Stalin were as incredible as Stalin's on Trotsky.[26] The French committee included Alfred Rosmer, who had once been on the Comintern's executive committee. He then became an admirer of Trotsky and visited him at Prinkipo in 1929. Trotsky's friend Victor Serge, the labor organizer Fernand Charbit, and the author Andre Breton also were members. Romain Rolland, who had backed Dimitrov, opposed the group.[27]

The Fractured American Left

The Depression of the 1930s drove many intellectuals leftward as they sought state-sponsored solutions for the West's catastrophic economic decline, while the Soviet Union had full employment and robust growth. Moreover, by encouraging communists to join liberals and socialists in an antifascist Popular Front following the rise of the Nazis in Germany, the Soviet Union strengthened its position as a bulwark against increasingly triumphant fascism. It was this enhanced position that enabled Moscow to frame the debate in the advantageous manner articulated on February 5, 1937 by American Communist Party General-Secretary Earl Browder, before an audience of fifteen thousand at Madison Square Garden in New York: "There is no issue merely between Trotsky and the Communist Party. It is the choice between war and fascism on the one side, or democracy and peace on the other side. Trotsky is the advance agent of fascism and war throughout the world."[28] Of course, demonstrating faith in the Soviet experiment and endorsing the validity of show trial charges inevitably led to the conclusion that many of the original founders of the Soviet Union were so opposed to Stalin that they had to resort to terrorism in collusion with fascist foreign powers.[29] Focusing on the external danger was surely an efficacious means of obscuring internal discontent.

Norman Thomas was among those refusing to accept that judgment, declaring: "The last thing I want to do is to escape from Trotsky by falling, or seeming to fall, into the arms of Stalin."[30] In August 1936, Thomas had reacted to the first show trial by calling for an investigation of Soviet charges. He soon joined the Trotsky defense committee and lobbied for asylum in Mexico. In February 1937 the Socialists and the defense committee cosponsored a meeting in Chicago addressed by Thomas. Undertaking Trotsky's cause provided committed Socialists like himself with an opportunity to save the Bolshevik Revolution by arguing that Stalin had diverted the Soviet Union from the Leninist path. The trouble was that Trotsky opposed not only Stalin but also the Popular Front, backed by many democratic socialists and liberals—thus adding to their natural reluctance to point out flaws in the Soviet system for fear that unity against fascism would dissipate.[31]

Moscow was defiantly vigilant. It hand-picked Columbia University philosophy professor and public intellectual Corliss Lamont to orchestrate a campaign against the Trotsky defense committee. He was a member of the editorial board of *Soviet Russia Today* and chairman of the American Friends of the Soviet Union. Lamont argued that the Moscow trials demonstrated that there were indeed efforts to overthrow the workers' state.[32] He gratefully welcomed the support of Malcolm Cowley, the literary editor of the leading liberal magazine *The New Republic*, who castigated the defense committee as divisive in the antifascist struggle. Cowley argued that politics had to supersede morality as "liberals who get mixed up in the controversy on moral grounds are stooges and suckers." *The New Republic*, which had called for involvement in the Reichstag fire case and the Spanish Civil War, advised liberals to stay out of the Moscow trials debate. This incurred the wrath of one of the magazine's most distinguished founders, John Dewey. He wrote to editor and president Bruce Bliven that his publication had strayed from "genuine liberalism" in its coverage of the Soviet Union. Liberals, Dewey insisted, had to fight for the right of free political discourse, which is an essential component of democracy and a counterweight to the violence and dictatorship of the proletariat evident in the Soviet Union. Dewey asserted: "I cannot understand how the Journal which identified liberalism with the spirit of full and free discussion could take the attitude of belittling in advance the attempt to give Mr. Trotsky a full opportunity for a hearing."[33]

Leftist periodicals did not embrace Trotsky. *New Masses* published a letter signed by fifty intellectuals (including Max Lerner and Louis Fischer) warning liberals that they were being used by the Trotsky defense committee. *The Nation* at first mildly criticized the August 1936 show trial, but then forced out editor Frieda Kirchway and became pro-Stalinist. *Partisan Review* was the most balanced, endorsing Marxism but not Stalinism. Petitions against the defense committee proliferated, the best known being the one signed by eighty-eight (including Theodore Dreiser and Lillian Hellman) anti-Trotskyists in the March 1937 issue of *Soviet Russia Today*.[34]

The effect of the clash between the Trotskyists and the rest of the left was best exemplified by the story of Mauritz Hallgren, a specialist on American history and an associate editor of *The Baltimore Sun*. In his 1937 book *The Tragic Fallacy* Hallgren predicted that the United States would go to war to protect capitalism and would succumb to a revolution or dictatorship, should it lose. The book was dedicated to Eugene Debs and Robert La Follette, former presidential candidates of the Socialists and Progressives, respectively, thereby indicating Hallgren's leftist ideological proclivities. By contrast, his analysis did not include any references to Soviet foreign policy interests nor to Stalinism.[35]

Hallgren joined the defense committee to help secure asylum for Trotsky and his January 27, 1937 decision to leave it was a powerful body blow to the organization. Hallgren's letter of resignation was printed in *The New York Times* and he then proceeded to write a pamphlet explaining his motivations. Hallgren pointed out that the goal of asylum had already been achieved once Trotsky got to Mexico. More important, he stressed his differences with the Trotskyists, as he claimed that the exile bore "moral responsibility" (similar to charges once leveled at Dimitrov, Kamenev, and Zinoviev) for an anti-Soviet conspiracy sparked by his writings and that he may have participated or have had knowledge of it. He maintained that the defendants in both show trials were guilty, and that those at the first trial had implicated Trotsky in the hope of securing lesser sentences for themselves. Hallgren condemned Trotsky for not providing any documents to support the accused (the Reichstag defendants had been saved by hard evidence) and concluded that Trotsky's failure to do so demonstrated that he was not a "disinterested party" concerned about abstract justice. Trotsky's aim was, "perhaps unwittingly," to undermine the Soviet system and socialism, and the defense committee was doing the same thing—not just supporting Trotsky. Hallgren decided that the Stalinist order was flawed, though said, "but I can and do overlook these faults in so far as they do not impair the work that is being done on behalf of socialism."[36]

George Novack responded in *The New York Times* that Hallgren should reconsider his resignation since a fair hearing was needed to determine whether Trotsky was guilty—as Hallgren, to some extent, had alleged. In a private letter to Dewey, he vented his anger by suggesting that Hallgren seemed to be "a plant." Suzanne La Follette also came to the committee's defense. Whereas Hallgren had asked why Trotsky had not provided evidence while the trials were in progress, she wanted to know why the Soviet government (as requested by the defense committee) did not stay the executions in order to await evidence supplied by Trotsky.[37]

Hallgren's resignation stung the defense committee more than those of other members, as he had announced it in *The New York Times* and had no known connection to the Soviet Union or communism. No substantiation ever surfaced to show that he had been pressured by the Soviets or bribed. A wounded committee then continued on its mission to provide a hearing for Trotsky—and eventually to confront another "Hallgren" in its midst.

The Commission of Inquiry

Two days after arriving in Mexico, Trotsky telegrammed the American defense committee and asked it to form a commission of inquiry, a sort of countertrial at which he finally hoped to get the opportunity to do to Stalin what Dimitrov had done to Goering.[38] Mexico City was far from the ideal venue, however, and, unlike Dimitrov, Trotsky would have no chance to confront his opponent in court nor demonstrate his courage on the enemy's turf.

Trotsky had been unable to stride the stage in Europe and the United States had refused to grant him a visa. His chances of entering the United States certainly were not improved when he threatened libel suits against communist publications if he were able to reach American soil. Mexico seemed to be willing to permit a public hearing, but it was geographically marginal. Trotsky and his supporters therefore decided to use modern technology to break out of their uncomfortable public relations straightjacket. By promising not to comment on American or Mexican politics, Trotsky got the U.S. State Department to approve an address by telephone hookup to a February 9 New York rally. Five hundred policemen were on duty as a crowd of sixty-five hundred waited at the Hippodrome to hear the passionate orator, but they were sorely disappointed when there was a mysterious problem with the transmission lines in Mexico. Pro-Soviet unionists aligned with the labor leader Vicente Lombardo Toledano seem to have been responsible for sabotaging the telephone connection. When Trotsky rushed to the central office of the phone company, workers there cited technical difficulties and did nothing to help him. Max Shachtman therefore had to read Trotsky's prepared remarks to the rally. At one point he stopped, made a futile attempt to phone Trotsky, but then went on reading.[39] Basically, Trotsky was calling for a commission of inquiry just as he had over the previous weeks since arriving in Mexico.

On February 14 the defense committee met to organize a commission of inquiry. By early March, a Joint Commission of Inquiry was in operation in conjunction with defense committees in Great Britain, France, and Czechoslovakia. The European committees were to have their own hearings on the Continent. The American committee was to prepare hearings in Mexico, with Trotsky as the prime witness. The American group, formally known as the Preliminary Commission of Inquiry into the Charges Made against Leon Trotsky in the Moscow Trials, scored a major coup when John Dewey agreed to chair the commission. One committee member, Dewey's former Columbia student, Sidney Hook, had convinced

Dewey to join the defense committee. Now another of his ex-students, George Novack, prevailed on him to chair the commission. Hence, it came to be known as the "Dewey Commission."

Moscow immediately understood the public relations danger this beloved public intellectual presented. Soviet envoys therefore temptingly offered him the leadership of the American delegation to the twentieth anniversary celebration in Moscow of the Bolshevik revolution. Dewey was also visited by Soviet embassy representative Jacob Urvanovsky and by pro-Soviet historian Louis Fischer, but he was determined to use the commission to prove the superiority of democratic liberalism and would not be moved. Interestingly, Trotsky worried about the effect Dewey's liberal agenda would have on the hearings. His supporters tried to calm his fears by explaining Dewey's value to the commission. James Burnham assured him that Dewey would be fair even though he wasn't a Marxist; he had a philosophical and logical approach that would prove beneficial to the inquiry. Novack promised Trotsky that the planned Dewey Commission hearings would help vindicate him in the eyes of world public opinion.[40]

Defense committee members La Follette, Stolberg, and Solow put together the commission in a manner, based on the Muenzenberg precedent, that would enhance the appearance of objectivity. This produced some intentional ideological distancing. For example, James Farrell was rejected because of his public pro-Trotsky pronouncements. Also, several of those appointed to the commission were not defense committee members. A nervous Trotsky kept after the organizers, urging them on and eliciting indirect assurances that he would have the "final word" on procedure and that changes suggested by him could be "put through." The commission secretary Pearl Kluger recognized that there would be criticism that the commission was being assembled and financed by the defense committee.[41] Still, the committee sent a lawyer named Albert Goldman to Mexico to assist Trotsky in preparing for the hearings.

The entire system in which committee members chose commissioners was rather free-wheeling, as appointed commissioners were then asked to recommend other commissioners. Sometimes, recommendations were made by individuals who were not yet commissioners, or never would be. Nor was there a special effort to select lawyers, because, as Stolberg argued, the Moscow trials that were under examination had historical and social, as well as legal, significance.[42] Consequently, the anti-Trotskyist *New Masses* was not alone in suspecting that the commission lacked credibility, since "Trotsky [would] try himself and declare himself not guilty."[43]

When Sidney Hook sought Albert Einstein's endorsement of Trotsky's right to asylum and a public hearing, Einstein responded that Trotsky, in his view, was seeking a propaganda forum and that there wasn't sufficient evidence to conduct a meaningful inquiry. Einstein suggested that he assist in looking into the charges against Trotsky, privately. Hook quickly realized that Einstein would not accept an invitation to be a commissioner, but he wanted his backing since it would encourage others. Hook and Stolberg then went to meet with Einstein in Princeton. The renowned scientist told them that the commission would appear one-sided and its judgment would be seen as arbitrary because witnesses could not be subpoenaed. Einstein remarked: "From my point of view both Stalin and Trotsky are political gangsters."[44]

Norman Thomas, a defense committee member, professed that he would not serve on the commission because he was not impartial. Novack deemed this explanation "specious," and wrote to Trotsky that Thomas was being pressured to join—especially since Dewey had already signed on. Thomas stuck to his guns.[45] The prominent American history expert Charles Beard had a rather sophisticated reason for spurning an invitation. Earlier he had declined membership in the defense committee on the ground that he preferred to "stick to matters of which [he had] some personal knowledge." He was skeptical about the Moscow trials confessions and the allegations against Trotsky, and believed that there was insufficient evidence to prove the Soviet charges. Trotsky was therefore to be considered innocent until the charges could be substantiated, but it was very difficult to demonstrate noninvolvement in a conspiracy. A negative is impossible to prove. Using this logic, Beard believed that the outcome—Trotsky being adjudged not guilty—was really known in advance, so he did not want to play any part in such a procedure. Once Beard had turned down an offer, George Novack contacted the historian Carl Becker, who begged off for health reasons. Felix Morrow then sent Becker a copy of Beard's letter of refusal, and Becker agreed with its reasoning. He also opined that Trotsky's political attitudes were consistent with the possibility of conspiracy, so his defense would have to be an effort to explain why he wasn't a conspirator.[46] After being rejected by Thomas and Beard, Novack wrote to Trotsky: "As you can see, the fetish of absolute impartiality has many worshipers in our high intellectual circles."[47]

The commission came close to including Arthur Garfield Hays and D. N. Pritt, stalwarts of the Reichstag international citizens' tribunal. They would provide experience as well as ideological balance, since they certainly were not Trotskyists. Novack asked Hays to serve, met with him, and secured his participation. However, Hays's letter to the committee sidestepped the idea of being a panel member and focused on the role of commission counsel. Hays indicated that he trusted the commission because of Dewey's major role, but was willing to take part only as a lawyer and not as a propagandist. He said that the purpose should not be to determine guilt or innocence, but to evaluate the Moscow trials. Trotsky would have to be cross-examined vigorously and evidence should be accepted from Stalinists as well as Trotskyists. Hays further suggested that a communist lawyer, Joseph Brodsky, should be invited to participate; if no communist lawyer were to agree to be involved, then Pritt should be invited.[48] Hays was laying out strict conditions that demonstrated once again his independence and attachment to due process, regardless of the circumstances. He wanted critics of Trotsky included, and clearly considered Pritt to be in that category, since he had found the Moscow trials to be fair. Pritt later wrote to Hays about the "genuineness" of these trials and remarked: "After all, practically no one any longer doubts it."[49] Basically, Hays offered to be the commission's counsel and wanted to influence the legal context of the hearings.

Dewey immediately answered Hays's letter. He thanked him for being willing to serve as counsel without fee, but noted that he had actually expected him to be a commissioner. He then went on with an explanation of the structure of the commission, and pointedly commented that procedures were to be determined by the Commission. Dewey agreed that Trotsky should be cross-examined, but differed with Hays on the issue of guilt and innocence. He also affirmed that he would invite Brodsky and did so that very day. Brodsky then decided not to take part. Pritt proved more controversial, as Dewey believed that his writings did not properly present evidence and that he was partisan. He maintained that Pritt could attend if designated as a representative of the Soviet side, but he was not acceptable as an "impartial observer."[50]

When Hays had asked to be the commission's counsel, Dewey was caught unawares as two other lawyers—Paul Hays and Frank Walsh—had already been approached in that regard. Once Arthur Garfield Hays had offered his services as counsel, Dewey quickly accepted and asked for his assistance in recruiting nonbiased commissioners from other countries and in encouraging Stalinists to present evidence to the commission. Nevertheless, Hays had to drop out of the picture, because a court date prevented him from participating in the Mexico hearings. John Finerty, a veteran of the Sacco-Vanzetti defense team who knew Dewey from that case, was then selected as counsel.[51]

Pritt was not invited to go to Mexico. Hays then pointed out that his absence made it more likely that the Soviet Union would not provide evidence. He also alluded to the hearings as covering only one side of the story and proposed that an international group of lawyers, including Pritt, should have their own investigation of the Moscow trials. After the Mexico hearings, Pritt informed Hays that he had been asked to be on the commission scheduled to meet in New York. He was unsure if he wanted to participate under such circumstances and also was unable to leave London at the time. Therefore, he responded "no."[52]

Once it became clear that neither Pritt nor Brodsky was going to be at the Mexico hearings, Dewey became concerned that there would not be any proponents of Soviet interests. Invitations were therefore sent out rather belatedly to the Soviet embassy in Washington, the Comintern, the American and Mexican Communist parties, and the leftist Mexican labor union, CTM. None responded. They did not want to legitimize a hearing expected to be favorable to Trotsky. The letter from Dewey and Finerty to the ambassador to the United States, Alexander Troyanovsky, asked him to send a representative to Mexico City who would be entitled to cross-examine Trotsky and other witnesses, and to supply records from the Moscow investigation. Troyanovsky publicly announced that he wouldn't even forward the request to his government. Alluding to the participation of three defense committee members on the subcommission, he declared: "Practically, it means that Trotsky will lead the inquiry about himself and afterward will probably be his own judge with the assistance of his advocates."[53] The Soviet Union thus acted similarly to Germany, which had refused to send a representative to the London countertrial.

When the Preliminary ("Dewey") Commission was finally organized, its six American members were Dewey; the labor journalist Ben Stolberg; the author and journalist Suzanne La Follette; the Latin American scholar Carleton Beals; the analyst of Russian affairs Edward Ross; and the former professor and literary critic of *The New York Times,* John Chamberlain. Joining them were the French Marxist Alfred Rosmer; the German biographer of Marx, Otto Ruehle; the former German Communist and Reichstag deputy Wendelin Thomas; the Italian anarchosyndicalist Carlo Tresca; and the Mexican labor journalist Francisco Zamora. None was an avowed Trotskyist, but Rosmer was close to Trotsky—and Stolberg and La Follette were guiding forces in the defense committee. There was no Stalinist, nor any highly prestigious non–American representatives. Efforts to recruit Russell and Gide failed.[54]

All of the commission members were not available to go to Mexico, so a subcommission was to represent them there. Dewey had a prior commitment to speak in St. Louis on April 21, and wasn't sure if he would be at the hearings. Sidney Hook and James Cameron, a leading Trotskyist, prevailed on him to go, and Dewey agreed because of his anger at Moscow for pressuring him and others not to do so. He stipulated, however, that sessions had to be concluded no later than April 19 so that he could get to St. Louis on time. Dewey was accommodated, but this meant that the international citizens' tribunal was scheduled a little earlier than originally planned.[55] This helps explain why so many invitations to panelists and observers were sent out at the last minute.

Finally, Trotsky was to get his public hearing. The focus thus shifted to Mexico City to await the interplay between the eloquent and fiery revolutionary and his methodical and judicious liberal interlocutor, John Dewey. The venue was to be remote, but a session featuring such intellectual giants could only produce an electric atmosphere filled with rhetorical sparks.

Chapter VIII

SOUTH OF THE BORDER

On April 2, 1937, a contingent from the defense committee left New York aboard a train bound for Mexico City. It included Dewey, La Follette, and Stolberg, who were members of the subcommission being sent to the Trotsky hearings, along with the committee secretary George Novack, the commission secretary Pearl Kluger, and the committee member James Farrell. The other two subcommissioners were to join them in Mexico. Carleton Beals was en route from California and Otto Ruehle lived in Mexico City. Dewey used the long journey to read transcripts of the two Moscow show trials and some of Trotsky's writings.

The unintentional composition of the group aboard the train was a portent of controversies to come. Beals was not accompanying the other Americans on the subcommission and therefore did not have an opportunity to develop any camaraderie with them, while Trotskyists Novack and Farrell, who were not subcommission members, did. Stolberg and La Follette worried that the inclusion of Novack would compromise the subcommission. Novack discussed the matter with Trotsky after the travelers arrived in Mexico City on April 6, and decided that it was best that he reside separately from the panelists.[1] Dewey, careful to present an image of objectivity in his role as subcommission chair, decided that he would not meet with Trotsky prior to the official sessions.

Dewey announced that Mexico was displaying its status as a "political democracy" and was being honored by hosting a hearing about a foreigner, conducted by other foreigners.[2] All seemed to be going well as the subcommission was about to start work, but some crucial questions remained: Could a subcommission with links to the Trotsky defense committee be perceived as impartial? Would the hearings uncover evidence that could undermine the credibility of the Moscow trials and vindicate Trotsky? Would the commission be able to withstand the Stalinist offensive against it, and would Dewey be able to press his concepts of liberalism in juxtaposition to Trotsky's revolutionary Marxism-Leninism? The answers would soon become known.

The Liberal Philosopher

The chairman of the "Dewey Commission" and its subcommission was the seventy-eight-year-old philosopher John Dewey, who had retired from his Columbia University professorship in 1930. During World War I, he had opposed communist advocacy of world revolution and had supported U.S. involvement. In 1928, Dewey visited the Soviet Union as part of an educational delegation sponsored by the American Society for Cultural Relations with Russia and was impressed with its social and pedagogical reforms. Nevertheless, he noted: "The phase of Bolshevism with which one cannot feel sympathy is its emphasis upon the necessity of class war and of world revolution by violence."[3] Dewey soon became increasingly critical of the Soviet system, due to its repressive dictatorship of the proletariat. As he later remarked, the failure of the Soviet experiment was a "bitter disillusionment to me personally." When Kamenev and Zinoviev were first put on trial in January 1935, Dewey had joined the International Committee for Political Prisoners which sent a petition of protest to Soviet ambassador to the United States Alexander Troyanovsky.[4]

Dewey viewed Stalinism as representative of the natural evolution of Bolshevism, whereas former Bolshevik Trotsky saw Stalinism as its perversion. Dewey had no affinity for Trotskyism, which he considered dogmatic. In fact, Dewey wasn't even a Marxist, despite the observation by his then-Marxist friend Sidney Hook that Dewey's pragmatic instrumentalism was compatible with Marxism. Trotskyist George Novack was closer to the mark when he described Deweyism as "middle-class liberalism" inconsistent with Marxism.[5] Dewey was open-minded about Trotsky's innocence and was anxious to investigate specific charges made at the Moscow trials to determine whether Trotsky had actually been a conspirator. For Dewey, Trotsky the individual was less important than the fact that many Americans admired the Soviet Union and there was a need to ascertain the truth about its system. Even Stalin deserved the same right to a hearing, were he to be in such a position. Neither ideological preferences, nor the Jewish issue, motivated Dewey's concern. His emphasis was on applying democratic modes of inquiry.[6]

Dewey argued that democracy was a process, not an end. Communists, by contrast, were too end-oriented and this produced dictatorship. He also was concerned that many American liberals were willing to accept aspects of Soviet behavior that they would not countenance at home, in part because of Moscow's success in combating the Depression. An analysis of means appropriate to societal change was imperative in the United States, as there was a danger that democratic values would be eroded. Dewey saw the conflict between Stalin and Trotsky as significant only so far as it affected American attitudes, and he commented shortly after arriving in Mexico City that the effect of the hearings on the Soviet Union was not as crucial as its impact on "the outside world." Dewey was out to save democracy in the United States. For him, the key was to understand that "it is the means that are employed that decide the ends or consequences that are actually attained," and that "the only ends are the consequences."[7]

Dewey argued that "the fundamental principle of democracy" was that means must accord with ends, and that ends were not "things beyond activity at which the latter is directed" but "terminals of deliberation, and so turning points in activity." Ends are not "termini of action at all." Those who contemplate fixed ends are seeking certainty and thus demand "guarantees in advance of action." This produces dogmatism, as truth turns into "an insurance company." There is really no such thing as "the single all-important end" that can be used to justify means.[8] Dewey therefore had a philosophical explanation for Trotsky's dogmatism that embraced class struggle as the means toward the end of communism. For Dewey, other means also were possible, and their justification had to be based on an analysis of their consequences.[9]

Dewey was essentially an educator and he believed that democracy was the first step toward enlightenment. On his ninetieth birthday, he explained that "democracy begins in conversation." This is exactly the way he viewed the role of the Dewey Commission, an exercise in the right to present evidence in search of some aspect of truth. There was no preconceived universal truth, only an unfolding educational process that is open to new situations.[10]

Mise-en-Scene

Trotsky, living at Kahlo's "Blue House" in Coyoacan, diligently prepared for his appearance before the Dewey Commission. He was assisted by the Chicago lawyer Albert Goldman; the writer Bertram Wolfe; a secretary from his Norwegian exile, Jean van Heijenoort; and his longtime aide, Jan

Frankel. George Novack was in Mexico for part of the time prior to the hearings. There also was the technical staff of the subcommission, organized by Herb Solow, which eventually included secretary Pearl Kluger and the verbatim reporter at the sessions, Albert Glotzer. Predictably, Trotsky proved to be a difficult client. Shortly before the hearings convened, Solow confided to a financial contributor: "I have had two violent fights with him and expect another tomorrow."[11]

From April 10 through 17, the Dewey Commission conducted its international citizens' tribunal hearings at the "Blue House." This was selected over a more public site for security reasons and to reduce the risk of embarrassment to the Mexican government. To prevent any attack, brick barricades were constructed outdoors to shield the windows. Attendees, including Dewey, were frisked on entrance.[12] Space constraints limited seating to about fifty nonparticipants, including the press. The subcommission, composed of Dewey, La Follette, Stolberg, Beals, and Ruehle then directed the hearings, which were in English. Some areas of possible bias were apparent, since Trotsky's lawyer had been recommended by the defense committee, and it also had selected the panelists. Critics pointed out that La Follette and Stolberg were admirers of Trotsky, and that they and Dewey were members of the defense committee. Ruehle became close to Trotsky after the hearings, but he was not a Trotskyist, ideologically.[13]

Also subject to scrutiny was the role of the Dewey Commission press agent, Charlie Walker, who spent two months in Mexico prior to the hearings, including considerable time with Trotsky. During the sessions, Dewey, Stolberg, La Follette, and Finerty lived in Walker's home and were transported daily to the "Blue House." Isolated again, Beals stayed in a hotel and had to make his own way. This arrangement enhanced Beals's feeling that he was being excluded.[14]

Adopting the position recommended by Hays, Dewey declared in his opening statement in Coyoacan that the aim was not to pronounce guilt or innocence, but to examine Trotsky's evidence regarding the Moscow trials. Trotsky diplomatically asserted that he would not say anything offensive to Mexican opinion.[15] Trotsky and Frankel were the only witnesses to appear before the subcommission, with the latter testifying briefly. Trotsky was not a defendant and was questioned by his own lawyer, Goldman. Members of the panel and their counsel, John Finerty, then engaged in cross-examination.

Finerty was acting more like an independent magistrate than a prosecutor. When questioning Trotsky, he referred to "alleged" acts—usage generally associated with the legal defense. When Finerty had agreed to serve as counsel, he had been assured that he could treat Trotsky as a hostile witness. Trotsky concurred. Finerty was so impressed with Trotsky during the hearings, however, that he came to treat him rather gently. Solow and Glotzer recognized that a pro-Soviet attorney was needed to conduct a proper cross-examination. Dewey later wrote in reference to Finerty: "It was my impression that he went there mildly prejudiced against T. and was more or less converted in the process of the hearings." The *Manchester Guardian Weekly* reported: "If in the Moscow trials there was, for Trotsky, no means of defense, in Mexico there was, on the other hand, no prosecutor."[16] This was to a considerable extent true, but was surely not part of the tribunal's design. It had clearly recognized the need for pro-Stalinist participation, but entreaties had been rejected by both Brodsky and Troyanovsky. This was similar to the Reichstag countertrial's failure to attract German government representation.

Trotsky finally had his opportunity to follow in Dimitrov's footsteps. According to *The New York Times*: "The thin gray man dominates the proceedings and Mr. Dewey, large and quiet, slow-spoken and quick-witted, in Yankee shrewdness lets him dominate." A British journalist agreed, writing that Trotsky "is a dramatist and plays his own title-roles; I doubt if his judgment has ever been objective. But, in exile, objectivity is about impossible. Its destruction is the worst damage that exile inflicts."[17]

Affecting such objectivity was the documentary evidence. Almost all of it was furnished by Trotsky, with some of it having been forwarded from Paris by his son Lev. It was examined carefully, especially by Otto Ruehle, but there was surely leeway for Trotsky to hold back anything incriminating and copies were frequently supplied, rather than the originals. When asked for specific documents that were not available, Trotsky cited the November 1936 theft at the Paris archive plus the need to hide originals so they would not suffer the same fate. His lawyer, Albert Goldman, stated publicly that Trotsky would be unable to produce all of his correspondence from the previous nine years because many of the documents were not in Mexico. Stolberg tried to focus attention on the full half of the glass, asserting: "The commission is concerned not with the paucity of the documentary material but with its overwhelming abundance."[18] For example, there was ample proof of Trotsky's activities that cleared him of meeting with other alleged conspirators on certain dates, and a hotel in Copenhagen cited at a Moscow show trial as a rendezvous location was shown to have burned down years earlier.

Dewey was alert, articulate, and logical despite his advanced age, but fireworks did not erupt between him and Trotsky. Dewey disagreed with many of Trotsky's ideological positions and made it clear that he would never endorse Trotskyism. As his friend James Farrell relates, "He said it was tragic to see such brilliant native intelligence locked up in absolutes."[19] However, he was always polite to Trotsky. Dewey observed in reference to Goldman: "He says that in T's interest as well as our own we must lean over backward whenever necessary in order to be fair." Actually, Trotsky was less concerned about the fairness of the procedure than he was about the opportunity to prove his innocence and advance his agenda. After the hearings, Dewey shook Trotsky's hand. He describes the scene as follows: "I broke down and came so near crying—perhaps it was actually crying—I had to turn away—and my tear glands don't work easily."[20] Apparently, those in attendance were affected similarly. Glotzer observes in regard to Trotsky's impact: "And when he finished, the audience, a singularly diverse one, burst out into applause, which was, believe me, spontaneous."[21]

Uncivil War

Considerable attention paid to Dewey and Trotsky was quickly diverted by Beals, who challenged the subcommission's credibility. Beals had been invited to serve because of his friendship with Stolberg. An expert on Mexico, he was at first reluctant to take part because he did not believe he was sufficiently knowledgeable about the Soviet Union, but once having decided to be a panelist, he read the Moscow trial transcripts as preparation.[22]

Beals arrived in Mexico City two days after other panelists. He was not involved in planning the hearings and had no input into the subcommission's opening statement, which was to be read by Dewey. Beals claimed that he wasn't consulted on the matter, but La Follette maintained that Stolberg asked him to look it over (after it had been written) and he responded that he was too busy. Once Dewey had made his presentation, Beals somewhat tactlessly pointed out publicly that there was a factual error in the text. Dewey had said that Trotsky could be extradited to the Soviet Union but, as Beals noted, there were no diplomatic relations between Mexico and the Soviet Union and no extradition treaty. Dewey graciously apologized to Beals for not making sure that he had given him the opportunity to read the statement in advance, and for erring factually. Trotsky retorted to Beals that the extradition issue wasn't germane since he had always been willing to appear in a Moscow court and that he had come to Mexico involuntarily after being expelled from Norway—surely not to avoid extradition to the Soviet Union.[23]

Antagonisms between Beals and other panelists then escalated. Beals moved out of his hotel and refused to divulge his new address. La Follette requested three times during the hearings that he stop chewing gum, and Goldman even asked Trotsky about his own opposition to gum chewing. Beals retorted that the chewing culprit was actually Frida Kahlo—not himself. Kahlo was indeed masticating, but this fact did not necessarily absolve Beals. Ruehle would writhe and groan whenever Beals asked a question. Beals wasn't too pleased with Ruehle's participation anyway, rudely claiming that Ruehle didn't know English.[24]

There also was the matter of inadequate clerical support, since Glotzer proved to be unable to keep up with the onerous task. Panelists were not furnished with transcripts as the hearings progressed, leading Beals to complain that he was unable to refer to relevant points. This problem was compounded as the cross-examination of Trotsky was to be at the end. It turned out that Trotsky gave testimony for approximately five and one-half days and was subsequently cross-examined for only one and one-half days.

Beals objected to what he described as the "chummy clubroom" atmosphere and was adamant about probing into Trotsky's political past. He also inquired rhetorically whether Trotsky may have destroyed documents unfavorable to himself. In an attempt to rein him in, the subcommission decided that all queries had to be cleared with counsel, John Finerty. Beals' failure to adhere fully to this stricture generated considerable friction with Finerty and basically turned his own role into that of a prosecutor.[25]

Beals grilled Trotsky about his role at the time of the Brest-Litovsk peace negotiations with Germany in 1918, arguing that since Trotsky had been prepared to cede Russian territory to Germany then, he would possibly advocate doing so again. This line of questioning was cut off by other panel members, and Beals was asked to stick to more relevant matters.[26] Beals appeared to be reintroducing the rather fantastic allegation made at the second Moscow show trial that Trotsky had colluded with Germany during the 1930s on a plan to turn over Soviet territory. Nazi Germany was certainly different from the Kaiser's Germany, and Trotsky would never have countenanced such a giveaway to his sworn enemy. Trotsky had not, in fact, advocated the relinquishment of land to Germany in 1918, although his "no war, no peace" policy while commissar of war did unintentionally produce the loss of Russian territory. When the Treaty of Brest-Litovsk was effected in March 1918, Trotsky refused to be the Russian representative to sign it.

Another flap also revolved around events from many years earlier. At issue was Trotsky's organization of a Fourth International. Beals wanted to trace Trotsky's advocacy of world revolution and so went back to the years 1919 and 1920. He asked Trotsky if he had promoted revolution in other countries and the reply was that it had been done by the Comintern. Then Beals, apparently armed with a document prepared years earlier by the Comintern agent Mikhail Borodin, asked Trotsky if he had dispatched Borodin to Mexico to ignite a revolution in conjunction with Mexican Communists. Trotsky declared that the insinuation was false, the document a lie, and the question was actually aimed at jeopardizing his status in Mexico. His position was backed by La Follette. Dewey adjourned the session and gathered his fellow panelists to discuss the matter. Beals then charged that this was an attempt to get him to "disclaim" his question. La Follette and Finerty maintained that the charge regarding Borodin was based on private information, not on evidence introduced at the hearing. La Follette stressed that the source was the problem, not the question itself, but made it clear that Trotsky's continued asylum could be threatened.[27]

Beals badgered Finerty mercilessly, accusing him of wasting time with nonconfrontational cross-examination techniques and of helping Trotsky fill in gaps in his testimony left open by the omissions of Goldman. Finerty thought that Beals's goal was to embarrass Trotsky. For Beals, Trotsky was a defendant; for Finerty, he was a witness. Beals was a scholar interested in history and ideology, whereas Finerty was a lawyer focused on guilt or innocence. Upset by Beals's interrogation about the role of Borodin, Finerty angrily remarked that he would quit should similar questions follow. Beals commented that Finerty was acting like Trotsky's lawyer and threatened to leave the subcommission if Finerty did not resign. La Follette advised Beals to apologize to Finerty, but he stormed out. Dewey later insisted that he had told Beals that his questioning could be continued at the next session.[28]

Walkout

Beals's showdown with other panelists and Finerty following the Borodin incident took place on April 16. The next morning, Beals withdrew from the Dewey Commission. He tendered a letter of resignation to Dewey, prepared a statement about his action, and spoke with journalists. Dewey had tried to head off Beals by suggesting that each subcommission member could submit a minority report to the full commission, but Beals responded: "For me to bring in any other minority report than that of my resignation would be to commit a grave injustice to Mr. Trotsky." He claimed that the hearings were not a serious attempt at investigation, only "a pink tea party with everyone but myself uttering sweet platitudes," and that he discerned a "hushed adoration" by subcommission members for Trotsky.[29] Dewey felt that Beals had prejudged the case, but Beals said that he couldn't judge Trotsky's role because of the subcommission's "intolerable methods." An editorial in *The New York Times*, which had been hostile toward the hearings, contended: "As the quarrel sharpens it will become hard to say offhand who is being denounced for staging travesties of justice, John Dewey or Joseph Stalin."[30]

Beals maintained that "if anything, I was predisposed in Trotsky's favor before I went to Mexico." He was not a proponent of Trotsky's views, but did believe that he deserved a hearing. During the sessions, he thought that Trotsky was at times untruthful. Nevertheless, he didn't think that the exile's guilt or innocence of Moscow's charges was really crucial, since conspiracy was the only possible method available against the Soviet system. Beals claimed that he had resigned purely as a reaction to the behavior of the subcommission, and that his act was unrelated to his perspective on the Moscow trials or Trotsky. He asserted that the procedures adopted at the hearings smacked of unfairness and had been more harmful to Trotsky than the Moscow trials. Trying to counter charges that he was a Stalinist, Beals wrote a year later: "Stalin for me is a menace to the world. Poor Trotsky reveals all the symptoms of a disordered temperament. I repeat: 'A plague on both their houses'."[31]

Beals's disaffection from the subcommission, provocative questioning of Trotsky, and resignation can be taken at face value, as no information has ever surfaced to demonstrate that he was biased against Trotsky or pro-Stalinist. Although he had been a Mexican correspondent for the Soviet news agency, Tass, he had also been a friend of Rivera, an admirer of Cardenas, and had wired the Mexican president to encourage the granting of asylum to Trotsky. Hook suspected that Beals had planned from the start to disrupt the Dewey Commission, but was unable to provide any evidence to substantiate such a charge. Trotsky implied that he was operating on behalf of the Soviet government.[32] One theory about why he bolted from the hearings was that he was swayed by Harry Block, the American son-in-law of the Mexican labor leader Vicente Lombardo Toledano. Dewey alluded to pressure on Beals after he got to Mexico and cited the influence of the Stalinist "Toledano faction," which wanted him to "keep away from us." Beals had enjoyed a long association with leftist Latin American trade unions and probably came to believe that the appearance on the scene of Trotsky was divisive and sure to weaken labor's cause.[33]

On returning to the United States after the hearings, Dewey said: "I have my own ideas about Beals, but they're not for publication." In a private letter, he wrote that "either Carleton Beals is lying or I am," and complained that the Communists were using Beals's statements to discredit the inquiry.[34] Dewey blamed Beals for spreading "false accusations" against the subcommission on behalf of "powerful interests" (ostensibly Stalinists) that were trying to disrupt it. He additionally pointed out Beals's lack of cooperation with other subcommission members and his failure to register complaints prior to his resignation. As for Beals's concern that the absence of some of Trotsky's documents was prejudicial, Dewey countered that those presented were "sufficient to justify the full commission continuing with its work."[35]

Dewey saw the subcommission as an agent of the full commission, so he intended to present his findings to the latter, which would hold additional hearings and then issue the final report. Beals challenged this procedure at the hearings, calling on the subcommission to act on its own in writing the final report. Speed was essential, maintained Beals, because lives in the Soviet Union could possibly be saved if Trotsky were to be found innocent and because the Soviet government deserved to be cleared of any suspicions, were Trotsky to be declared guilty.[36] After all, the London countertrial in the Reichstag fire case intentionally reached its conclusions in time to secure the release of four Leipzig defendants.

The simplest explanation for Beals's behavior is that he developed personal differences with the subcommission members, felt like an outsider, and then compounded this resentment with what to him appeared to be a lack of integrity on the part of the panelists in regard to their treatment of Trotsky. Beals's biographer, John Britton, points to his inherent distrust of "established authority" and cynicism toward "intellectual dogma." In Britton's interpretation, Beals rebelled against what he perceived to be "an organized power structure" around Trotsky.[37]

In any case, when Beals published his analysis of the Coyoacan hearings in *The Saturday Evening Post*, an outraged Finerty considered filing a libel suit against Beals for damaging his professional standing. A concerned Dewey immediately sent two letters to Hook on the matter. Hays was brought in for advice and concluded that a lawsuit would be too time-consuming and would produce little in the way of a settlement. He suggested that Finerty should instead write to *The Saturday Evening Post* and give it a choice of publishing a counterstatement from the Commission or of facing a libel suit. Finerty then wrote to the magazine demanding the right to have an article published with a "correct statement of facts," to be paid for "at your usual rates." Otherwise, there would be a possible lawsuit. La Follette thought that Finerty's hint of libel action was "foolish" and the whole affair seems to have dissipated at this point.[38]

Back in Coyoacan, the Dewey Commission had finished taking testimony. It had suffered a setback as a consequence of the Beals fracas, which had diverted media attention from the strong evidence and provided ammunition to opponents of the tribunal process. Remaining for the commission were the difficult tasks of compiling transcripts of the hearings and preparing a final report on the Moscow show trials and the charges against Trotsky. As *The New York Times* indicated, what really mattered in the long run was "the printed record."[39]

Chapter IX

DELIBERATIONS AND RECRIMINATIONS

Following the big bang of Beals's departure, the Mexico hearings ended with a whimper. No interim judgment was issued as at the Reichstag countertrial. Members of the panel quickly dispersed, with Dewey heading for his planned address to the American College of Physicians in St. Louis and La Follette and Stolberg returning to New York. Ruehle remained at his home in Mexico City.

The next tasks were for the commission to evaluate the evidence derived from the hearings, consider additional documents furnished by affiliated European committees, and to assess materials to be submitted by Trotsky. One problem was that Trotsky supplied many affidavits from Europeans who had not been available at Coyoacan for cross-examination. The commission asked the French subcommission to carry out this responsibility, but it did not reply. La Follette assumed correctly that it would not be done, as it was difficult to arrange and expensive. A second problem was that many documents were not forwarded to New York, but instead left in Mexico to be translated into English by Trotsky's staff. There was therefore a possibility that their content could be distorted. Finally, supplemental materials to be submitted by Trotsky could easily be selected in a self-serving manner.[1]

Despite such deficiencies regarding evidence, the hearings in Mexico were gaining credibility. Trotsky had finally been able to testify and the procedures of the Moscow trials had been opened up to public scrutiny. Trotsky's testimony had made a powerful impact on an initially skeptical media and the genuineness of the show trial confessions was increasingly being questioned. Contributing to this evolving perspective was the June 11, 1937 execution of eight Soviet generals, including former chief of staff

Mikhail Tukhachevsky, for supposed conspiracy with Germany. This far-fetched charge undermined Stalin's image because he was weakening Soviet military capability in face of a strengthening Axis alliance. Dewey observed that it had become apparent that the Soviet regime's veracity was in doubt. He added astutely that these executions would do more to undercut Stalin than had his own subcommission's hearings.[2]

Feedback

Press coverage of the hearings was limited because Mexico City was not a major media center and because the "Blue House" had little room for journalists. Interest in the proceedings came mainly from the United States, where the defense committee had the support of many prominent intellectuals. The whole endeavor was largely an American show, since four of the five subcommission members were from the United States. The British and French committees sadly reported scant attention in their countries.[3] Published accounts were mostly negative, due to a reluctance to give credence to Trotsky's charges against the Soviet Union at a time when fascism was seen as the prime danger. An article in the influential journal *Foreign Affairs* conceded that Trotsky may not have conspired with the defendants against Moscow, but concluded that his Coyoacan testimony was not sufficiently convincing in regard to his claim that he would not resort to terror or sabotage in his anti-Soviet struggle.[4]

The New York Times had a reporter, Frank Kluckhohn, on the scene and his articles during the hearings tended to accentuate their alleged lack of impartiality. He was critical of the Dewey Commission but did, by contrast, cite considerable evidence backing Trotsky. Dewey protested Kluckhohn's coverage to the journalist's managing editor, Edwin James. The response was that the newspaper would look into Dewey's complaint and in the meantime, advised Kluckhohn not to editorialize in his news reports. In a letter to Roberta Lowitz Grant, Dewey quipped: "If K wasn't paid by the GPU he missed a chance."[5]

The Stalinists waged a no-holds-barred attack on the Commission, with Soviet Ambassador Troyanovsky labeling the hearings a "flop." He claimed before the National Press Club that they were one-sided, dealt hastily with events far away, and relied exclusively on the testimony of Trotsky. Dewey then condemned Troyanovsky for smearing his commission.[6] The pro-Soviet Communist press in the United States denigrated Dewey as dishonest and not in possession of his senses and even reversed course by attacking his philosophical works that had earlier been praised.

The *Daily Worker* called Dewey a "Charlie McCarthy for the Trotskyites" and described Ben Stolberg as an "ordinary low-priced street-walker ready to peddle himself in parks, alleys, or hallways to any chance customer." Stalinists also went after James Farrell, who had supported the defense committee and traveled to Mexico with Dewey. His writing ability was questioned, and he was criticized by twenty-five intellectuals in *The New Republic*.[7]

Waldo Frank, the chairman of the League of American Writers, also ran into trouble with the Stalinists. He had once been asked to serve on the Dewey Commission. Then, after the hearings, he had proposed an international commission of British and American communists and socialists to investigate the Moscow trials and Trotsky's countercharges. Under Moscow's pressure, Frank prevaricated, with the explanation that he was not anti-Soviet, that Trotsky's allegation of a frame-up at the show trials was unreasonable, and that clarifications were needed because the Soviet image had been tarnished by the Moscow trials. His effort was to no avail, as Stalinists brought about his ouster from the chairmanship of the League of American Writers.[8]

Trotsky and the Dewey Commission were forced to the defensive as a result of the Mexico tribunal, but they had publicized their causes. Even if Trotsky had not aroused liberal opinion (there was surely no hope of converting pro-Soviet communists), he had made his views known and basked in the attention afforded. *Time* insightfully declared: "Whatever the Dewey investigation might prove in the end, there was no doubt that it had shown Leon Trotsky, . . . a disowned and virtually impotent revolutionist, to be now the most important revolutionary extremist in the world."[9] Dewey had shown that the right to a hearing and adherence to the democratic process were paramount irrespective of ideology. His emphasis on means rather than ends had been duly noted.

Dewey's Stance

Among those discrediting the Mexico hearings was Malcolm Cowley of *The New Republic*. He had been a thorn in the side of the defense committee for several months, so in May 1937 a combative Dewey resigned as a contributing editor of *The New Republic*, a position he had held since 1914. He charged that the magazine had claimed impartiality but actually was sympathetic to the Soviet Union. Impressed by the recantations of old Bolsheviks at the Moscow show trials, Cowley had indeed written to the noted literary critic Edmund Wilson that very month: "I think that their confessions can be explained only on the hypothesis that most of them were guilty almost exactly as charged."[10]

Dewey disagreed that the Soviet Union was, in Cowley's words, "moving in the right direction," for this could not be so if claims about Trotsky's role as a conspirator were false. Dewey stressed that he was not a Marxist, and was not prepared to defend Trotsky from attacks on his political views, but he was particularly concerned about the Soviet Union serving as a model for some Americans. The heart of the matter, according to Dewey, was "that the sooner American radicals cut loose from the influence, direct and still more indirect, of Soviet Russia, the better it will be for the radical movement in this country."[11] Cowley responded that *The New Republic* did publish anti-Trotsky editorials, so it tried to balance opinion by giving preference to pro-Trotsky letters to the editor. He confirmed that he disliked Trotsky, and remarked: "I wouldn't ever say it in print, but my personal conviction is that he is touched with paranoia, with delusions of persecution and grandeur." Cowley insisted that he was not a Stalinist and did not accept Soviet one-man leadership and repression, but that the Soviet Union had to be defended from the fascists. He tried to appease Dewey by professing "deep respect for your own work and for its spirit of inquiry, and fair-mindedness."[12]

Dewey also engaged in an ideological minuet with Alex Gumberg, an American who represented Soviet trade interests in the United States. Gumberg met with Dewey prior to the latter's May 9 "Truth is on the March" speech at the Mecca Temple in New York to warn him about the implications of his commission's activities. After the speech, he wrote to Dewey that ascertaining the truth is noble, but "the possible temporary injustice to one individual" (i.e., Trotsky) was not so important. He indicated that Dewey would end up with "strange bedfellows" with whom he would become increasingly uncomfortable. Dewey countered with the explanation that he knew how to apply "objective intellectual analyses," and could not easily be deceived even if he was somewhat ignorant of leftist factional intrigues.[13]

The fullest explication of Dewey's views on the Commission took place in December 1937 in an interview by Agnes Meyer, his former student and the wife of the publisher of *The Washington Post*. The elderly philosopher did not mince words as he opined that "personally, I have always disagreed with the ideas of Trotsky and I disagree with him now, if possible, more than ever." He rejected Trotsky's continuing commitment to violent revolution and class dictatorship and explained that "this is the reason why I said earlier that Communists and their sympathizers among liberals cannot solve the problem which the current debacle in the Soviet Union puts to them, by turning to Trotsky." Dewey equally condemned Soviet means of effecting social change and referred to proclaimed Soviet democracy as a "farce." He stated: "We must stop looking to the Soviet Union as a model for solving our own economic difficulties and as a source of defense for democracy against fascism." Like Trotsky, Dewey interestingly concluded that the Soviet Union was becoming more like Germany, another totalitarian state—and he correctly predicted that the two countries would become allies.[14] Nothing could have irked his Stalinist opponents more.

Ongoing Process

The Commission of Inquiry was responsible for producing the transcript of the Mexico hearings, evaluating the evidence assembled by the subcommission, organizing additional sessions in which witnesses could testify, and preparing a final report on Trotsky and the Moscow trials. As Pearl Kluger reported to Trotsky, however, the commission "is just broke, and has been since the Mexican hearings." La Follette informed Dewey that Glotzer could not be paid what was promised (apparently for his work on the transcript) and Dewey was unsuccessful in getting the Philadelphia art collector and philanthropist Albert Barnes to provide money for Trotsky's preparation of documents.[15] There also was friction between the defense committee and the commission, with Dewey upset about the committee's interference with his work, as well as about plans to resign by commissioners who felt that most of their task had already been accomplished.[16]

Another problem was the collapse of the tactical alliance between Trotskyists and Socialists. Even before the hearings in Mexico, Trotsky had told Glotzer that events in Spain necessitated revolutionary action and that cooperation with the Socialists in the United States was no longer justified. Norman Thomas then returned from the Soviet Union in June with negative comments regarding the Kremlin's use of violence and intrigue, but Trotsky was insistent on orchestrating a split despite a common anti-Soviet platform. There was a crucial difference, however, in that Thomas continued to view the Soviet Union as essential to the antifascist front. Trotskyists fomented dissension within the Socialist Party, to which they formally belonged, leading to their expulsion in August 1937. This affected collaboration in the Trotsky defense committee as Socialists began to leave. They claimed that the committee was only serving Trotsky's interests, as the original concerns about asylum and a hearing had already been resolved.[17]

The commission forged on, with most of the input provided by sub-commissioners Dewey, La Follette, and Stolberg. To replace the departed Beals, Angelica Balabanova was added. She was a Russian living in France who had once served as secretary of the Comintern and had been a leftist agitator in Italy. The commission hoped to arrange hearings in Oslo, Copenhagen, and possibly London, but did not manage to do so because European defense committees were not very active. The French committee was an exception, and it lay behind the subcommission that held eleven sessions in Paris from May 12 through June 22, 1937. The French did not have a good relationship with the commission in New York, lacked funds, and were not adept at attracting press coverage (France was a Soviet ally at the time), but they were successful in securing the testimony of Lev Sedov and in cross-examining four witnesses whose depositions had been presented at Coyoacan.[18] Hearings in New York then took place on July 26 and 27. Among the eleven witnesses were Herb Solow and Max Shachtman. Commissioners attending were Suzanne La Follette, Alfred Rosmer, Carlo Tresca, and Wendelin Thomas. Finerty and Goldman again served as counsel.[19]

In September, the commission met in New York for three days to produce a "summary of findings" and the transcript of the Mexico hearings in a volume entitled *The Case of Leon Trotsky*. John Chamberlain did not attend, nor did Angelica Balabanova, who feared that her participation could lead French Stalinists to press for nonrenewal of her residence visa. Consideration was given to having Trotsky attend, but action was not taken on this because the U.S. government was unlikely to issue him a visa. On September 21 the commission released the transcript and issued a statement that Trotsky's guilt or innocence would be investigated further. This was in accordance with the original plan to release evidence first and to arrive at judgment afterward.

The commission's endeavor did not garner much publicity in the United States and got even less in Europe, since there was a general impression that the subcommission had been sympathetic to Trotsky. Although many questioned the fairness of the Moscow trials, the Dewey Commission was seen as the other side of the coin—favorable to the defense rather than the prosecution.[20] Also pertinent was the undermining of Trotsky's image after Coyoacan by revelations about his role in suppressing the Kronstadt uprising of 1921. Sailors in Petrograd were pressing for democratic reforms within the Communist-ruled system, so Trotsky's authoritarian response made him appear similar to the Stalinists and linked him to the regime he had come to oppose.[21]

Dewey, La Follette, and Stolberg prepared the evaluation of the evidence and the conclusions, with most of the text being written by La Follette. On December 12, Dewey announced the verdict at a meeting in New York at which attendees paid 25¢ admission. The $625 raised was to be used to help pay publishing costs for the book *Not Guilty*. The commission found that Trotsky and his son Lev Sedov had not conspired with Moscow show trial defendants, and that the trials "served not juridical but political ends." They were "frame-ups," and Trotsky was not guilty. No evidence, the commission asserted, demonstrated that the defendants had conspired with Trotsky and Sedov, although their possible guilt otherwise was not assessed.[22]

The night after Dewey released the commission's final report, he engaged in a radio debate with Corliss Lamont, who was national chairman of the American Friends of the Soviet Union. Lamont charged that Dewey was bringing false charges against the Soviet Union. He emphasized the legitimacy of confessions made at the Moscow trials, but didn't directly try to refute Dewey's evidence. Basically, Lamont attempted to defend Soviet actions and to argue for restraint by Americans in trying to influence Soviet affairs. This approach was rather hypocritical, as pro-Soviet Communists had often called for involvement in the fight for justice around the world.[23] Dewey, ever mindful of teaching the American public an anti-Soviet lesson, proclaimed: "A country that uses all the methods of Fascism to suppress opposition can hardly be held up to us as a democracy, as a model to follow against fascism."[24]

The verdict on Trotsky was more positively received in the American press than had been the Mexico hearings or the September release of the transcript. Dewey duly recognized that press support had been growing since the commission had started its work. *The Nation*, which had flirted with Stalinism, had predicted after Coyoacan that "the only verdict which would be generally accepted from such a Commission would be a verdict of guilty." It also referred to "amateur efforts of an unofficial commission however well-meaning." *The Nation* then changed its tune somewhat after the final commission report was released. Although derisively citing "one of the greatest political interviews ever published" and reiterating its long-held position that Trotsky's innocence could not be proven, the leftist periodical acknowledged the thoroughness of the investigation and the commission's presentation of "an impressive defense." In a later review in *The Nation* by the liberal theologian Reinhold Niebuhr, there was a much more favorable assessment of the findings in *Not Guilty*: "Some of us who regard Trotsky's political theories as fantastic, his messianic ego as pathetic, and his present political influence as confusing will be willing to be regarded as 'Trotskyists' while we stand up for that vote."[25]

Trotsky, of course, was elated with the Commission's judgment and exclaimed that "nowhere and never is progress fed on lies." In a letter to Dewey, he described the verdict as "a terrible—better to say insufferable blow to the Kremlin clique."[26] Of course, Trotsky knew that the verdict was a substitute for any opportunity to defend himself in a Moscow court, since Soviet authorities recognized that he would not confess to any acts and would probably challenge the chief prosecutor Andrei Vyshinsky. Predictably, the Soviet ambassador, Troyanovsky, deemed the verdict a "farce" and posited that "it was clear from the beginning that the committee of Trotsky's advocates would find what they wanted to find."[27] George Novack, the Trotskyist driving force behind the American defense committee, appreciated the verdict but had philosophical differences with Dewey and was perturbed that the commission chairman had combined his exoneration of Trotsky with the comment that his ideas were no better than Stalin's.[28]

Red Graffiti

On February 16, 1938 Trotsky's son Lev died under mysterious circumstances in a French clinic at the age of thirty-two. It is unclear if he was murdered by Soviet intelligence operatives, perhaps in retaliation for the Dewey Commission's verdict on his father.[29] What is patently evident is that the Dewey Commission was unable to moderate Stalin's behavior or provide a chilling effect on state-sponsored terror. On the contrary, in March 1938, there was another show trial at which twenty-one defendants were accused of complicity with Trotsky in crimes including the planned assassination of Soviet leaders. Trotsky claimed that this event was "Stalin's dramatic answer" to Dewey.[30] Nikolai Bukharin, Aleksei Rykov, and Genrikh Yagoda were most prominent among those charged, and they and fifteen others were executed. Foreign press reaction was more negative toward the Soviet Union than it had been during the first two show trials, in part because of the influence of the Dewey Commission's verdict.[31]

The American defense committee asked to be represented at the trial but was turned down. More important, the commission had become generally inoperative after the release of its final report in December and had not constituted itself as an ongoing permanent body. It therefore did not investigate the third major show trial, nor attempt to rally to Trotsky's defense one more time. Dewey did condemn the trial before it had opened, leading Lamont to criticize this allegation of a frame-up before any testimony had been presented. Dewey countered that his advance evaluation of the trial was consistent with his philosophy, since the "scientific method demands application of knowledge previously had by its use to judging related present and future conditions" (more simply put, the "walks like a duck" argument). The almost-defunct Dewey Commission continued in existence, but even Dewey resigned from it in November 1939, maintaining that it was no longer necessary because Stalin had been so severely discredited by the Nazi-Soviet pact.[32]

Trotsky reacted to the 1938 show trial by finally establishing his Fourth International to challenge the Comintern. In September, twenty-one delegates from eleven countries gathered outside Paris at the home of the commission member Alfred Rosmer. It was a modest grouping and it included the as-yet-unmasked Soviet agent Zborowski and a soon-to-be notorious Spanish Communist named Ramon Mercader. The Fourth International was a weak organization, but its anti-Soviet stance rankled the Kremlin leadership.[33]

So, too, had Trotsky's testimony at Coyoacan, which had driven Stalin to initiate a plot to kill his exiled rival. It was developed by Soviet intelligence with the cooperation of the Comintern and aimed at silencing a vocal critic who was not being politically restricted by Mexico. Trotsky's fears for his safety were indeed justified and his personal life was also becoming complicated. Because of a dalliance with Frida Kahlo, Trotsky became estranged from his wife, Natalya, during the summer of 1937. His relationship with Diego Rivera also became increasingly acrimonious, precipitating a move out of the "Blue House" in May 1939. Meanwhile, Stalin's effort to murder him was being carried out by Ramon Mercader, who had gained entree into the Trotsky entourage by becoming the lover of an American Trotskyist, Sylvia Ageloff. She had been a philosophy student of Hook, and her sister Ruth had worked briefly as a secretary for the Dewey Commission. Ageloff had also introduced Mercader to Alfred Rosmer and his wife, Marguerite, who had relocated to Mexico to live with Trotsky. On August 20, 1940, Mercader assaulted Trotsky with a pick and the exiled revolutionary died the next day. Stalin had secured his revenge. Trotsky's American backers tried to arrange for his burial in the United States, but the government would not issue a visa for his body. He was then cremated in Mexico.[34]

The impetus for the commission had come mainly from Trotskyists on the defense committee, but control by liberals was soon asserted by Dewey, whose main concern was the furtherance of democratic values rather than partisanship in intraleft ideological battles. There was thus a similarity with the Reichstag countertrial, in which Hays and other liberals came to the fore, even though Muenzenberg and the Communists had provided the initiative. Unlike the first international citizens' tribunal, which was successful in pressing for the acquittal of four defendants in a German court, the Dewey Commission was unable to head off the third Moscow show trial, with its continuation of the executions of Bolshevik leaders and its aspersions against Trotsky. Also pertinent was a change in emphasis in comparison with the earlier tribunal, in which members were all lawyers. The Dewey Commission was less legalistic, perhaps because its basic aim (despite Beals's complaint) was to reassess Trotsky, not to gain the freedom of the show trial defendants.

In retrospect, the Dewey Commission provided valuable evidence of a Moscow frame-up and Trotsky's noninvolvement in a nonconspiracy. At the time, however, this was not so apparent, as there was considerable support for the Soviet Union's role in a Popular Front against fascism—and the commission's pronouncements were not widely publicized. The commission was nevertheless effective in exposing the hypocrisy of leftist noncommunists who did not want to delve into Soviet misdeeds because they had conveniently deflected their moral outrage elsewhere. Andre Malraux, for example, would not even give a deposition to the commission because he claimed that the Moscow trials did not detract from the Soviet Union's communist dignity. He compared the situation to the Inquisition, which he maintained did not detract from Christianity, regardless of its negative function.[35] Also emanating from the commission was Dewey's strong commitment to democratic procedures and the warning to American liberals not to accept the communist philosophy that the means should be subordinated to the end.

The Dewey Commission had withstood considerable pressure from the Soviet Union and its proponents and had produced evidence that cast doubt about the charges made at the Moscow show trials. Its sympathy for Trotsky—if not for his ideology and revolutionary design—detracted from its appeal and press coverage, however, and contributed to the resignation of Carleton Beals. Also problematic was the inability to secure the participation of any Stalinists at Coyoacan. James Farrell, certainly a proponent of Trotsky, wrote to Dewey after the hearings that the absence of a Stalinist had been detrimental. His interesting analysis was conditioned by the Beals incident, as he argued that a Stalinist on the commission would have been compelled to take a position on Beals and, if he had disavowed him, the commission's image would have been enhanced. He concluded that future tribunals should include a Stalinist as protection against another Beals or Hallgren.[36]

When Trotsky was still in Norway, Malcolm Cowley acutely observed that his real tragedy was not being removed from power and being pilloried by the Soviets, but being discarded in the dustbin of history. Cowley, certainly no advocate of Trotskyism, stressed Trotsky's focus on justice and stated: "It is history that has been his forum and stage, his purpose in living, one might almost literally say his God."[37] In Coyoacan, Trotsky had emerged from the dustbin and vigorously demonstrated his essence of being. The Dewey Commission furnished him with that opportunity. Ultimately, it reaffirmed the liberal notion that justice for individuals, objectionable as their ideologies may be, is critical even in the worst of times.

The Vietnam War Crimes Case

Chapter X

THE ACTIVIST PHILOSOPHER

John Dewey was an objective scholar who agreed to chair an investigatory commission in an effort to ascertain the truth. He had no commitment to Trotskyism. Bertrand Russell, the eminent British philosopher, was engaged in a passionate mission to organize a tribunal that would prove that the United States was guilty of war crimes in Vietnam. His goal was to alter an American policy while it was in progress, not to redress a previous miscarriage of justice. Russell wanted to assign guilt, not seek exoneration, as had taken place at the Reichstag fire and Moscow show trial tribunals. He believed strongly in the accountability of leaders, so he applied the Nuremberg legal principles to the process of international citizens' tribunals and took on Lyndon Johnson and the world's predominant superpower—-the United States.

Lord Russell's Vision

Bertrand Russell's philosophy incorporated mathematical logic, but his politics evolved from heartfelt emotions. Russell was a perpetual adolescent in the sense of seeking new experiences and causes and he took great pleasure in the role of a gadfly who could attract the media's attention and shock the sensibilities of the political establishment. The historian Arnold Toynbee accurately observed: "The impulse to annoy, combined with a generous passion to make all things new, is a well-known mark of youth, and in this sense Russell remained youthful to the end. His insatiable relish for getting into trouble kept him always young in spirit."[1] Russell surrounded himself with keen-minded intellectuals less than half his age and he consistently sounded off on issues of international concern and sent blunt messages to heads of state. The tone was highly charged, rather than dry and legalistic, but Russell felt that they embodied his conception of truth that was based on "the relation between beliefs or assertions, and the facts which beliefs or assertions express."[2]

Russell was virulently anti-Soviet during the early years of the Cold War, and not a pacifist. He feared an invasion of Western Europe and wrote: "Even at such a price, I think war would be worthwhile. Communism must be wiped out, and world government must be established. . . . I do not think the Russians will yield without war."[3] Stalin's death in 1953 transformed Russell's thinking as a de-Stalinized Soviet Union, in his view, was no longer the aggressor. The United States, he believed, was becoming hegemonic and it constituted the prime threat to peace. While imperialistic, the United States also had the capability to enact beneficial changes in the world system, so the onus was placed on Washington rather than on a less flexible Moscow. Russell castigated the U.S. for taking the wrong path, but he was certainly not an admirer of the Soviet system. He endeavored to keep communists out of the peace movement, and he did not permit the pro-Soviet World Peace Council to use his name.[4]

Russell did not expect much from the Soviet Union, and therefore directed his petulance at the more responsible United States. He criticized American policy during the Cuban missile crisis, condemned the treatment of blacks, and played an active role in trying to refute what he saw as the Warren Commission's whitewash of the Kennedy assassination.[5] To him, the United States coveted power and wealth. Ideology was not important, as "nationalism is the greatest danger in world politics." Russell had earlier averred: "I think the ideologies are merely a way of grouping people, and that the passions involved are merely those which always arise between rival groups."[6] The competition between nationalisms could produce a nuclear holocaust, so his anticommunism had to be subordinated to his quest for peace. As the psychoanalyst Erich Fromm observed: "He warns the world of impending doom precisely as the prophets did, because he loves life and all its forms and manifestations. He, again, like the prophets, is not a determinist who claims that the historical future is already determined; he is an 'alternativist' who sees that what is determined are certain limited and ascertainable alternatives. Our alternative is that between the end of the nuclear arms race—or destruction."[7] To further his mission, Russell in September 1963 established the Bertrand Russell Peace Foundation (BRPF).

Escalation of the Vietnam War came to be Russell's main global concern. In late 1964 he dispatched senior staffer Chris Farley to observe the effects of American bombing. In February 1965, his letter to Lyndon John-

son accused the United States of preventing South Vietnamese independence and warned that there was a growing risk of war with the Soviet
Union and China.[8] Russell perceived a morally justified liberation struggle
in South Vietnam and a nationalist, rather than communist, National Liberation Front (NLF). He did not link the National Liberation Front to
North Vietnamese designs, nor advocate the unification of Vietnam.

Russell was perturbed by Britain's backing of the U.S. war effort. On
the same day in February 1965 that he wrote to Johnson, the energetic
philosopher complained to Prime Minister Harold Wilson: "It is intolerable that the British Labour Government should support a policy involving
such dangers through a cowardly desire to support the United States whatever that power may decide to do." Wilson responded that there indeed
was a precarious situation in Vietnam, but it was created by North Vietnam and the Vietcong.[9] In July, Wilson denied visas for three NLF representatives who wanted to speak in Britain; he said that such a visit was not
in the national interest. Russell sought a meeting with Wilson but was
turned down. He then publicized Wilson's refusal and continued to press
the issue via a fund drive and petitions.[10]

Russell relied heavily on Ralph Schoenman, a young American who
went to Britain in 1958 to participate in the nuclear disarmament movement. They met in July 1960 and Schoenman became Russell's secretary.
Like Russell, Schoenman was critical of U.S. policy in Vietnam and he
exuded a vigor that quickly endeared him to the eighty-eight-year-old
philosopher. In many ways, Schoenman and Russell complemented each
other, as the American was a hard worker, indefatigable organizer, and
inveterate traveler, whereas the elderly Russell devoted much of his time
to the broader picture and enjoyed staying at his home in Wales instead of
near the London headquarters of his foundation. Beginning in the summer
of 1965, Schoenman served as Russell's proxy on matters related to Vietnam and met frequently with NLF representatives.[11] Schoenman was more
of a revolutionary than Russell but less of a moralist. He also could be
abrasive, whereas Russell was usually only brash. Schoenman's attitudes
and behavior were to become highly controversial and cause divisiveness
when an international citizens' tribunal finally was assembled.[12]

Start–up

Bertrand Russell was very familiar with both the Dewey Commission and
the Nuremberg tribunal. Then, in 1959, a professor at the London School
of Economics (LSE) named Norman Birnbaum suggested a mock trial of

world leaders. It would be based on the Dewey precedent in terms of procedure, and on the Nuremberg principle of the accountability of government officials for crimes against humanity. Russell was not supportive, as he preferred to focus on the misdeeds of the West and he thought that duplicating the Dewey Commission would have anti-Soviet overtones. Russell turned down Birnbaum's proposal with the comment, "I am afraid that, if a committee were formed to point out faults on both sides, it would quickly divide into two factions, each critical of only one side, and that any debate between them would only exacerbate differences."[13]

The Vietnam War caused Russell to reconsider the tribunal concept. One influence on his thinking was Ralph Miliband, an LSE professor of politics, who was close to both Russell and Schoenman. Another was the radical American journalist M. S. Arnoni, who in 1965 had called for a tribunal similar to Nuremberg that could evaluate American war crimes in Vietnam. Russell had said that he was too busy and short of funds, but early in 1966 he reconsidered and started to organize a tribunal under the umbrella of his Bertrand Russell Peace Foundation.[14] In essence, he was repeating the pattern of the partisan Trotsky defense committee, which had spawned the Dewey Commission. The BRPF was clearly pro-NLF, but Schoenman, according to then staffer David Horowitz, thought it was possible to combine "an impartial tribunal and a revolutionary forum."[15] By April, Russell was set on his path and wrote the draft of a letter to many potential recipients about forming "a highly representative, independent, and respected international tribunal to hear full evidence concerning these crimes against humanity on the part of the U.S. government."[16] Copies were not mailed out until June 16.

Nuremberg shaped Russell's perception of the planned tribunal. He wanted to revive the process, which had been ad hoc rather than permanent, but to do so not in the form of victors' justice, but as an exercise in having private citizens sit in judgment of a great power. In an "Appeal to the American Conscience," Russell wrote: "With the exception of the extermination of the Jews, however, everything that the Germans did in Eastern Europe has been repeated by the U.S. in Vietnam on a scale which is larger and with an efficiency which is more terrible and more complete."[17] Schoenman, a Jew, was anxious to compare American policy to that of the Nazis. The German playwright Peter Weiss, living in Sweden, similarly saw an ominous development in South Vietnam's policy of moving villagers into fortified areas. He lamented: "The plan included nine million people, a figure that corresponds to the number of Jews that were imprisoned by Hitler in concentration camps."[18]

Russell's "Appeal to the American Conscience" included the tribunal's intention to "try" leaders for war crimes before a court of world opinion. The same position was taken in a Russell tape supplied to Vietcong radio. The main defendants were to be Lyndon Johnson, Dean Rusk, Robert McNamara, Henry Cabot Lodge, and William Westmoreland, with Russell hoping to force the removal of the American president, whom he portrayed as a "mouthpiece" for an "invisible government" based in the Pentagon and the Central Intelligence Agency (CIA).[19] Arnoni's newsletter used the Nazi analogy while declaring: "The tribunal will pair off for external infamy the names of Hitler and Johnson, Goering and McNamara, Ribbentrop and Rusk, Heydrich and Lodge."[20]

Russell had frequent contact with North Vietnam. In February 1966, he dispatched Schoenman and the BRPF's New York director, Russell Stetler, to Hanoi, where they met for two and a half hours with President Ho Chi Minh and Prime Minister Pham Van Dong. They also visited five provinces in North Vietnam. Russell had earlier informed Ho that Schoenman was authorized to speak for him on all matters pertaining to a tribunal.[21] In May, Russell sent four broadcast tapes to North Vietnam. They accused the United States of waging an "unjust war" and of committing war crimes. American troops were encouraged to terminate their involvement and to submit evidence.[22] On June 8, Vietcong radio announced the planned tribunal. The NLF offered to assist with investigations and the provision of witnesses and Russell thanked chairman Nguyen Huu Tho for his cooperation.[23] In a message to Ho, Russell suggested that the tribunal coincide with a North Vietnamese trial of captured American pilots.[24] Clearly, Russell was prepared to discard any pretense of political objectivity as he moved to activate his tribunal.

Despite concerted action with North Vietnam and the Vietcong, friction nevertheless surfaced. Russell was perturbed when the North Vietnamese called for a separate international commission on Vietnam, pointing out that there was no provision for Russell's tribunal to help select its members or have input into its "mode of procedure." There also was an implication that Hanoi was trying to influence the tribunal, since Russell warned Ho that the tribunal "must be seen to have full responsibility for its proceedings."[25] In a similar vein, Russell complained to the North Vietnamese representative in London, Nguyen Van Sao: "Recent developments have disheartened me. . . . I regard the Tribunal as an independent body dedicated solemnly to the service of the Vietnamese struggle for national liberation and true independence. To have the proper effect on Western opinion the procedures of our Tribunal must be exact and unimpeachable. The broad base required cannot be a mask for external control."[26]

Russell was firmly committed to an NLF victory in South Vietnam. While condemning American policy in Vietnam, however, he held no brief for the Soviet Union. Russell's protégé Ralph Schoenman had offended Moscow at a July 1965 peace conference in Helsinki by adopting a pro-Chinese stance, and Schoenman then wrote about the Soviet "revisionists": "I am very anxious to expose them because they are slandering us, but I have to weigh up whether I am able to do this without damaging the Vietnamese, who cannot afford, at this stage, to antagonize the Russians."[27] Russell criticized the Soviets for not providing sufficient support for the Vietcong and for not using their own air force to defend North Vietnam.[28] In letters to Prime Minister Aleksei Kosygin, he asked for "an early demonstration of Soviet intentions" and argued that more Soviet aid to North Vietnam would reduce the danger of American aggression. "May I appeal to you," implored Russell, "to issue a solemn warning to the United States of firm Soviet action." A response prepared on behalf of Kosygin defensively retorted that Moscow had "been doing everything it possibly [could] to give assistance to the heroic Vietnamese people fighting against U.S. aggression, and it [would] continue to do so in the future."[29] Russell's advocacy of deeper Soviet involvement was consistent with his commitment to an American military defeat, even at the risk of the very superpower confrontation that Russell had been seeking to prevent through his nuclear disarmament campaign.

The Soviet Union was wary of Russell's plan for a tribunal and lent it very little publicity. It recognized that Russell and Schoenman were sympathetic toward Third World liberation movements and the Chinese perspective, and also feared that there were Trotskyist anti-Soviet sentiments in the BRPF.[30] After all, Russell had expressed his admiration for Trotsky—but also had pointed out the Communist dissident's participation in a system that had repeated the evils of the tsarist regime.[31] Russell was also close to Trotsky's biographer and advocate, Isaac Deutscher, and made him the first appointee to the tribunal. Schoenman, at the encouragement of David Horowitz, had just read Deutscher's trilogy on Trotsky and had been favorably impressed. The name of the Trotskyist activist, Vanessa Redgrave, appeared on the BRPF letterhead. Senior staffer Ken Coates, who had headed the Labour Party in Nottingham, explained his leanings as follows: "I don't think my Trotskyist friends would be happy to have me described as a Trotskyist, but at the time, I was certainly Trotskysant."[32]

On the American Front

Russell believed that the key to changing Washington's policy toward Vietnam lay in the United States and that the tribunal should promote the role of the American antiwar movement. One aspect of his critique was racial. In January 1966, the Student Nonviolent Coordinating Committee (SNCC) proclaimed that it was hypocritical for blacks to fight for freedom in Asia while they were suffering from oppression domestically. The SNCC exhorted black Americans to oppose U.S. actions in Vietnam and to refuse military conscription. The SNCC's approach was strongly influenced by that month's Tricontinental Conference in Havana, in which the emphasis was on a Third World racial coalition against imperialism. Russell agreed, urging those engaged in combat in Asia to go home to fight American injustice. He also drew parallels between the conditions of American blacks and the Vietnamese.[33] Russell later invited SNCC leader Stokely Carmichael, who had been a delegate to the Havana conference, to be a member of the tribunal.

Russell's other major concern was the David Mitchell case, which he saw as an important test of the American conscription system. Mitchell claimed that the United States was committing crimes against humanity and war crimes in Vietnam, and therefore he would not fill out required draft board forms nor report for induction into the military. At first, Mitchell's legal team stressed his unwillingness to participate in preparations for a nuclear war. Afterward, it shifted the focus to the Nuremberg theme of personal accountability for carrying out criminal orders. This argument dovetailed well with the tribunal's plan to charge Johnson and other American leaders with war crimes, so the Mitchell case became a test in U.S. courts of a principle that Russell intended to apply at the tribunal. In a letter to the French feminist author Simone de Beauvoir, the British philosopher emphasized the centrality of the Mitchell case in terms of the Nuremberg precedent, pointing out that Mitchell was neither a pacifist nor a conscientious objector.[34]

Mitchell's defense strategy proved unsuccessful. At his second trial, his attorney, Mark Lane, cited Nuremberg, but the judge would not permit it to be the legal basis for an acquittal. Schoenman, who was in attendance, was not allowed to testify on American war crimes in Vietnam. Mitchell was then sentenced to a five-year term for draft evasion. The Supreme Court declined to act on Mitchell's appeal, although William O. Douglas's dissenting opinion argued that a Nuremberg defense should have been allowed.[35]

Russell initiated a petition drive on the Mitchell case and sent a cable of support to Mitchell.[36] He also directly connected Mitchell to Vietnam. A letter to the NLF representative in Prague sought cooperation on the case, and Schoenman was sent to Czechoslovakia to coordinate action. Another letter on the matter went to Ho Chi Minh.[37] Schoenman collected evidence in North Vietnam to use at Mitchell's trial, and he wanted the tribunal to be timed to coincide with it. In a letter to a tribunal member, Schoenman wrote: "It is my hope that at the conclusion of the Tribunal David Mitchell will be singled out as an example which the Tribunal will urge all to follow."[38]

Although the Nuremberg defense had not been validated in the Mitchell case, those planning the tribunal recognized its potential importance. Jean-Paul Sartre, who later presided at the tribunal, asserted that if the United States was to be found guilty of war crimes, then young Americans would be able to cite Nuremberg precedents in order to refuse military service.[39] Undercutting American military capacity was therefore chosen as a prime goal, as Russell and his colleagues prepared to take on the government of the United States.

Chapter XI

PLAN OF ACTION

Russell was the guiding force behind the creation of the International War Crimes Tribunal, often dubbed the "Russell Tribunal," but it soon gathered a momentum of its own and became divided over issues related to format, legal precedent, bureaucratic structure, and the clash of personalities. Not only did the British philosopher provide the overall conceptual framework, but also the prestige attached to his name brought publicity and induced many prominent intellectuals to become tribunal members. Russell financed the tribunal's activities with funds from loans and an advance on his autobiography. In a manner reminiscent of the Trotsky defense committee, the BRPF infrastructure served the tribunal, as well. Russell was initially the benefactor and the will, the energetic Schoenman the facilitator and instrument acting on the elderly man's behalf. Soon, Russell's declining involvement (due to age) and Schoenman's dynamism rendered the latter's role so prominent that he became widely accused of using the "old man's" name to advance his own positions.

The tribunal optimistically planned to examine American policy pertaining to charges of aggression, usage of banned weapons, bombing of civilian targets, inhumane treatment of prisoners, resort to forced labor and deportation, and possible genocide.[1] A reality check then set in as more practical matters, such as determining the tribunal's membership and securing a location for the hearings, became the predominant concerns.

Invitations

Russell anticipated twelve weeks of hearings in Paris, divided into separate segments that could arrive at preliminary conclusions. He gained the approval of the president and prime minister of North Vietnam for this procedure, thereby permitting a belligerent to have a say in the tribunal's process. As sessions were to be so lengthy, Russell did not expect tribunal members to attend all of them, so he advocated a prearranged system of substitutes.[2]

Some of the early appointees to the tribunal formed a core group that helped shape it. Isaac Deutscher, resident in Britain, was the eminent biographer of Trotsky. Vladimir Dedijer, a Yugoslav dissident, was an expert on international law. At first he leaned against participating in the tribunal so he could concentrate on his writing. His dismayed son asked: "Haven't you become a little tired, haven't you begun to lose touch with the pulse of the new generation?" When his son soon died, Dedijer committed himself to the tribunal.[3] Jean-Paul Sartre, the French existential philosopher, and his companion, Simone de Beauvoir, the feminist social critic, were enticed to join by Schoenman. He went to Paris and convinced them with the promise that the sessions would be held in the French capital, they would only have to attend for two or three days when the final judgment was being considered, and that they would regularly be supplied with the transcripts of the hearings. Sartre and de Beauvoir agreed because they had opposed French military actions in Indochina and Algeria and saw parallels with American policy in Vietnam.[4]

Another key member was Gunther Anders, a Jewish philosopher living in Austria who had lost several friends at Auschwitz. Laurent Schwartz, a French mathematician, was also influential, as was Peter Weiss, the German playwright. Weiss turned down membership on the tribunal, urging that lawyers be appointed, but he agreed to help and indeed contributed significantly.[5] Russell invited Stokely Carmichael to serve, but the SNCC leader responded that he could not find sufficient time. Favoring the prosecution of Johnson, Carmichael indicated that he expected a Nuremberg trial at the end of the war. He pledged the support of his organization for Russell's tribunal but not necessarily his personal participation.[6]

Invitations to join the tribunal were turned down by Che Guevara, Vyacheslav Molotov, and the journalists Tom Wicker, R. W. Apple, and Harrison Salisbury, among others. The British theater critic Kenneth Tynan was concerned about the expected absence of defense witnesses, while the American cultural historian Lewis Mumford declined because he did not think that the tribunal could be an effective court of justice without the presence of the defendants. Mumford also argued that it would be unwise for Americans to serve, since this would undermine their antiwar position with the U.S. public. The playwright Arthur Miller made the very same observation, and called for a less partisan tribunal. Russell countered that Americans who failed to speak out against the war were condoning it through their silence.[7] Clearly, the tribunal had an image problem in the United States. The gadfly journalist I. F. Stone had a different reason to refuse an invitation. He asserted that Schoenman had no tact, and was "just the man to ruin that verdict and save U.S. from its full effect." New Left idol Herbert Marcuse feared the potential loss of his academic position at San Diego State University. Russell remarked that such a fate could only assist the tribunal by raising American consciousness.[8]

The composition of the tribunal remained fluid. Sartre, who was to preside, was upset about new additions and he chided Russell over the matter. Russell, apparently in a combative mood, proceeded to send letters to tribunal members requesting the inclusion of Melba Hernandez, a Cuban, and indicating that the issue could be discussed in Paris. That same day, however, he sent an invitation to Hernandez.[9]

The Process

Russell intended to pattern the tribunal after Nuremberg, and that is the reason why he chose the term "tribunal." As *Le Figaro* observed, "using the word tribunal forces one to recognize an analogy of the actions and of the guilt." By contrast, his hearings had no legal standing and could not really carry out the functions of a court, such as determining guilt or innocence. Furthermore, the tribunal members were all critical of U.S. policy in Vietnam and were what Schoenman called "a partial body of committed men."[10]

When Russell's letter of invitation referred to a "tribunal," Deutscher immediately stated his preference for a commission of inquiry modeled on the Dewey Commission. He also emphasized a need to assert moral and political independence and to secure fair representation of both sides.[11] Mumford also suggested a court of inquiry, while Anders and Russell corresponded about a hybrid procedure that wouldn't be a "mock trial," but would permit tribunal members to make accusations and question witnesses. Anders felt that such an activist role, particularly by members who were not lawyers, could help clarify the moral issues.[12] Russell basically adhered to this middle position, recommending that members act as judges who formulate conclusions based on their inquiries. There would not be a court or a trial, but those with legal expertise would assist other members. No formal legal structure was possible, as there would not be an adequate defense nor an assured presence of the accused. In the absence of a legitimate adversarial procedure, no sentence would be pronounced. Russell privately proposed that the tribunal would really be an "international investigation commission."[13] At the same time, he was publicly threatening to "try" Johnson and other American leaders.

Russell's concept of linkage to Nuremberg evoked memories of the Holocaust and analogies equating Jewish and Vietnamese resistance. Gunther Anders pressed the symbolism most strongly. He proposed that a session of the tribunal should meet at Auschwitz, but due to the lack of proper facilities there, it should then move to Cracow. He also advocated the participation of the former U.S. Supreme Court justice and Nuremberg prosecutor Robert Jackson. By contrast, he argued that no tribunal sessions should be held in Germany or Austria for fear that neo-Nazis would use revelations about American transgressions to belittle Nazi crimes.[14] Schoenman, too, was eager to compare Americans to Nazis and to cite Nuremberg legal precedents, and both he and Russell applied a Warsaw Ghetto analogy when commenting on what they considered the Vietnamese uprising against American occupation. They also decided that Vietnamese war crimes would not be considered by the tribunal, since who would try Jews for resisting the Nazis?[15]

Such references to Nuremberg as a symbol of the Holocaust produced considerable controversy when applied to Vietnam. A letter to *The New York Times* from seventeen faculty members at Western Reserve University maintained that the Nuremberg precedent did not go far enough in assigning guilt to Americans perpetrating war crimes in Vietnam because Nuremberg dealt with ex post facto laws, while the United States was violating existing laws. An American Jew, who had lost many relatives in the Holocaust, complained that comparing it to Vietnam was not appropriate, as the latter situation had ambiguity.[16] More important, Deutscher had written to Russell that Nuremberg should not be the focus, since international law and war crimes had been defined by the military victors; the emphasis should instead be on the right of self-determination. Russell replied that Deutscher had presented a strong case.[17] Mumford also looked askance at the Nuremberg war crimes approach. He felt that rather than moderate U.S. policy, it would only harden Johnson's resolve. Mumford predicted that the American public would rally behind LBJ against international criticism.[18]

It was unlikely that the American government would agree to take part in a tribunal so obviously bent on finding it guilty of war crimes, or even genocide. If Russell was attempting to seduce Washington with assurances that it could present defense witnesses and evidence, and by inviting Johnson, Rusk, and McNamara to the hearings, he certainly went about it in a strange manner. Russell's letter to the president asked Johnson to appear "in [his] own defense" to face charges regarding acts performed "on [his] instruction." Nuremberg was cited, as Russell stated that standards applied by the United States to Germany had to be adhered to by the United States, as well. Russell then rhetorically queried: "Here, then, is the challenge before you: Will you appear before a wider justice than you recognize and risk a more profound condemnation than you may be able to understand?" The Johnson administration predictably wanted no part in this process and did not authorize any defense. Russell had already dismissed an alternative procedure by maintaining that only U.S. government-approved witnesses could testify; others could be disavowed or deemed inadequate by Washington.[19]

The U.S. government reacted to plans for the tribunal with disdain. Russell's letters to Johnson and others went unanswered and an internal memo indicated that the United States took "no official cognizance" of the tribunal. To some extent, this was bravado, as there surely was concern. The Dewey Commission was acknowledged to be a legitimate precedent and top advisers George Ball and Averell Harriman participated in deliberations on the issue.[20] Johnson blamed Hanoi for the Vietnam quagmire and believed that a unilateral bombing pause would be tantamount to abandoning America's fighting men on the battlefield. "I think I'm going to be tried not by Bertrand Russell, but by Mrs. Goldberg for killing her boy without giving him the weapons to protect himself," mused the president. When the U.N. ambassador Arthur Goldberg responded that "Bertrand Russell has become a nut," Johnson retorted: "No, but do you heed my point, sir? I think my great danger is how can a commander in chief stop his men from fighting unless the other side is just willing to do something."[21]

Dissenting Opinions

Organizers of the Russell Tribunal were soon challenged by two unlikely sources, an American antiwar activist and a group of African sponsors of the Bertrand Russell Peace Foundation. The first was Staughton Lynd, a history professor at Yale and a leading advocate of nonviolence. He turned down an invitation to serve on the tribunal and went public with his criticisms. Lynd had strong radical credentials; he was on the editorial board of the peace movement journal *Liberation* and was a major organizer of the National Coordinating Committee to End the War in Vietnam. In

December 1965, he had traveled to North Vietnam with American Communist Party theoretician Herbert Aptheker and Students for a Democratic Society founder, Tom Hayden.[22] Although firmly opposed to American policy, Lynd did not favor an NLF victory; he preferred a coalition of the NLF and South Vietnamese neutralists. Lynd opined that were he Vietnamese, he might himself be a neutral Buddhist rather than a backer of the NLF. Also, while he believed that the NLF cause was more just than that of the United States, he endorsed equal condemnation of war crimes committed by the contestants.[23] Lynd was surely an advocate of nonviolence, but he recognized that there were just wars and was not an absolute pacifist. He had the status of a noncombatant when in the U.S. Army in 1953–54, and did not claim to be a conscientious objector. Lynd explained his nuanced position as follows: "I don't believe that in any conflict situation both sides are equally responsible in all instances, and I don't believe that violence never accomplished anything good."[24]

What troubled Lynd about the Russell Tribunal was that criteria being applied to American behavior were not being applied to the Vietcong. In a letter to Russell, he asked whether the NLF was "completely innocent" and declared: "I consider this to be a very dangerous position. I believe it amounts to judging one side (the NLF) by its ends, the other side (the United States) by its means. Precisely this double standard is what I had thought all of us, in this post-Stalin era, wished to avoid."[25] Schoenman parried with the observation: "It is the automatic assumption on your part that violence in itself is a crime which is not shared by the tribunal and many people outside of it." He cited Jewish resistance to the Nazis. Schoenman argued: "It is fatuous to call a tribunal of this kind into existence and then to retreat ten steps behind the moral and intellectual level necessary to reach that point, and to re-open the possibility that the victim is a criminal." The issue of violence, Schoenman defiantly insisted, would be viewed more from the perspective of Che Guevara than from that of American pacifists. In a slap at Lynd, he avowed that tribunal members would be drawn from "the more emancipated section of the American intelligentsia."[26]

The second criticism came from African leaders, who withdrew as sponsors of the BRPF because of its overlapping role in organizing the tribunal. This was a severe blow to the tribunal's credibility in the Third World. The men involved were Julius Nyerere of Tanzania, Kenneth Kaunda of Zambia, Haile Selassie of Ethiopia, and Leopold Senghor of Senegal. Nyerere had become a BRPF sponsor in 1964. In October 1966, his personal assistant, Joan Wicken, informed Russell that Nyerere was withdrawing and wanted his name removed from the BRPF's letterhead. Nyerere was not in agreement with all of its activities, and no longer wanted to be identified with an organization over which he had no influence. The real problem was that the BRPF was planning the tribunal, and was doing so through letters written on BRPF stationery. Nyerere's name was on the letterhead with his approval, but he had never authorized its use in conjunction with the tribunal. Schoenman disingenuously responded that the tribunal was autonomous, and was not being organized under BRPF auspices. Russell angrily prepared a reply to Nyerere in reference to Wicken's letter, in which he fumed: "The terms of the letter are arrogant and offensive. I feel confident that, had you intended to communicate with me, you would do so personally and courteously."[27] He never mailed it.

Nyerere went public, decrying BRPF's use of his name and declaring: "I object to a serious matter like the Vietnam situation being dealt with by trickery and dishonesty." Russell continued to claim that the tribunal was not under BRPF control and that Nyerere's name had not been used improperly. Nyerere wrote that even if he had been a proponent of the tribunal, he would have objected to the way his name had been used, but in fact, he was indeed critical of a tribunal that would not contribute to peace and would only "make anti-American propaganda."[28] Coming from Nyerere, such an assertion was a hard blow to the tribunal, since he was Africa's most respected statesman and had strongly denounced American policy in Vietnam. He did, however, favor a Vietnam settlement under provisions of the 1954 Geneva accords.

Setting the Stage

Preparations for the tribunal were handled through the BRPF's London office and included active roles for members already selected. The problem was coordination, as these members lived in different countries and basically stayed in touch by mail. Gunther Anders complained to Russell that he had seen many prospective dates for the tribunal, and needed some clarification. Also, as a tribunal member, he was unsure as to his function: Was he to act as a judge, a juror, or as an expert on current events? Anders also pointed out that he had never received a response to a query about the tribunal's aims. Because of such confusion, he recommended a preparatory meeting of tribunal members.[29]

Simone de Beauvoir was concerned as well, and Russell apologized for not keeping her well-informed. Hoping to keep tight control over the tribunal, he opposed a preparatory meeting on the ground that organizational work had to be carried out by "a tightly-knit and integrated team." Russell informed Isaac Deutscher that there wouldn't be a meeting, since the BRPF would take care of the preparatory work, but the growing concern of tribunal members forced the British philosopher to quickly reverse course. He wrote to Peter Weiss that there was a "need" for such a meeting and he commented to Isaac Deutscher that members considered it "essential."[30] Russell then asked Deutscher to serve as chairman. Deutscher agreed, but asked Russell to "lend credibility" by his attendance. Russell proposed that teams gathering evidence in Vietnam should report their findings to the preparatory meeting, which would then publicly release the information. Deutscher vehemently rejected the idea, observing that such a procedure would prejudice the tribunal.[31] Unlike Dewey, the aging philosopher failed to appreciate the importance of at least appearing impartial.

The November 13 through 15 preliminary meeting in London was aimed at planning a timetable, developing an administrative structure, and stating the tribunal's aims. Deutscher, Dedijer, and Schwartz were leading participants, as was the Italian lawyer and parliamentarian, Lelio Basso. Also involved were the Austrian philosopher Gunther Anders, the Sicilian poverty expert Danilo Dolci, the Pakistani Supreme Court advocate Mahmud Ali Kasuri, and the Turkish lawyer Mehmet Ali Aybar. Sartre arrived a day late. Weiss did not attend because he had decided not to serve as a tribunal member. Russell made the opening statement and departed, leaving Schoenman to represent him. Russell was appointed honorary president of the tribunal (physically he was not equal to the burden of playing a more active role), Sartre the executive president, Dedijer the chairman and president of the sessions, and Schoenman the secretary-general.[32]

The gathering outlined the questions to be addressed by the tribunal, reinvited American governmental participation, and decided that evidence would not be bound by traditional legal standards and would thus be accepted as long as it was of probative value. Schoenman said that the tribunal would be separate from the BRPF, and two French lawyers then delineated the tribunal's structure and guidelines. Deutscher made it clear, however, that the BRPF's secretariat would continue to assist the tribunal and that Schoenman would be deeply involved, even though formally not a tribunal member. Schoenman's hands-on approach was the complete opposite of Muenzenberg's hidden-hand at the time of the Reichstag fire countertrial.

Schoenman indicated that there would not be a trial, only an investigation, and Basso declared that he was able to investigate without prejudgment whether or not there were war crimes, even though he was partial in regard to the war. There were some linguistic problems at the meeting over usage of English and French, and procedural irregularities were aired. Dolci even resigned for not having been consulted sufficiently. Kasuri quipped: "Mr. Dolci's difficulty is that he feels that some decisions have already been taken. My difficulty is that I do not know of any decisions which have been taken."[33]

After the meeting Russell appeared at a press conference to publicize the tribunal. He was forty-five minutes late and left after his opening statement without taking questions from journalists. Russell said that he wanted to "reawaken the world's conscience" and, paraphrasing the Cuban national hero Jose Marti, he declared: "May this tribunal prevent the crime of silence." He also argued that the tribunal's lack of legal standing was an advantage, as it couldn't be influenced by any state.[34] Reaction to Russell was decidedly mixed. When he opened the preliminary meeting, Deutscher (as described by David Horowitz) enthused sycophantically about "what a magnificent and courageous task he had undertaken, what light to the oppressed, and what a debt of gratitude was owed to him. The old man nodded, visibly moved, and then turned again to make his slow way out." From the other side, the British journalist Bernard Levin wrote in reference to Russell's press conference: "The man who has now become the holiest relic the international left possesses is to be unwrapped and shown to the populace."[35] Ideological battle lines were clearly being drawn.

After the preliminary meeting, Russell stopped playing a guiding role in the tribunal and turned over most responsibilities to Schoenman. At the same time, the tribunal's executive committee (in which Dedijer was prominent) operated rather autonomously out of Paris. Cooperation was difficult. The executive committee made decisions without informing Schoenman, and it did not always pass along information to Sartre. Sartre was often too busy to participate and so was represented by his protégé, the journalist Claude Lanzmann. There also were difficulties both with fundraising for the tribunal and allocating financial resources between London and Paris. Sartre conferred with Schoenman in London in January 1967, but these difficulties persisted.[36] The bifurcated administrative structure was problematic, but so, too, was the resentment of some tribunal members toward Schoenman. Claude Cadart of the Paris office reminded the cantankerous American that the tribunal was autonomous of the BRPF, and Dedijer questioned whether Schoenman was really expressing Russell's viewpoint.[37]

Tensions also arose between the London office and American support-ers. Schoenman complained to Dave Dellinger, a pacifist critic of U.S. pol-icy who became a tribunal member, that Americans failed to focus on such essential tasks as raising funds, increasing the number of U.S. tribunal par-ticipants, and recruiting investigators for missions in Vietnam. Moreover, he claimed to BRPF's New York director Russell Stetler that the tribunal was perceived in the United States as "immature, superficial, and antago-nistic."[38] American activists were excluded from European preparatory conclaves, but hoped that a tribunal session could be held in the United States in order to stimulate the war resistance movement.[39]

Getting Settled

Russell was jittery about scheduling the tribunal, aware that potential hosts would be reluctant to offend the United States.[40] Washington was indeed applying pressure, and Schoenman's passport was revoked for unautho-rized visits to North Vietnam. Paris was expected to be the venue for the first round of hearings, with later sessions anticipated in New York, Tokyo, and Auschwitz, and then a final one in Paris again.[41] Paris was an attractive location because de Gaulle's government was firmly opposed to the American role in Vietnam.

Arranging a March 1967 opening session in Paris proved highly prob-lematic. On November 25, 1966 Russell wrote to President Charles de Gaulle, requesting assistance in the issuing of visas for witnesses from both North and South Vietnam.[42] Control over visas was clearly in the hands of the French government and, according to French law, even public meet-ings required official approval. Since there was an 1881 law forbidding insults to foreign heads of state, the organizers had to drop plans to charge Lyndon Johnson with war crimes.[43]

Hoping to avoid a direct confrontation, de Gaulle signaled his displea-sure by failing to answer Russell's letter. At first, tribunal organizers hesi-tated, but they then decided to press on by renting a hall, effective April 10, for two weeks. The French government couldn't ban a private gather-ing, but the tribunal wanted journalistic coverage and this implied a public session even if members of the media were invited individually. Rather than formally reject the tribunal and bring the right of free speech into question, the French government got the hall to cancel. The same thing happened when a hotel was booked as the site for a tribunal session com-mencing on April 26. Finally, a theater in the "red belt," outside of Paris at Issy-les-Moulineaux, was lined up, and April 29 was set as the new opening date.[44] The French bureaucracy was not prepared to give up. Dedijer secured one-day transit visas several times, but was denied a visitor's visa. Schoenman was detained at the Orly airport while on his way from London to Hanoi via Cambodia. On another occasion, traveling from London to Prague via Paris, he was picked up at the airport by French police and escorted to another airport to catch his ongoing flight. They made sure that he would not use the opportunity to enter Paris.[45]

On April 10, Sartre wrote to de Gaulle requesting visas for tribunal participants (especially Dedijer). On April 19 the French president responded, telling the tribunal that it could not meet in France. His reasoning was legalistic: Justice may only emanate from the state, and the tribunal intended to warp that authority by acting in a juridical manner and issuing a verdict. The tribunal lacked any legal mandate and its moral weight and arguments would not be enhanced by "assuming robes borrowed for the occasion."[46] After all, de Gaulle was a confirmed statist who did not see any advantage in helping to set a dangerous precedent—not to mention causing further deterioration in Franco-American relations.[47]

Realizing that securing a location for the tribunal might prove difficult, the organizers pursued several tracks simultaneously. On November 25, 1966, the same day that he had contacted de Gaulle, Russell also wrote to the British Home Secretary Roy Jenkins about plans to hold the tribunal in London and requested assistance in arranging visas for North Vietnamese witnesses. Jenkins turned him down, citing inconsistency with Britain's national interest. Russell then called on Prime Minister Harold Wilson to reverse the decision, sarcastically observing that failure to do so would indicate that free speech was not in Britain's national interest. Wilson retorted that "the one-sided character of the International War Crimes Tribunal you are proposing to hold would make the government's peace-making efforts substantially more difficult."[48] An angry Russell quickly accused Wilson of being "arbitrary" and of failing to speak out against American atrocities. He went on: "You still maintain a series of military and diplomatic links with the aggressor which positively abets his aggression. . . . The principle difference between yourself and the members of the War Crimes Tribunal appears to be that they are not prepared to abandon their fundamental convictions in order to secure temporary preferment." Predictably, Wilson refused to budge.[49] Britain, a close ally of the United States, clearly did not want to cause offense. Moreover, even the British left did not rally behind the tribunal. This was in part because it didn't want to criticize a Labour government's policy, and in part out of sympathy for the Soviet Union, which was not shared by Russell and the tribunal's members. Isaac Deutscher, therefore, referred to the left's "wall of hostility" and "conspiracy of silence."[50]

Although turned down by France and Britain, there were other potential rabbits in the tribunal's hat. Switzerland was approached on hosting a session in Geneva, but its Federal Assembly decided that it would not contribute to the peace process and was not a judicial authority recognized by states. Danish supporters were told to check on the rental of a meeting hall in case plans for Paris didn't work out, and in the long run, the tribunal did have hearings near Copenhagen.[51] More immediate was the Stockholm option. The Swedish government had been asked to approve a session in Stockholm and Schoenman had announced that it was the main alternative to Paris.[52] When France rejected the tribunal and the Swedish government reluctantly agreed to Stockholm hearings, a home had finally been found. Sartre was completely surprised by this turn of events, thinking that de Gaulle's refusal was the coup de grace for the tribunal.[53] Sartre and other tribunal members then reluctantly packed and headed for the Swedish capital. It was a peripheral location, distant from major media centers, but at least the tribunal would be able to convene. Parallels with Mexico City and the Dewey Commission were apparent.

Chapter XII

BEHIND THE SCENES AT STOCKHOLM

The tribunal conducted hearings from May 2 to 10, 1967, in the relative backwater of Stockholm. The Swedish support committee worked feverishly to carry off the event successfully, in the hope of buttressing Sweden's New Left by humbling the mighty United States. A carnival atmosphere prevailed in the Swedish capital. There were protribunal demonstrators, counterdemonstrators, and even the threat of a countertribunal organized by the Swedish Committee for a Free Asia. The tribunal's impact on the host state was considerable, but this was not necessarily the case in regard to the rest of the world, despite the prominence attached to Russell's name.

There had been delays in convening the tribunal, in finding a meeting site, in raising funds, and in securing visas for North Vietnamese and NLF witnesses. A despondent Russell commented on May 1: "Well, I suppose this tribunal is going to be a great fiasco. I don't suppose most of those eminent people we have invited will turn up."[1] These "eminent people" certainly did not appreciate that their personal calendars were being thrown asunder, as a delay of the tribunal's opening from April 30 to May 2 forced them to hastily alter travel plans. Isaac Deutscher did not arrive until May 6, and Schoenman observed that "until the first session took place, the effort to produce the session was great and had to be conducted against the hesitance and vacillation of many of the leading members of the tribunal."[2] Most important, when the International War Crimes Tribunal finally convened in the Folkets Hus (People's House) of the Social Democratic Party, the elderly Russell did not journey to Sweden.

Fundamentals

Sartre, de Beauvoir, Deutscher, Dedijer, Basso, Anders, Kasuri, Aybar, Dellinger, and Schwartz, plus Lawrence Daly (head of the Scottish mineworkers' union), Kinju Morikawa (Japanese lawyer), and Shoichi Sakata (Japanese physicist) made it to Stockholm, while the tribunal panelists Stokely Carmichael, James Baldwin (American author), Lazaro Cardenas (former Mexican president), Amado Hernandez (Filipino poet and politician), and Wolfgang Abendroth (German law professor) did not.[3] Courtland Cox (American lawyer) represented Carmichael and Sara Lidman (Swedish novelist) stood in for Abendroth. There were also some last-minute additions: Melba Hernandez, the Cuban activist for solidarity with Vietnam; Peter Weiss, whose Swedish group had been essential in making arrangements; and Carl Oglesby, former chairman of Students for a Democratic Society. Leo Matarasso and Gisele Halimi ran the tribunal's legal commission.

Executive president Jean-Paul Sartre presided over the tribunal sessions and provided the basic legal and ethical framework. De Beauvoir assisted him, encouraged other panelists to treat him reverentially, walked slightly behind him, and said little at the hearings.[4] Sartre believed that the role of the tribunal was to assess whether the powerful United States was behaving criminally toward Vietnam, a small weak state. It was with some irony that he wrote: "Our tribunal today merely proposes to apply to capitalist imperialism its own laws."[5] Since the United States had helped formulate international law, it would have no choice but to accept its dictates. Even though many members of the tribunal were Marxists who looked at international events through the prism of class struggle and revolutionary ethics, Western-style jurisprudence was to be emphasized, for Sartre intended "to reintroduce the juridical notion of international crime."[6] This was a tall order for a tribunal with only a minority of lawyers, chaired by a philosopher.

Sartre wanted Stockholm to be another Nuremberg, in which international law would not only be used to hold an undefeated major power responsible for war crimes, but also make Nuremberg-style tribunals a permanent fixture.[7] Stockholm, however, lacked Nuremberg's legal standing, enforcement capabilities, and even a mandate to determine individual guilt. Swedish law prohibited offensive statements about the chiefs of state of friendly foreign countries. Indeed, the tribunal's very presence in Stockholm was conditional on its adherence to this law. Neither Lyndon Johnson nor any other individual could be "tried," found "guilty," or assigned a punishment. Although Russell compared Johnson to Hitler in a media appearance, the fact was that the tribunal would only be addressing the role of the United States as a country.[8]

In a taped press conference prior to the opening session in Stockholm, Russell counterproductively lambasted the United States for its commission of war crimes. The Swedish support committee was aghast, since it had promised the government that there would be an objective commission of inquiry, not a biased kangaroo court. Fact-finding was to be emphasized, not preconceived judgments. How else could Sweden justify its permission to hold the tribunal? Comments by Schoenman and Daly added further fuel to the fire, since these men, too, looked at a Nuremberg process as a means of assigning personal guilt to American leaders. Fearing that the Swedish government would cancel the hearings, the support committee member Peter Weiss disavowed remarks by Daly. Mahmud Ali Kasuri, presiding at a pretribunal press conference, also carefully distanced himself from rash public statements, as did Sartre.[9] They hoped to demonstrate the tribunal's credibility through the introduction of evidence and the application of international law.

Evidence

Much of the evidence was based on investigations carried out prior to the tribunal in North Vietnam and NLF-controlled zones of South Vietnam. Areas under the Saigon government were not included. Vietnamese enemies of the United States were not only eager to offer assistance, but also were particularly focused on using the "race card" against the United States. That is why they encouraged an investigatory role for Stokely Carmichael, and that is why Julius Lester and Charlie Cobb, Jr., were sent to North Vietnam as part of an SNCC mission to photograph the effects of American bombing raids. Hoping to cultivate connections to the U.S. antiwar movement, Hanoi permitted biochemical investigator John Neilands to be the first American to talk to U.S. prisoners of war in North Vietnam.[10]

The U.S. media, which did not have access to North Vietnam, tried to piggyback on the investigatory missions. NBC, CBS, *Time, Newsweek,* and *US News and World Report* all had contacts with the tribunal organizers. Schoenman demanded that the media help fund the missions in return for the tribunal's assistance in the acquisition of visas. He additionally wanted to exercise some control over film footage and to have it turned over for use at the hearings. Chafing at such restrictions on their journalistic integrity, news organizations stepped away from the whole affair.[11] This experience badly tarnished the tribunal's image with the media.

The tribunal addressed three questions: 1. Did the US violate international law by committing aggression? 2. To what degree were civilian sites bombed? And 3. Did Australia, New Zealand, and South Korea act as American accomplices and commit aggression in Vietnam?

The eight days of hearings opened with the reading of a speech prepared by the absent Russell. Sartre followed with introductory remarks, Matarasso contributed some legal background, and American historian Gabriel Kolko examined U.S. involvement in Vietnam. Witnesses then described the use of fragmentation bombs, the bombing of civilians, and the destruction of dikes. Four of the witnesses were Vietnamese. Another witness, in a questionable legal procedure, was the tribunal member Lawrence Daly. Thought was given to using U.S. servicemen captured in Vietnam as witnesses, but this idea was rejected during the course of the tribunal on the ground that personal responsibility should not be assigned.[12]

Medical, scientific, and legal evidence was introduced. There were physical exhibits and eyewitness accounts pointing toward U.S. violation of war crimes statutes. It was claimed that schools, hospitals, and populated areas had been bombed. Graphic photos and a movie featured mutilated civilians, especially children. Four Cuban investigators and Schoenman charged "genocide."[13] Sartre and Dedijer did much of the cross-examining, focusing on facts and endeavoring to keep out personal opinions of the witnesses.[14]

Most effective was the evidence regarding fragmentation bombs and other antipersonnel devices used against civilians, and the destruction of North Vietnam's irrigation system. The U.S. government, anxious not to publicize the tribunal, nevertheless felt the need to respond publicly, so the Department of Defense asserted that civilians had not been targeted for fragmentation bomb attacks and that there had been no intentional bombing of dikes or dams. Moreover, it had to admit that defoliants had been used, but it would not agree to characterize them as chemical weapons.[15] American refutations may have been generated by a perceived need for public relations self-defense, but the points made also served to blunt some of the tribunal's evidence.

Delegates from North Vietnam and the NLF attended the Stockholm sessions. The North Vietnamese president Ho Chi Minh was invited to address the tribunal, but he did not do so. He did send an ill-advised telegram calling it "a strong encouragement for us, the Vietnamese people."[16] Lyndon Johnson had been asked to attend back in August 1966, but he had no desire to act like a defendant in a criminal case. After hearings had already commenced, Sartre tried to counteract charges of unfairness by inviting the Secretary of State, Dean Rusk, to provide testimony or send representatives to "present the defense of the United States government." Rusk replied, via a journalist, that he would not "play games with a ninety-four-year-old Briton." Annoyed with Rusk's slight to the Frenchman, the French daily *Le Monde* quipped that Rusk should have found a better argument to use against the tribunal than Russell's age. Sartre responded in kind: "I find that the response of Mr. Dean Rusk indicates the total mediocrity of this poor man."[17]

A Swedish lawyer, Frank Hallis Wallin, offered to defend the United States for free—arguing that there could not be a meaningful verdict in the absence of defense representation. An American lawyer practicing in Germany, George Bronfen, also offered his services at no charge. There also was the case of two American journalists covering the tribunal who proposed that they give testimony on behalf of the United States. Their credentials to cover the tribunal were ripped up, and a Swedish organizer claimed that they had been issued without his authorization.[18]

Fissures

Tensions among tribunal members ran high. Considerable irritation was directed at Ralph Schoenman, who organized the Stockholm session in coordination with the Swedish support committee, but who generally kept tribunal members in the dark. Simone de Beauvoir observes that when she arrived for the hearings, she had no idea about who else would be serving on the tribunal.[19] Schoenman held frequent press conferences in Stockholm prior to the tribunal's opening, thus usurping the authority of its members and particularly irking Sartre, Dedijer, Schwartz, and de Beauvoir. The French feminist accused him of wanting "to exercise a positive dictatorship over the tribunal" and revealed that she had received phone calls while still in Paris, informing her that Schoenman was talking "wildly" before journalists.[20] Schoenman's comments touched on three sensitive areas: 1. He accused the United States of war crimes, and called for an indictment even though evidence had not yet been introduced; 2. He portrayed the tribunal as a court that would render judgment, rather than as a commission of inquiry (as promised to the Swedish government) that would ascertain facts; and 3. He challenged, inappropriately and incorrectly, the meaning of a message sent to Russell by Prime Minister Tage Erlander, thereby publicly offending the tribunal's host.[21]

Tribunal members forced Schoenman into apologizing before the press about his lack of veracity on Erlander's letter and they undercut him by appointing their own spokespersons to speak to the media. In general, they viewed Schoenman as two-faced in regard to his relationship to Russell. On the one hand, he represented the British philosopher and pointed out that the results of the tribunal would have to be made to please Russell because he was paying the costs. On the other, whenever queried regarding one of Russell's positions, he said that he couldn't speak for Russell. Sartre got so angry about this equivocation that he cried out: "You can't hide behind Russell and keep him in your pocket at the same time."[22]

Isaac Deutscher tried to promote internal peace by saying that the feelings that members had toward Schoenman should not be allowed to affect their treatment of Russell, and they indeed were careful not to offend the elderly philosopher. Schoenman afterward remarked that the tribunal had been a public success, but that "privately, it was very unpleasant." The American radical journalist Robert Scheer aptly summed up Schoenman's situation: "He is the sort of political organizer who determines the purity of his organization by its ability to resist members."[23]

Antagonism between Schoenman and tribunal members reached a high point when an infuriated Dedijer lifted and shook him, and then pushed him to the ground. Sartre and Dellinger pulled Dedijer off the hapless Schoenman. Ken Coates observes that Dedijer was "schizophrenic" and "capable of outbursts when provoked, or when he thought that he was being provoked." He could be "extremely erratic and unpleasant" and it was impossible to engage in a "restrained and civilized" disagreement with him. Dedijer, according to Coates, was "as unreasonable as Ralph, but in a far more frightening way, because he was a very big man, and out of control, he was overbearing."[24]

Dedijer's temper was not helped by the recurring pain he suffered from an old war injury. In addition to the Schoenman incident, he assaulted Quentin Hoare, managing editor of *New Left Review*, and he was accused by Russell of threatening violence against staffers Chris Farley and Russell Stetler. Dedijer also irritated Carl Oglesby. When the latter said that he was an "American," Dedijer objected and suggested that Cubans, Peruvians, and Mexicans were also "Americans."[25]

Another problem within the tribunal was an emerging split between Schoenman, with his London BRPF, and the Paris office. Sartre, as executive president, chaired the Stockholm sessions, and he chose Schwartz and Dedijer to act as his assistants. For all practical purposes, Dedijer was identified with the Paris group, even though he was a Yugoslav. Dedijer also became the self-appointed editor-in-chief in charge of publications emanating from the hearings. While the tribunal was in progress, the members voted (three against) to move its secretariat to Paris. The intent was to undercut Schoenman's administrative authority, but they also knew that based on past experience, he would probably be unable to secure entry into France for meetings.[26] Russell correctly interpreted these actions as a French attempt to take over the tribunal. Deutscher, who was close to Russell and Schoenman, labeled Sartre "irresponsible and tactless," and Dedijer "inept and rude." Anders, who was not present at the end of the Stockholm session, wrote to Schoenman that he would like to learn more about the differences between the "Russell group" and the "Sartre group." Asian tribunal members were upset from the start about the intra-European wrangling and had to be convinced to remain in Sweden.[27]

The London-Paris split may have contained some element of geography and language, but it was mainly about Schoenman, bureaucratic interests, and contrasting perspectives. The Londoners wanted to use the tribunal as part of their revolutionary agenda. Their rhetoric was inflammatory, including denunciations of new "Hitlers." The Paris group stressed international law, focused on procedural matters, and issued more sober pronouncements. Although the Londoners had set the whole tribunal process in motion, their approach tended to be counterproductive in terms of being taken seriously by the major media. The Paris group understood this problem and it also sought to establish precedents that could be used by future tribunals. Anders wrote to Schoenman that the two groups should not be viewed as "hawks" and "doves," with the difference being who was more critical of the United States. Both were equally opposed to American conduct of the war.[28]

The American members of the tribunal shared the British approach, more because of ideology than Anglophone loyalty. None were lawyers; they rejected French efforts to apply international law and they advocated world revolutionary change. For them, too, the Stockholm tribunal was aimed at furthering the cause of revolution. As Julius Lester, a SNCC member in attendance, suggested, establishing a moral conscience was not sufficient; caring meant a willingness to die. Intellectual commitment didn't mean much. It could only serve as salve for European radicals, not help end the war. Lester afterward reflected: "I couldn't help but feel that Sartre was as much my enemy as LBJ."[29]

Lester saw the French as dominating the proceedings, and their legalistic approach as having no practical validity because spotlighting illegalities could not transform political realities. Similarly, the tribunal member Carl

Oglesby declared: "To say that America commits war crimes in Vietnam is merely to elaborate legalistically the simpler fact that America is fighting in Vietnam. From the decision to fight that fight, the necessity of war crimes follows irresistibly." War crimes existed whether the tribunal so stipulated, or not. The real issue should have been to prevent the defeat of Vietnam's revolution. "After all," he commented in an allusion to the struggle against fascism, "it is not Auschwitz which is being judged again by the Russell tribunal; it is Guernica, which is an entirely different matter."[30] Oglesby clearly risked giving public offense by remarking: "I get the feeling that only the Americans on the tribunal are really concerned. The others are just going through the motions. But you better not quote me. No, go ahead. I don't care."[31]

Lester believed that the U.S. peace movement received insufficient attention, and resented Sartre's comment that America was "not the center of the world." The SNCC delegate viewed the tribunal as a European affair and felt that the Europeans were stridently anti-American. He thought that Americans were wasting their time in Stockholm and observed: "America is the country waging the war, and the tribunal should have addressed itself more to that element in the country opposing the war. Instead, it acted as if the war was going to be stopped on Boulevard Saint Germain-des-Pres." Who were the French, asked Lester, that they could assert moral authority? They created the mess in Vietnam in the first place. Also, the Holocaust had taken place in Europe, so how could its intellectuals put Asia's affairs in order? According to fellow SNCC member Charlie Cobb, Jr., "Europe was one big graveyard."[32]

Schoenman, like the Chinese, had a revolutionary Third World perspective that incorporated race as a crucial element. It was not fortuitous that he had been eager to recruit Stokely Carmichael and James Baldwin as tribunal members, since he considered the war against Asians to be racist and he hoped to encourage American blacks to refuse military service. Schoenman's assessment was attuned to that of Malcolm X, who had said that the white man was sending the black man to kill the yellow man. Just after Stockholm, Schoenman wrote to Carmichael: "I still am convinced that we have a chance to make this tribunal an effective and even revolutionary vehicle for the struggle." He asked him for ideas on how to focus on the use of "black cannon-fodder."[33]

The Americans at Stockholm were aligned with Schoenman on racial matters and were at odds with most of the Europeans. When Courtland Cox, a black lawyer, questioned a Japanese witness about race, Gunther Anders interjected: "I hope you are not trying to say that a war waged by white people against colored people is worse than a war waged by whites against whites. You forget that war was waged in Europe by white people against white people." Cox also elicited from Tariq Ali, a Pakistani, that Canadian members of the International Control Commission had made derogatory remarks about Vietnamese. Isaac Deutscher then said: "I trust, gentlemen, that we will not inject race into the discussion."[34]

Europeans may have been downplaying race to assuage their guilty white colonial consciences. More than that, they were attempting to further the emancipation of Third World peoples. They seemed to have cared more about their intellectual commitment than about the fate of Third World peoples, leading Lester to resent their "air of unapproachability."[35] Sartre had written the introduction to Frantz Fanon's *The Wretched of the Earth,* in which he described Europeans being decolonized mentally for "the settler which is in every one of us is being savagely rooted out." Sartre maintained: "Our victims know us by their scars and by their chains, and it is this that makes their evidence irrefutable. It is enough that they show us what we have made of them for us to realize what we have made of ourselves. But is it any use? Yes, for Europe is at death's door." Sartre's deep concern about the victimization of Vietnam was accompanied by a rejection of moral equivalence regarding war crimes. Whereas he condescendingly described the Vietnamese as a "horde of poor peasants," he blamed the colonialists for such a condition and thus deemed the Vietnamese not accountable for possible violations of international law committed in the cause of revolution.[36]

Verdict

After the presentation of testimony was completed on May 9, the tribunal members met for ten hours until 4:00 A.M. the next day to render their verdict. Deutscher refers to disagreements, but says that they were resolved via a majority rule principle. Nevertheless, there were no recorded negative votes on any point of the verdict, and only one abstention. Sartre was convinced that there was ample evidence of war crimes and crimes against humanity, and he pressed for a quick decision. When it was suggested that postponing the verdict for two weeks could disarm critics who claimed that it had been arrived at in advance, Sartre threatened to resign, go back to France, and issue his own statement.[37]

The May 10 verdict was close to unanimous. The first count was that the United States had violated international law through its aggression, as "in defiance of the Geneva Agreements, the United States has, since 1954, introduced into Vietnam increasing quantities of military equipment and personnel and has set up bases there." Considering the American argument that it was defending South Vietnam from North Vietnamese aggression, the tribunal rather politically decided that Vietnam was one country, so it "cannot be seen as an aggressor against itself." There were also two subdivisions to the first count: South Korea, Australia, and New Zealand were found to be accomplices in the American aggression, and the United States, Thailand, and South Vietnam were guilty (with one member abstaining) of aggression against Cambodia. The second count regarding the targeting of civilians and the use of prohibited weapons also produced a guilty verdict. The United States was condemned for war crimes based on "intensive and systematic bombardment" of hospitals and schools and for using fragmentation bombs.[38] Note that genocide, treatment of prisoners of war, and the role of Japan were not addressed.

Russell's closing statement to the tribunal, read by Schoenman, declared: "We will be judged not by our reputations or our pretenses but by our will to act." You must defy "the powerful rulers who bully and butcher with abandon" since one hundred thousand tons of napalm cannot be compared to a peasant holding a rifle. Furthermore, American policy was "comparable" to Nazism, so the tribunal was able to reveal truths while the injustices were still being committed, something that was not possible in regard to Nazi crimes.[39]

Press coverage of the tribunal was greater in Europe and Asia than it was in the United States. French and Italian accounts were generally more positive, British ones more negative. The Soviet Union, China, and most other Communist-ruled states paid scant attention, in part out of concern that the tribunal could establish a precedent that could eventually be used against them. The Soviets certainly noted that demonstrators carried a placard with the words "What About Budapest?," and that Hungarian exiles had written to Sartre, requesting a tribunal on the 1956 Soviet intervention.[40] Yugoslavia was an exception, in part because of its role in the Nonaligned Movement and Dedijer's participation.

North Vietnam—appreciating the role of tribunals in protecting the interests of a small state—applauded the Stockholm hearings, with Hanoi radio trumpeting: "The Bertrand Russell international tribunal actually is a new Nuremberg Tribunal, the first international tribunal of the masses to try the crimes of aggression committed by U.S. imperialism in Vietnam and to condemn it politically and morally."[41] Only one East European journalist attended the tribunal, Ladislaw Mnacko of Czechoslovakia. His citizenship was then revoked in August, but restored the following year, once Alexander Dubcek became the Communist party leader. Mnacko's citizenship most likely was taken away less for his role in Stockholm than because of his sharp disagreement with Czechoslovak policy during the June war in the Middle East when he sided with Israel.[42]

Overall, the tribunal failed to capture the media's imagination—in part because of the eruption of the Middle East crisis. After the opening session, National Security Adviser Walt Rostow sent Johnson a memorandum on what he considered to be the rather negative reaction of the world's press. The American consul-general in Stockholm, Turner Cameron, Jr., cabled Secretary of State Dean Rusk with the same interpretation and advised that there was no need for Washington to consider a countertrial on Communist actions or economic sanctions against Sweden.[43] The tribunal's ineffectiveness in influencing public opinion had diminished its role as a threat to American interests.

The Soviet Union had been criticized by Russell for insufficient military support for North Vietnam—and Moscow also was suspicious about the revolutionary Marxists who planned the tribunal. By contrast, attacks on American policy and backing for Hanoi and the NLF could only be beneficial to Soviet interests. A middleground position was thus taken, in which there were no Soviet delegates or journalists at the tribunal, but its activities were covered by the Soviet media in a low-key and terse style summarizing the evidence. Analysis was eschewed, as was commentary on the individuals serving on the tribunal.[44] The Soviets surely realized that overt enthusiasm could only be counterproductive, making it appear that the tribunal was an exercise in pro-Soviet propaganda. Also, many of those who were there to condemn the United States would not have attended the tribunal, had the Soviet Union played a prominent role.[45]

American reports on the tribunal were generally negative. Lester says that he knew in advance that this would be the case because public opinion had not yet turned against the war. When SNCC had adopted an anti-administration posture in 1966, it proved to be a major tactical blunder, as considerable white support was lost.[46] Dave Dellinger ruefully commented after Stockholm: "The truth, once revealed so clearly, is bound to become known—even in the United States. The question is whether, given the resistance of the American people and the distortions of the liberal press, it will be known soon enough to avert even greater catastrophe."[47] Morley Safer was in Stockholm for CBS. His derisive commentaries included attacks on Sweden's alleged self-righteousness, its hatred toward the United States, and its professed neutrality. During one of CBS's presentations, Eric Sevareid strongly condemned Russell. When Lester ran into

Safer in Stockholm, the newsman commented that nothing important had come out of the tribunal. When Lester said what about the American use of napalm, Safer retorted that it was not a significant issue.[48] Meanwhile, Russell's book *War Crimes in Vietnam* received few reviews in the United States, with the publisher remarking that even *The New York Times* wouldn't touch it.[49]

Some of the attacks on the tribunal were ad hominem assaults on Russell for being old, feebleminded, and a puppet of Schoenman. David Horowitz, who worked in London for the BRPF, later concluded that the tribunal had humiliated and isolated the prestigious philosopher and "deprived him of being regarded affectionately as a remarkable antique from the Victorian era, to be trotted out for annual celebrations."[50] Another charge leveled at the tribunal, rather accurately, was that it had overstepped the bounds of legal propriety. The procedure was aimed at convicting the United States, not trying it; the purpose was propagandistic rather than judicial, and the verdict had been predetermined, irrespective of whatever evidence would be produced.[51]

Even harsh critics of American Vietnamese policy weighed in with castigatory comments. Richard Falk was at that time the chairman of the Consultative Council of the Lawyers' Committee on American Policy Toward Vietnam, an organization that denounced the United States for legal violations. However, his two-volume study of international law and the Vietnam War labeled the hearings "a juridical farce." The tribunal member Carl Oglesby viewed the tribunal as an anti-American public relations exercise based on polemical testimony, which would impress outsiders as "a stretched-out and fancified party rally." Julius Lester, an SNCC delegate, explained to Schoenman that he had written judgmentally about the tribunal in an effort to analyze it—but he did not want to jeopardize its future. Despite his reservations, he praised the tribunal's verdict: "They had not been silent, as had the citizens of Germany when the smoke from the crematoria had filled their nostrils."[52] Lester was attuned to the Nazi analogy that permeated the tribunal, but recognized that its moral saliency undermined the tribunal's credibility through an exaggerated parallel to extermination camps.

The Reluctant MD

An important aim of the Russell tribunal was to attempt to provide a legal basis for draft resistance. Dedijer announced that he would offer evidence and witnesses to Congressional committees, since substantiation that the war was illegal could have a dramatic impact on cases before U.S. courts. A draftee could possibly refuse induction, a soldier could conceivably refuse to serve in Vietnam, and federal taxpayers could potentially withhold the percentage earmarked for the war effort.[53]

The court-martial of Dr. Howard Levy, which started at Fort Jackson, South Carolina, on the same day that the Stockholm verdict was rendered, was an opportunity to provide an important link between the tribunal and Americans challenging the legality of the war. Levy had requested support and the tribunal then furnished him with evidence. It also offered the testimony of witnesses, some of whom had been on investigatory missions in Vietnam. Captain Levy, who maintained that he did not want to assist those whom he believed were killers of Vietnamese, was charged with disobeying an order to teach in the dermatology program for Green Beret medics. He was also charged with offensive political remarks, with a witness asserting that he had compared Johnson to Hitler, and the Special Forces to the Nazi SS. Levy's attorney, Charles Morgan, Jr., at first concentrated on proving that the Green Berets had been ordered to kill. He argued that, under the Nuremberg precedent, they had borne individual responsibility for such acts and therefore should have refused to obey orders. Morgan was not maintaining that war crimes had been committed, but he wanted to "create an aura of Nuremberg" because Levy was Jewish.[54]

It was the chief officer of the court, Colonel Earl Brown, who said that the defense could present evidence pertaining to Green Beret war crimes and crimes against humanity. This was the first time that a Nuremberg defense had been permitted in a U.S. domestic trial, and it had not been introduced by Morgan. Also it was the Green Berets, not Levy, who allegedly were ordered to commit war crimes. Levy was only ordered to abet them by providing medical training. Morgan was given a recess to prepare the new line of defense, and the Supreme Court decided that the Levy court-martial could continue on that basis. Levy then claimed that Green Berets had committed war crimes, crimes against humanity, and even genocide. The doctor contended that he was not accusing the United States of these crimes, only the Green Berets, and that he was not challenging American foreign policy.

A curious twist was soon evident. Brown, in an out-of-court hearing, ruled that while there was evidence against the Green Berets, there was none to show that Levy's training of them would lead them to commit war crimes. The Nuremberg defense was deemed inadmissible, and Levy had to resort to a medical ethics argument. On June 2, Levy was found guilty on five charges—but Brown overruled on two of them. He was sentenced to a three-year term for one count of refusing to obey an order and for two counts of criticizing government policy. Morgan compared Levy to the wrongly convicted French officer Alfred Dreyfus and claimed that the army was biased against him because he was Jewish.[55] Just as in the David Mitchell case, an American court had refused to validate a Nuremberg defense in reference to actions in Vietnam so the Russell Tribunal's attempt to undercut the U.S. military system resulted in failure.

Internal Crisis

Tensions apparent at Stockholm became more severe afterward, as tribunal operations centered in Paris, thus representing a bureaucratic defeat for Russell and Schoenman. Sartre, Schwartz, and Dedijer constituted themselves as a working committee that was to carry out tribunal business between official sessions. They basically usurped the powers of the London office in an attempt to "rescue" the tribunal from what they perceived to be Schoenman's grasp.[56] Displaying his financial clout, Russell hit back by accusing the Paris faction of drawing on funds of the BRPF, and then not honoring its debt. The money had been a loan, so, if the tribunal couldn't repay it, the BRPF should have received the rights to publish tribunal materials in return. From Paris, the view was that the tribunal had to assert its financial independence from the BRPF, particularly from Schoenman. Dedijer had put himself in charge of an editorial board to deal with publications, but Russell charged that he had agreed to contracts "for pitifully small sums."[57] Just as Schoenman had been targeted by the Paris group, the Londoners were turning Dedijer into their selected enfant terrible.

Following his confrontation with Schoenman in Stockholm, Dedijer had gone to the press with criticisms of the tribunal and had even raised the issue of removing Russell's name. Schoenman wrote to Melba Hernandez: "Publicly we will try to say nothing and try to preserve unity." Russell immediately sent a letter to Dedijer (with copies to all tribunal members), however, complaining about his public comments and his "long and unpalatable history of private behavior." The abusive incidents at Stockholm were cited, and Dedijer also was chided for revealing internal tribunal matters. The upshot was that Russell asked Dedijer to resign as chair of the tribunal.[58] Russell then explained to Sartre and Schwartz that Dedijer could continue to serve as a tribunal member, just not as the chair. He also implied that Sartre and Schwartz were party to Dedijer's public comments by propounding: "If you are seeking my resignation from the tribunal I think it would be better if you said so explicitly." Russell suggested to Anders that someone more calm and rational should replace Dedijer as chair, perhaps the Italian attorney Lelio Basso. Chris Farley of the BRPF also contacted Anders with the same proposal, but Anders replied that replacing Dedijer was premature. Farley called Dedijer a "disaster" as the chair.[59]

The Paris office wanted to retain Dedijer as chair. Sartre proposed a reconciliation meeting to discuss the issue; Russell replied that he would meet with Sartre and Schwartz only if advance clarifications were made in writing. Russell did not mention any inclusion of Dedijer. Deutscher then tried to mediate by placing some of the blame on Schoenman. He wrote to Schwartz that the Paris faction should not treat Russell so shabbily, for he should not be made responsible for Schoenman's actions. Deutscher also attempted to build up Schwartz as an interlocutor by telling Russell: "He is, as far as I can judge, the only member of the tribunal in Paris who really works for the tribunal."[60] Prospects for a meeting were improving. Farley wrote to Anders: "Lord Russell has never been unwilling to see Professor Schwartz or monsieur Sartre. He has only tried to clarify certain matters in writing before any such meeting were held." A hopeful Russell explained to the former Mexican president, and original tribunal appointee, Lazaro Cardenas: "The tribunal's internal difficulties have not, unfortunately, been resolved as yet, but I have exchanged a number of letters with Professor Schwartz and feel that some progress has been made in any case."[61]

A reconciliation session between Russell, Sartre, Schwartz, and Deutscher appeared probable until Deutscher's sudden death on August 17. A Russell-Schwartz meeting was then scheduled for late September, but Russell fell ill and it was canceled.[62] In the end, Dedijer remained the chair. The Paris group had in effect secured a victory, and plans for new hearings would become the focus of tribunal activities.

Chapter XIII

THE SWEDISH CONTEXT

Sweden was a neutral non-North Atlantic Treaty Organization (NATO) state with an active antiwar movement and strong governmental criticism of U.S. policy in Vietnam. Schoenman, in January 1965, had mailed articles to Prime Minister Tage Erlander on "the true nature of the war in Vietnam" and it was rather natural that Sweden was one of the countries approached in late 1966 as a possible backup location for the tribunal.[1] When Paris and London were nonreceptive, Stockholm became the venue, through the efforts of Peter Weiss and the Swedish support committee. Such an outcome proved to be highly controversial, creating antagonisms between Erlander and the tribunal organizers and polarizing Swedish public opinion. Even the issue of neutralism became a significant factor in Swedish internal politics.

The Permission Controversy

In November 1966, Russell wrote to Erlander that the tribunal was planning to meet in Stockholm and he requested assistance in arranging visas for Vietnamese witnesses. The message was the standard one sent to de Gaulle and other leaders whose countries were being considered as tribunal venues. The Swedish prime minister responded on December 9 that a tribunal would not contribute to a peaceful solution in Vietnam, and he added: "I urge you not to choose Sweden as a site for such meetings." Erlander did not want to jeopardize Swedish neutralism, nor did he want to serve as host. Then, to his chagrin, Russell published the letter and thereby provided potent ammunition for the prime minister's left-wing opponents.[2]

Swedish opinion was critical of the U.S. role in Vietnam, as were many prominent members of Erlander's Social Democratic Party. Assurances given by tribunal supporters in regard to two key legal matters further undercut Erlander's options. One was a promise to abide by a Swedish law prohibiting offense to a foreign chief of state, in this case Lyndon Johnson. The other was a commitment to fact-finding and investigation, rather than a formal war crimes trial. Erlander told U.S. national security adviser Walt Rostow that Swedish leftists had agreed to drop their endorsement of the tribunal, should it try to operate as a quasi-legal forum.[3]

Erlander was especially concerned about a tribunal's effect on Sweden's secret mediation between the United States and North Vietnam, not to mention potential American trade retaliation. Still, the prime minister noted that he was coming to terms with the growing probability that Stockholm would end up as the tribunal's venue.[4] Thus, on April 24, 1967, he announced that his government "[did] not wish the tribunal to hold its session in Sweden." The next day, he admitted that he had no legal basis to prevent such a meeting. Russell cabled him on April 26 with thanks for upholding the freedom of expression.[5] An annoyed Erlander focused on damage control. He went on American television to explain that Swedish law was incapable of stopping the tribunal, while simultaneously sending a letter and a cable to tribunal organizers about planning for the hearings.[6] The foreign committee of parliament unanimously opposed the tribunal on the ground that it would jeopardize prospects for peace. Swedes objecting to the tribunal then greeted its opening with protests, which included banners condemning NLF supporters for agitating against Erlander. On the other side of the issue, the Aliens Commission voted four to three to issue visas for North Vietnamese witnesses, despite the absence of diplomatic relations between the two countries.[7]

At the Bonn funeral of the former German Chancellor Konrad Adenauer, Erlander tried to talk to Johnson at an April 25 dinner hosted by de Gaulle. He had earlier that day announced that the tribunal would take place in Stockholm, apparently calculating his timing so that he would not have to reject the American president's entreaties directly, and he wanted to explain his action. Former Prime Minister David Ben-Gurion of Israel was engaging Johnson in discussion, so Erlander never managed to speak his piece.

After the meal, Johnson dispatched national security adviser Walt Rostow to Erlander's room with a strong message. Rostow cited LBJ as calling a Stockholm tribunal "highly regrettable." Erlander explained that he personally opposed the tribunal, but was being pushed by his own political left. Moreover, he could not keep tribunal members out of the country except on the basis of national security. The prime minister promised that Johnson would not be personally attacked and that the tribunal was merely an investigatory body. He also said that were he to prevent the tribunal, it would appear that neutral Sweden had succumbed to U.S. pressure. His own political image also would be tarnished. In fact, university students in Uppsala had already distributed a cartoon portraying him as an American puppet. Rostow pointed out that Sweden's acceptance of the tribunal was inconsistent with its neutralism. When questioned on Swedish television about his conclave with Rostow, Erlander was asked about American warnings in regard to the tribunal. He coyly responded, "I cannot say."[8] The U.S. chargé d'affaires in Stockholm, Turner Cameron, Jr., declared that the tribunal would "not improve Swedish-American relations."[9]

At a press conference prior to the hearings, a tactless Schoenman denied that Erlander had written to Russell indicating his opposition to the tribunal. This contradicted the prime minister's public statements, as well as his December 9, 1966 telegram to Russell. When the Swedish foreign ministry produced the text, Schoenman refused to accept its authenticity. Swedish newspapers complained about this insult to Erlander and Schoenman was forced by tribunal members to apologize once the original copy from London showed that he was wrong. Dedijer expressed the tribunal's regret, Schoenman was harnessed as a spokesperson, and the Stockholm session opened after a rocky preliminary round.[10]

Internal Politics and the Vietnam War

The Social Democrats dominated Swedish politics, with Tage Erlander having served as prime minister since 1946. Erlander, his Foreign Minister, Torsten Nilsson, and Olof Palme were the key figures determining policy toward the Vietnam War. Palme had been Erlander's private secretary since 1954. He had been appointed minister without portfolio in November 1963, and then minister of transportation and communication in November 1965. Despite his relatively minor official posts, Palme enjoyed the confidence of Erlander and was instrumental in the area of foreign policy.

Erlander argued that American actions in Vietnam conflicted with democratic values and, in any case, that major powers should not intervene in the affairs of small ones. The U.S. vice president, Hubert Humphrey, warned Johnson while Erlander was visiting Washington in November 1965 that the Swede had been critical of LBJ's policies. Ever anxious to maintain deniability and avoid antagonizing the United States directly, Erlander let Nilsson and Palme take the lead on Vietnam pronouncements.[11]

In September 1964, and again in May 1965, foreign minister Nilsson had called for great power restraint in Vietnam. It was Palme, an opponent of earlier French policy in Indochina, who in July 1965 used a stint as acting prime minister during Erlander's vacation break to say publicly that the Social Democrats should side with the oppressed, and favor the Vietnamese over the Americans. Such a position differed from Nilsson's comments in May, since the foreign minister, while critical of the bombing of North Vietnam, nevertheless had called for reconciliation rather than an American defeat. Sven Weden, deputy leader of the Liberal Party, attacked Palme's anti-American attitude because he was concerned that Sweden would be at the mercy of the Soviet Union were it to cause a rift in relations with the United States. American Ambassador J. Graham Parsons protested Palme's speech and called for an explanation, but Erlander would not apologize or reprimand his closest aide.[12]

In August, Nilsson endorsed Palme's declarations, affirming that the Social Democrats had for long been in favor of economic and social change in the Third World and that the amelioration of conditions cited by Palme was linked to his advocacy of peace. Nilsson blamed the Vietnam conflict for an increase in world tensions, and found the cause in U.S. behavior: "Any policy that uses force to suppress national aspirations is a dangerous international explosive force." He called on the United States to use its influence over allies not to act contrary to "the laws of humanity," and stated: "We welcome this process of colonial liberation." Nilsson condemned the division of Vietnam, thus implying the illegitimacy of South Vietnam. He certainly was more militantly anti-American than he had been previously, as the United States had increased its troop strength, started to carry out large-scale offensive land operations against the NLF, and had been joined by forces from Australia and New Zealand. Nilsson nevertheless tempered his remarks by observing: "We are fully aware that the continuation of the war in Vietnam cannot be held to be the one-sided responsibility of one party."[13] At the United Nations the following month, Nilsson supported a halt to U.S. bombing of North Vietnam, the inclusion of North Vietnam in negotiations, and consideration of a timetable for American troop withdrawal.[14]

Indubitably, Swedish criticism of U.S. policy in Vietnam was facilitated by the fact that it was not a member of NATO. However, domestic considerations were operative as well. The rise of the New Left during the

1960s had radicalized Swedish youth, and they were several years ahead of their American counterparts in their degree of vehemence against the war. In part, they were trying to atone for a sense of guilt over Sweden's neutrality during the Nazi era. More immediately, Social Democrats were afraid of being outflanked on the left. Their concern only increased with the results of the September 1966 local elections, when their share of the vote dropped 7 percent from four years earlier, while that of the Communists rose 2.8 percent. There were calls for Erlander's resignation and the scheduling of new national elections. The prime minister then moved to appease his leftist critics by giving asylum to American draft evaders and defectors and by increasing parliamentary cooperation with the Communists, who were acting independently of Moscow.[15]

Historian Fredrik Logevall accurately noted: "Americans and opposition leaders were certainly correct in charging that the Social Democratic government used the Vietnam issue to gain domestic political advantage, particularly among the young. The war mobilized a whole generation of Swedish youth to a degree not seen since the Spanish Civil War, and the government plainly saw the electoral benefits that an antiwar position could bring."[16] Even prior to the Stockholm tribunal, anti-American demonstrations were commonplace. In February 1967, the U.S. embassy was attacked and protesters burned an American flag.[17] Erlander's decision to let the Russell Tribunal proceed was therefore attuned to the sentiments of a growing segment of Sweden's population—and it did come to pay domestic political dividends.

Foreign Policy Perspectives

Based on its efficacy during World War II, Sweden maintained its neutralism during the Cold War. To provide this choice with an appropriate foundation, it advocated an ideological "Middle Way" based on democratic socialism, economic egalitarianism, and racial equality. Sweden also advanced itself as an alternative model for Third World development. It did not join NATO (as had Norway and Denmark, which had experienced Nazi occupation) or the European Economic Community (EEC). Instead, it concentrated on Nordic unity as a means of deflecting the Cold War from Northern Europe. Seeing detente as ensuring small states against a superpower clash in its region, Sweden enthusiastically supported Willy Brandt's "Ostpolitik" once he became West Germany's foreign minister in December 1966. This did not mean that Sweden was oblivious to the fact that, in a strategic sense, it was the Soviet Union—not the United States—

that represented its prime military threat. This was due to geography more than ideology, since Russia had controlled neighboring Finland until late 1917, and Soviet forces had occupied Finland during World War II.[18] Consequently, Sweden's neutralism included a commitment to self-defense, including the development of nuclear weapons. This principle was certainly crucial, once U.S. forces became bogged down in Vietnam. Palme, who was so vocal an opponent of the American war in Vietnam, was consequently a strong advocate of a nuclear Sweden. His outlook, like that of Erlander, was strategic, not moralistic.[19]

Sweden feared that the Vietnam War undermined detente in Europe, and thus jeopardized small states. Its anti-American stance evolved out of concern for detente, and Sweden similarly castigated the Soviet Union in 1968 for its intervention in Czechoslovakia.[20] One means of seeking superpower reconciliation was through the United Nations, but Sweden's influence there was in decline because Third World states were becoming major actors. U Thant, of Burma, was the secretary-general. The first two holders of that post had been Scandinavians: Trygve Lie of Norway and Dag Hammarskjold of Sweden.

The second Swedish method was to serve as a peace mediator in Vietnam. The ambassador to China, Lennart Petri, established contacts with the North Vietnamese government in mid-1966. In November, with Erlander's encouragement, Nilsson had met with Hubert Humphrey in Washington. They discussed Sweden's ability, not available to the United States, to talk to the North Vietnamese. Humphrey asked if he could speak unofficially, and then suggested that North Vietnam and the NLF should reduce the level of hostilities in order to facilitate an American withdrawal. Afterward, the Communists could take over Vietnam.[21] Sweden agreed to be a mediator, and Operation ASPEN was launched that month. Erlander's government then toned down its condemnation of American policy in order to sustain U.S. faith in Sweden's role as a liaison. According to the foreign policy analyst Lars-Goran Stenelo, neutral Sweden had never been such a vocal critic previously, and there was some contradiction in being a critic and a mediator simultaneously.[22]

Connections

Shortly before the Swedish government permitted the Russell Tribunal to assemble in Stockholm, it downgraded relations with South Vietnam. The ambassador to Thailand had previously been accredited to Saigon as well, but a new ambassador was posted solely to Bangkok. Nilsson charged that the South Vietnamese government did not represent a majority of its people. Richard Hichens Bergstrom, Director of Political Affairs at the foreign ministry, claimed that "Hanoi might listen to us more" in expediting peace negotiations. The U.S. Department of State, in a communication to the American embassy in Stockholm, expressed "disappointment" on the accreditation issue and was skeptical of Bergstrom's explanation. Washington predicted that Hanoi would probably harden its response to Swedish mediation. Chargé d'affaires Turner Cameron Jr. observed that Bergstrom and Jean-Christophe Oberg, first secretary of the political division of the foreign ministry, were becoming more receptive to the view that North Vietnam would further entrench, due to the ambassadorship flap and the decision to host the tribunal.[23]

Swedish public opinion tended to view the U.S. as an arrogant superpower committing aggression against a small state. The majority of Swedes, however, did not support the Russell Tribunal—and the media was polarized along ideological lines. Despite Moscow's lukewarm attitude, the Communist organ *Norrskensflamman* favored the hearings. *Aftonbladet,* voice of the Social Democrats, was also supportive and it accused American and British reporters of slanderous coverage that did not properly reflect the evidence. At the same time, the paper expressed concern about the use of terms such as "trial," "tribunal" and "court." *Dagens Nyheter,* a Liberal People's Party newspaper, criticized the hearings as a prosecution case that endeavored to present an image of being juridically authorized. This was portrayed as an "abuse of the freedom to congregate." *Expressen,* also Liberal, accused the tribunal of disguising political protest in the form of a court procedure and of rendering its verdict in advance. It also bemoaned Sweden's deteriorating image in the United States, with Swedes being described as "meddlesome," "righteous," American-hating "little people." Predictably, the Conservative outlet *Svenska Dagbladet* was the most negative. It called the tribunal a "miserable gimmick," and an editorial stated: "The freedom of assembly is one thing; its misuse is another."[24]

The tribunal, although not warmly received, seems to have had a strong impact on Sweden. Causality is difficult to determine, and Foreign Minister Nilsson does not help elucidate the evolution of attitudes, since his memoirs strategically skip the period from November 1966 to September 1967. What is evident, however, is that a countertrial to cover alleged crimes committed by North Vietnam and the NLF was scheduled for just after the tribunal, but it was canceled when the four political parties expected to participate all pulled out.[25] In July 1967, a conference on Vietnam organized by peace movements convened in Stockholm. There were 350 delegates, thirty-three of them American. By the fall, the Swedish government was increasing its attacks on U.S. policy, apparently seeking support from young voters. Nilsson told U.S. Secretary of State Dean Rusk that Sweden wanted the Vietnam War ended because it was producing a deterioration in superpower relations.[26]

North Vietnam, partly emboldened by the Russell Tribunal, had little interest in a negotiated settlement. On May 18, Permanent Undersecretary of State Leif Belfrage met in Warsaw with Hanoi's ambassador to Poland, who cited growing criticism of the American role and what he interpreted as an upsurge of the U.S. antiwar movement. The ambassador must have implied endorsement of a military solution, because Belfrage later related that he had to repeat several times that Johnson still had strong public backing and had not lost his determination. Belfrage warned that a lack of progress in negotiations would intensify the war. When Sweden's ambassador to China, Lennart Petri, visited Hanoi in late June, Foreign Minister Nguyen Duy Trinh expressed his "appreciation" for the Stockholm tribunal.[27] North Vietnam withdrew from peace diplomacy, and Sweden had no choice but to end the secret ASPEN program of contacts in February 1968. The Stockholm government then challenged the United States more vocally, chiding it publicly ninety-three times from February 1968 through 1972. There had been only ten such attacks during the period from January 1965 through January 1968.[28]

In February 1968, coinciding with the termination of ASPEN, the Swedish Vietnam Committee staged an anti-American demonstration in the capital. Olof Palme, then the minister of education, participated and marched alongside the North Vietnamese ambassador to Moscow, Nguyen Tho Chanh, even though there were no diplomatic relations between the two countries. The American ambassador William Heath quickly complained to Erlander, but the prime minister would not admonish Palme or dissociate from his pro-NLF remarks. Erlander argued that Palme was merely trying to prevent Communist domination of the event. Washington protested by recalling Heath for "consultations," but he returned six weeks later.[29]

Erlander's catering to the left contributed to a landslide Social Democratic victory in the September 1968 elections, his last as party leader. The Social Democrats garnered a majority of seats in the Riksdag for the first time since 1940. In January 1969, Nilsson announced the establishment of full diplomatic relations with North Vietnam, making Sweden the first Western country to take such a step. In October of that year, Palme succeeded Erlander and extended $40 million in humanitarian aid to Hanoi.[30]

The Russell Tribunal played an integral role in Swedish politics, helping to galvanize the New Left and providing impetus to Erlander's effort to attract younger members of the electorate. Internal opposition to the Vietnam War grew, so the tribunal's impact on the host government was clearly salutary from that perspective. Sweden also had become more of a player on the world scene. The tribunal itself was not as fortunate, since positive international reaction was limited. The Russell Tribunal therefore had much work remaining after Stockholm.

Chapter XIV

SECOND WIND

Ralph Schoenman continued to frustrate tribunal members interested in projecting a more objective image. Emulating Trotsky, he became enmeshed with North Vietnam and Cuba in organizing a Fifth International based on Che Guevara's guerrilla warfare concepts and designed to defeat the United States by creating many Vietnams. As his colleague David Horowitz later pointed out, there was a serious logical contradiction, because more Vietnams would inevitably produce an upsurge in war crimes.[1] When Regis Debray—a French contributor to Guevara's revolutionary effort—was arrested in Bolivia, Schoenman attended his October 1967 trial and was himself apprehended on the charge of aiding the guerrillas. Finally, he was expelled for failure to hold a valid passport.[2]

These sideshows did not prevent the tribunal from forging on and holding hearings in Japan and Denmark. The organizers were determined to reduce the level of distractions so detrimental to the tribunal's success.

The Japanese Venue

A chapter of the Bertrand Russell Peace Foundation was organized in Japan in October 1966 and there were two Japanese tribunal members at Stockholm. The Japanese had an obvious interest in the Vietnam War, in terms of American actions against fellow Asians, and there was also some residual guilt about the Japanese occupation of Vietnam, deriving from a pacifist streak in reaction to Japan's militarism and defeat in World War II. In fact, Japan had only just completed paying reparations to South Vietnam in January 1965. Japanese opinion was split over the war, but the major media outlets were generally critical of U.S. policy and there was a power-ful antiwar movement known as Beheiren (Citizens' Federation for Peace in Vietnam). Opponents of the war were deeply concerned about Japanese assistance to the American military, fearing that their country would be drawn more deeply into the war, and believing that Japan had not suffi-ciently learned its lesson from the post–World War II Tokyo war crimes trials. The Japanese, who had themselves been subjected to atomic attack, were particularly sensitive about the burning effect of napalm on Viet-namese civilians.[3]

The European-based Russell Tribunal was glad to extend its operations to Asia, so hearings were scheduled in Tokyo from August 28 to 30, 1967. Japanese supporters of the Russell Tribunal joined with the Japanese Com-munist Party to form the Japan Committee for Investigation of U.S. War Crimes in Vietnam, and sent two investigatory missions to North Vietnam. Prime Minister Eisaku Sato, a Liberal Democrat in office since November 1964, realized that public opinion was increasingly turning leftward against his cooperation with the American effort in Vietnam. Sato's party con-trolled 277 of the 486 seats in the Diet. The antiwar Communists and Socialists held only five and thirty seats respectively. Tokyo had elected a leftist governor in April, however, and the Communist Party's popularity was expected to rise following its July break with China. At the time, the Cultural Revolution was seriously tarnishing China's image in Japan.

By August 1967, Sato came to recognize that mild criticism of the United States would contribute to his popularity.[4] He agreed to a Tokyo tribunal, but tried to cut down its effectiveness by stipulating that only Japanese could participate officially as tribunal members and witnesses. Foreigners could attend, but a language barrier further limited external publicity. Dave Dellinger was there, but other non-Japanese Stockholm tribunal members were not present in Tokyo. Influential newspapers such as *The New York Times* gave it scant coverage. Sato therefore succeeded in having his cake and eating it, too.

The Tokyo tribunal had twenty-eight members and was presided over by a university president, Hiroshi Suekawa. There were thirty-six wit-nesses, but no defenders of Japanese actions in Vietnam. The testimony included a considerable amount of information previously unreported in Japan.[5] Basically, it focused on Japan's provision of a rear base for Ameri-can forces, and on its direct military and economic roles in the war. The 1959 reparations agreement with South Vietnam also was criticized for not covering North Vietnam, thereby signifying tacit Japanese endorsement of the permanent division of Vietnam.[6]

Japan hosted 264 U.S. bases for the purposes of combat, logistics, repairs, intelligence, and training. It profited from weapon components manufacturing, repair and maintenance contracts, and from the R&R provided to American troops. Self-Defense Forces carried out joint exercises with the United States, and also took over some functions in order to free Americans for duty in Vietnam. Troops from Thailand, South Korea, the Philippines, and South Vietnam also trained under U.S. command in Okinawa. In Vietnam, Japan furnished air and naval transport units, including LSTs (landing ships tanks) with Japanese crews that operated as part of the U.S. military, flew U.S. flags, and carried munitions and napalm for the war. Japanese firms helped produce this napalm. Economically, Japan earned about $1 billion per year on the sale of goods and services to American and South Vietnamese forces, including materials for port construction in South Vietnam. Based on this evidence, the tribunal found Japan guilty of aggression and of being an accomplice to U.S. aggression. A copy of the August 30 verdict was forwarded to the Russell Tribunal office in London.[7]

Japanese critics of the war questioned the 1960 treaty that permitted the United States to maintain military facilities in Japan to preserve peace and security in the Far East. The government argued that the Vietnam War could be interpreted as a threat to peace and security in the Far East, but opponents retorted that Vietnam was not itself in the Far East and therefore was not covered by the treaty's provisions. In April 1966, Foreign Minister Etsusaburo Shiina had acknowledged that Vietnam was not part of the Far East, but claimed that the security treaty could be applied to threats from an adjoining area such as Southeast Asia. Shiina stated that Japan would not intervene in Vietnam, but would permit the United States to operate out of Japanese bases in accordance with the treaty. Opponents also questioned the freedom of U.S. troop movements in Japan. No redeployment in terms of new divisions or naval task forces was allowed without Japanese approval, but otherwise, U.S. troops could move in or out of Japan. Difficult to enforce was the stipulation that orders for American assaults on other states could not be issued in Japan. It is clear, however, that U.S. troops based in Japan could be conveyed into combat elsewhere, as long as they did not directly attack from Japanese territory. B-52 bombers based in Okinawa did carry out missions in Vietnam, since this island was not under Japanese administration.[8]

When Prime Minister Sato visited Washington in January 1966, he endorsed American backing of the Saigon government, but kept Japanese (as compared to South Korean) direct involvement in the war limited. As the August 1967 tribunal session approached, however, Sato tactically catered to his political opponents by mildly speaking out on U.S. policies. Once the hearings were over, he reversed course, apparently calculating that he had shored up his left flank sufficiently. In this regard, the tribunal's impact on the government had been temporary.

After observers from Sato's Liberal Democratic Party announced that South Vietnam's September 3 presidential election had been fair, the prime minister undertook two extensive trips to the region. He adopted a pro-American position but did not increase Japan's role. While in Saigon, he met with President Nguyen Van Thieu and Vice President Nguyen Cao Ky and justified American bombing of the North. In Bangkok, Sato said that a bombing halt would not end the war. On both occasions, he stated that North Vietnam had to provide a meaningful response to peace overtures. Sato tried to use his embrace of the United States to help recover Japanese islands under American control. He was successful in the case of the Ogasawara Islands, but Washington balked on Okinawa because it was central to the war effort in Vietnam.[9]

On to Roskilde

In the course of preparations for another tribunal session, Russell discovered that he was not in the driver's seat. Erlander had informed Dedijer that a second set of hearings couldn't be held in Sweden. When Russell heard this news, he suspiciously remarked: "I hope that the close personal relationship between Mr. Dedijer and Mr. Erlander has not affected this decision." The Paris office of the tribunal assured Russell that it had played no role. The Paris faction, which included the tribunal's executive committee, also informed Russell that Copenhagen was its choice as the next site and that Schoenman had been notified. Russell was unaware of this matter and thought it "strange" that Erlander's wish should be honored this time around. He also doubted whether Danish supporters would be equal to the Swedes in their activism. The United States had already dropped out of consideration as a site because of the poor public and media response to Stockholm.[10]

Denmark did in fact have a well-organized group backing the Russell Tribunal. In November 1966, Schoenman had sought its financial assistance and public action with an appeal to the country's glorious past: "The Danish Resistance is an heroic chapter in the history of this century, and so I am sure that the resistance of the Vietnamese will find an echo amongst the Danish people."[11] When plans to meet in Paris ran into difficulties in April

1967, Denmark had been considered as a backup. It is therefore not surprising that it was later suggested by the executive committee as the venue.

On September 20, most of the tribunal's members met in Brussels to organize the next round of hearings. They discussed the Tokyo session, and endorsed the Copenhagen site. They also noted that if Denmark did not extend visas for all of the witnesses, then arrangements were already in place to take testimony in a neighboring country.[12] Dave Dellinger explained his plan for a giant demonstration in Washington on October 21, which he hoped would encourage U.S. servicemen to appear as witnesses in Denmark. He asked that hearings be delayed until a month from that date, and members readily agreed. Addressing the crowd in Washington, Dellinger proclaimed that it was time for active resistance and confrontation; peaceful protest was passé. He advocated "nonviolent militancy." That same day, antiwar activists rallied in Copenhagen. On October 31, 1967, a month after returning from a fruitful visit to Washington, Danish Prime Minister Jens Otto Krag agreed to let the tribunal meet in his country.[13]

Danish supporters of the BRPF were anxious to organize a tribunal session, more because of its expected impact on Denmark than on Vietnam. They saw their fellow citizens as smug, affluent, and morally noninvolved. Hearings could energize their society out of its complacency. Denmark was rich and stable enough to absorb any vibrations, they argued. Protest was not enough; there had to be a legalistic basis for "the dawning of global human experience."[14] Danish organizers gallantly committed themselves to financing the tribunal session, but soon discovered that execution was not quite so simple.[15]

Danish tribunal advocates sought to compete with the Swedes. They admired Palme for redirecting Swedish society by emphasizing atonement for a sense of collaborationist guilt regarding the Nazi period, and felt that the Stockholm tribunal had contributed to Sweden's humanitarian transformation. If Palme could do it, so could they. Sweden had asserted its independence of the United States, but Denmark was still tied to the American apron strings. It was time to break loose.[16]

The Danish government approved the tribunal, but wanted it to be low-key. It rejected hearings in Copenhagen, but permitted them in sleepy Roskilde, which was twenty miles from the capital. They were to take place at a union building within a hall generally used for Saturday night dances. The sessions were scheduled for November 20 through December 1. Conspicuous by his absence in this whole endeavor was Stockholm's major domo, Ralph Schoenman. When he tried to get into Denmark on

November 20, he was refused entry at Copenhagen's airport on the ground that he did not possess a valid passport. He flew to Amsterdam and Helsinki, hoping to remain in the region so he could make another attempt at Copenhagen, but was turned away unceremoniously. He was even detained temporarily in Stockholm. Schoenman gave up and returned to the United States on November 24. His appeal pertaining to the American confiscation of his passport was rejected by a federal court.[17]

Simone de Beauvoir was not displeased. Commenting on Denmark's refusal to admit Schoenman, she remarked: "So much the better—our discussions would be much less stormy without him." The journalist Ebbe Reich, a dynamic force behind the Danish support committee, described Schoenman as "crazy," "a strange man," and "difficult to work with."[18]

The Third Round

Deutscher died in August, so a bridge between the London and Paris offices had been lost. The Paris group of Sartre, Dedijer, Schwartz, and de Beauvoir then ran the Roskilde hearings—with Claude Lanzmann substituting for Sartre for a few days. There was a much more trusting and cooperative atmosphere than there had been at Stockholm. The panelists were able to concentrate on the evidence, but the press was continuously distracted by the somewhat antic peregrinations of Ralph Schoenman.

The Roskilde hearings concentrated on napalm and chemical warfare; the treatment of prisoners and civilians; military action against Laos; the roles of Thailand, the Philippines, and Japan; and, most important, genocide. More attention was paid to South Vietnam than at Stockholm, where the focus had been on the North. The United States again chose not to present a defense. Hence, the tribunal heard only one-sided testimony, which emphasized "collateral damage" to the Vietnamese land and people caused by the U.S. military. Actions by the North Vietnamese and NLF were not considered, as the emphasis was on whether American forces had used weapons forbidden by the rules of war.

Testimony was presented on napalm, phosphorus bombs, chemical defoliants, and cluster bomb units (CBUs). Evidence about CBUs had a particularly powerful impact on the tribunal, since they release pellets (such as guava bombs) that kill people but spare property. Vietnamese witnesses displayed the crippling effects of napalm on their own bodies and film footage compiled by American soldiers also was shown. Former servicemen provided a moral tone as witnesses, since they had previously backed the U.S. war effort. Racial and class issues within the U.S. military structure were portrayed as endemic, with the black infantry veteran David Tuck charging that blacks, Puerto Ricans, and "hillbillies" were assigned to combat units because they were "expendable." Russell had encouraged the boxer Muhammad Ali to offer testimony about the racial aspects of the war, but he indicated that he could not do so inasmuch as his right to travel had been taken away.[19]

Distracting from the hearings was the case of four airmen from the carrier *Intrepid,* who had served in operations in Vietnam. They had deserted in Yokosuka, Japan, on October 17, after Dave Dellinger and the political scientist Howard Zinn had advocated such action in leaflets passed out to the crew. The airmen arrived in Moscow on November 20, just as the tribunal was commencing, where they denounced the United States on Soviet television. Efforts were made to bring them to Roskilde as witnesses, but this did not happen, because the Danish government refused entry because of their lack of passports. They then went to Sweden on December 29, where they were soon given asylum on a humanitarian basis, not as political refugees.[20]

Stokely Carmichael was supposed to serve as a tribunal member at Stockholm, but he sent a replacement and never attended. Russell Stetler, head of the BRPF New York office, prevailed on him to participate at Roskilde, but the young SNCC leader preferred fiery rhetoric to careful deliberations over evidence. He did appear briefly, but angered tribunal members by leaving hastily to deliver a speech in Copenhagen. The panelists therefore decided to strip him of his right to vote, for not having been present to hear most of the testimony. After speaking in Oslo, Stockholm, and Uppsala, Carmichael was detained at Orly airport and held for fourteen hours before being permitted to proceed to an antiwar rally in Paris. He told the crowd: "We don't want peace in Vietnam! We want the Vietnamese to defeat the United States of America!" When he returned to the United States on December 11, his passport was confiscated on the basis of unauthorized visits to North Vietnam and Cuba.[21]

The heart of the hearings, as pointed out by de Beauvoir, was the issue of possible genocide. The chief legal specialist Leo Matarasso prepared a report on the historical background, and tried to accentuate the victimization of minorities in order to justify a charge in accordance with the Genocide Convention. Lelio Basso correctly observed that nonratification by the United States was irrelevant to the matter of whether or not it had committed the crime. Sartre had a more philosophical interpretation and used the French role in Algeria as a precedent. He maintained that the American antiguerrilla strategy had genocide as its objective. Assuming that U.S. forces would not pull out of Vietnam, the Vietnamese were forced to choose between capitulation or extermination.[22]

Tribunal members tried to develop a context for their deliberations in terms of whether previous acts of genocide should be cited as analogous and, if so, which ones. Although the Genocide Convention did not go into effect until 1951, members viewed a Vietnam parallel with Nazism and frequently referred to Hitler. They also commented on the Nuremberg and Tokyo tribunals that dealt with war crimes and crimes against humanity. Jews were identified as victims of Nazism, but controversy prevailed on the question of a unique Jewish experience. It had just been accentuated as a vital frame of reference in regard to Israel's experience during the June 1967 Six Day War.[23] The decimation of Armenians at the hand of the Turks from 1915 through 1916 was not mentioned, apparently in deference to the Turkish tribunal member Mehmet Ali Aybar.[24]

Vladimir Dedijer led the charge on the genocide issue. Simone de Beauvoir was skeptical, going so far as to consider bypassing it altogether. She thought that there was no point in asking the question about genocide if the answer was to turn out to be "no," and she was wary of a Holocaust analogy. Sartre was in the middle. He impressed the Danish support committee member Ebbe Reich as an old man torn between a brilliant de Beauvoir and an overbearing Dedijer. In the end, Dedijer won out with the help of graphic testimony about chemical defoliation, the bombing of civilian targets, and the forcing of Vietnamese into strategic hamlets where health conditions were poor. Carl Oglesby, too, was at first concerned that a finding of genocide would be viewed by the public as rhetorical overkill. He then shifted to Dedijer's position, in part because of the Yugoslav's persuasiveness and in part as a consequence of evidence suggesting that the United States was trying to demoralize Vietnamese civilians by targeting hospitals and using cluster bomb units.[25]

The tribunal's December 1 verdict was unanimous on American guilt for using illegal weapons, maltreating prisoners of war and civilians, and for aggression against Laos. There also were unanimous decisions on Thai and Filipino complicity in U.S. aggression against Vietnam, but three negative votes were registered on Japanese responsibility on the ground that Japan provided assistance to the United States but did not participate in the aggression. On the genocide charge, the tribunal unanimously voted guilty.[26] This decision on genocide had little impact on the American public and was generally viewed by the press as verbal excess. The My Lai incident in March 1968 soon contributed to an attitudinal shift against U.S. involvement.[27]

The foreign press generally was dismissive of Roskilde. American and British media coverage was scant, but that on the Continent was more substantial and helped move public opinion further in an antiwar direction. Simone de Beauvoir noted: "The distressing side of it all was that because of the negligence of the press there were so few of us to profit from this impressive collection of documents, evidence, and explanations."[28] As at Stockholm, the North Vietnamese viewed the verdict as "an inspiration" conducive to their prospect for achieving outright military victory. They gave rings to tribunal members, which were fashioned from downed American aircraft, and the chief NLF delegate presented a Vietcong flag.[29]

The Danish Dimension

The Danish frame of reference was strongly conditioned by history. Denmark had experienced a border dispute with Germany over Schleswig-Holstein and had been occupied by the Nazis. The Holocaust had threatened Jewish Danes, who fortunately were aided by their fellow citizens in escaping to neutral Sweden. Fear of a powerful German neighbor was endemic, and the two countries were uncomfortable military allies within NATO. The Vietnam conflict therefore came to be viewed through a Germanic prism. In Sweden, by contrast, Germany was often seen as a protector against Russia, so superpower detente's effect on Scandinavia was the main concern of the Swedes. The centrist press argued that the United States should be thanked for its past help against the Germans by having the Danes endorse its actions in Vietnam. Also, when a group of students who attended the tribunal charged that the Americans were behaving like Nazis in Vietnam, they were quickly challenged by an electrician from Jutland who proclaimed that the students had never been at war and didn't understand that the Vietnamese were using young soldiers in their battle with the Americans, just as Hitler had done. The United States was not in Vietnam to seize any land, and had to be supported just as it had aided Denmark against the Nazis.[30]

Denmark's minority Social Democratic government was critical of U.S. policy in Vietnam. It opposed a military solution, favored a halt in American bombing of North Vietnam, and called for a Vietcong role in peace negotiations. Danish public opinion was split, but a plurality regarded American actions negatively. Antiwar activists were well organized, and an appeal from 227,000 Danes to stop the bombing appeared in the June 26, 1967 edition of *The New York Times*.[31]

The Social Democrats had lost strength during the 1960s, polling 42.1

percent of the vote in 1960 but only 38.2 percent in 1966. At the same time, the Socialist People's Party (SPP) saw its share grow from 6.1 percent to 10.9 percent and it was especially powerful among the educated elite in the capital city of Copenhagen. The SPP favored the Russell Tribunal. These two parties reached a cooperation agreement in March 1967, in which the SPP promised to support the Social Democrats in parliamentary votes without formally becoming members of the ruling coalition. They agreed on the Vietnam issue, but the SPP stood well to the left of the Social Democrats. It rejected Danish membership in NATO, objected to military cooperation with West Germany, advocated Danish disarmament, and opposed joining the EEC. Aksel Larsen had formed the SPP after he was expelled from the Communist Party for questioning the 1956 Soviet intervention in Hungary. His party pushed for Danish withdrawal from NATO by using the treaty provision permitting a member to pull out after twenty years (effective August 24, 1969) if giving one year's notice.[32] The Social Democrats were pro-NATO.

From their immediate right, the Social Democrats were being challenged by the Radical Party, which was wary of the American commitment to Denmark. Many Danes feared that U.S. promises were fragile and had been extended only to secure NATO's operational rights in Greenland. Commitment of the Americans to South Vietnam was thus a test case of Washington's resolve. The Radicals therefore backed NATO tentatively and endorsed a reevaluation of Denmark's membership. They also were concerned that antiwar sentiments generated by the Stockholm tribunal would further galvanize the Danish left.[33]

Consequently, the minority Social Democrats were ideologically squeezed on the Vietnam issue, so Prime Minister Jens Otto Krag tried to play both sides of the fence. While criticizing the American role and asking Johnson to consider a bombing pause, he conversely tried (in the manner of Erlander) to prevent a tribunal session in his country. In June 1967, he indicated that the tribunal was not welcome and that legal means, such as the denial of visas, would be used against it.[34] Krag realized that stopping the tribunal would nevertheless be difficult, since obstruction by him would probably inspire Danish demonstrators. In fact, U.S. Secretary of State Dean Rusk backed out of a planned visit to Denmark for fear of provoking protests embarrassing to Krag—and, of course, to himself.[35]

On October 30, Krag convened with Ebbe Reich and members of the tribunal support committee. They assured him that the tribunal would act as an investigatory commission, not a court, and stressed their right to freedom of speech. The next day, Krag told his cabinet ministers that he could not stop the tribunal. They concurred. On November 1, a government press release asserted that the tribunal would have a "different character" than previously believed. Krag permitted the tribunal, but did not lend any enthusiastic assistance. According to Reich, the Americans knew that they could count on the prime minister to exercise effective "damage control."[36]

The Danish left portrayed Krag as "gagged and bound, hand and foot" by Denmark's NATO membership. These antiwar activists claimed that their support for the tribunal was not anti-American, but rather, an effort to cooperate with the American opposition.[37] After all, the impetus and organizational skills behind the Danish protest movement had been furnished by American Quakers who had gone to Denmark for that very purpose. Criticism of U.S. actions in Vietnam, leftists tried to argue, was not meant to encourage U.S. isolationism, but to terminate the presence in Vietnam in order to enhance American credibility elsewhere.[38]

Ebbe Reich maintained that it was more important for the tribunal to be heard than for Denmark to have the ear of the U.S. government for, in any case, Washington would never seriously listen to Copenhagen on matters pertaining to Vietnam. As for Denmark's possible mediation in the war, Reich argued that his country had not been able to play a significant role because it was a member of NATO. This obstacle could be overcome by hosting the tribunal, an act that would please Hanoi and thereby facilitate Danish mediation.[39]

The Radical, Liberal, and Conservative parties did not favor the tribunal. On the day before it convened, demonstrators noted that North Vietnamese witnesses could not be reliable because their families were being held hostage. The chairman of the union that owned the Roskilde meeting hall feared a one-sided hearing, as the United States was not provided with a defense.[40] The Conservative newspaper *Berlingske Tidende* warned against an "anti-American farce" even before the Danish government gave a green light to the tribunal. Then, just prior to the tribunal's opening, it editorialized about the "unwanted guest," the "untasteful anti-American propaganda rally," and the aura of "political carnival." Witnesses and panelists were viewed as biased, and there was an objection to war crimes charges against American military personnel "from units whose names are written in the history of the liberation of Europe and Denmark." The editorial cautioned about a retaliatory U.S. boycott of Danish goods, and it charged that the tribunal was a "war-lengthening conspiracy" that would encourage North Vietnam to continue to fight rather than negotiate.[41] *Berlingske Tidende* also published a critique of its own editorial, which minimized the possibility of American retribution against Denmark, since no Danes served on the tribunal. It also pointed out that the U.S. government did not accept an invitation to provide defense witnesses. The hearings were justified, but the term "tribunal" was unfortunate, because members were indeed self-appointed.[42]

Danish newspapers carefully evaluated each day's evidence and the juridical demeanor of the panelists. They applauded the decision to exclude Carmichael from the final vote and were aghast when Dedijer exclaimed "Long live free Vietnam!" The verdict came under considerable scrutiny by the liberal publication *Information* because of a "lack of proper deliberations" and for avoiding any mention or censure of South Vietnamese actions. All offenses were attributed to the Americans. By contrast, testimony about the emotional suffering of victims was praised, as were "precise" charges regarding the use of fragmentation bombs. Some American methods were deemed by *Information* to be "uncivilized."[43]

The immediate impact of the tribunal in Denmark was mixed. The antiwar movement gained credibility from the presentation of evidence and was no longer portrayed as motivated primarily by anti-Americanism. Still, Danish voters had other priorities, so Krag, unlike Erlander, was not rewarded at the polls for his attempt to accommodate the left. In fact, Krag had to resign two weeks after the tribunal ended because six SPP allies in the Folketing broke with him on the issue of a wage freeze. In the ensuing January 1968 elections, the Social Democrats lost seven seats, but remained the largest party. They were unable to form a majority coalition, so the Conservatives, Liberals, and Radicals established a government under Radical Prime Minister Hilmar Baunsgaard, thus ending forty years of Social Democratic rule. Domestic economic issues dominated the campaign, but a key event took place just one day before balloting, when an American B-52 crashed in Greenland, causing the release of plutonium from its hydrogen bombs. The Social Democrats were greatly embarrassed, since U.S. nuclear equipped aircraft were not officially permitted over Danish territory. Suspicions that Social Democratic governments had secretly allowed an exception for Greenland have yet to be fully allayed.[44]

After-effects

After the tribunals, Russell continued to be a political activist. He campaigned for Soviet Jews and for British withdrawal from NATO. When Soviet intervention in Czechoslovakia was looming in 1968, the elderly philosopher cabled Prime Minister Kosygin to warn against such a course.

After Soviet troops invaded, he lodged a protest with General-Secretary Leonid Brezhnev and released a statement asserting that Moscow had "disgraced itself and the principles it invokes." When he feared that the new Czechoslovak government might stage show trials for backers of the overthrown Dubcek government, he threatened to counter with a tribunal of his own.[45] Russell demonstrated that he opposed the arrogance of power and was not a critic of U.S. policy in Vietnam because of any pro-Soviet proclivities.

Russell persisted on the Vietnam issue. On December 1, 1969, he wrote to U.N. Secretary-General U Thant that there had been "considerable ridicule or indifference" when he organized tribunal sessions, but that the record that had been developed through these procedures had since been "vindicated." Russell also asked for the establishment of a war crimes tribunal because he feared that the United States was planning a countercommission of its own. U Thant replied that it wouldn't be proper to act until after the outcomes of such a body were known.[46]

In July 1969, Russell broke with Schoenman. Schoenman was removed as the executor of Russell's will and as an occasional personal secretary, and then expelled from the BRPF. On December 8, Russell prepared a lengthy memorandum attacking Schoenman, which was not released until Russell's own death on February 2, 1970. Schoenman was accused of being untruthful, tactless, offensive, and arrogant in trying to impose his views on others.[47] After Russell's passing, the BRPF and Schoenman became embroiled in recriminations. Schoenman charged the BRPF with misappropriating funds. The BRPF claimed that it was Schoenman who had pocketed the U.S. advance on the third volume of Russell's autobiography.[48]

The Russell Tribunal on Vietnam surely had procedural defects in terms of selection of members, the lack of an American defense, the absence of clear rules of evidence, and an unwillingness to apply the same standards to both sides in the conflict. It also did not galvanize the American antiwar movement, for, as viewed by Julius Lester, it took place one year prematurely, before American antiwar sentiments had begun to surge.[49] The ninety-four-year-old Russell had been unable to repeat the performance of the seventy-eight-year-old Dewey. He did not personally attend the sessions, and undercut the tribunal's credibility with his biased public statements. Dewey had been passionate about applying objective means, but he held no brief for Trotskyism. Russell was oriented toward his desired end: an NLF triumph and American military disengagement from Vietnam.

The Russell Tribunal did reintroduce the concept of international citizens' tribunals after a thirty-year hiatus, but in contrast to earlier efforts to assist maltreated individuals, it targeted the war policies of a superpower. This opened the floodgates to requests for additional hearings related to charges of alleged injustices such as the Greek military's violation of human rights, Salazar's authoritarian practices in Portugal, Egyptian war crimes in Yemen, Iraq's treatment of its Kurdish minority, and Israeli actions toward the Arabs.[50] There was clearly no infrastructure that could handle such an assignment, and it took more than a decade for Russell Tribunal veteran and attorney Lelio Basso to come up with a solution.

Chapter XV

PROLIFERATION

The Russell Tribunal spawned many others with various foci of inquiry. They were mainly issue-oriented (human rights and "global capitalism"), rather than organized to impact the fate of specific individuals (as in the case of the London countertrial and Dewey Commission). In that vein, some sought to highlight past injustices and were not related to contemporary state behavior.

While the purview of tribunals broadened to include charges against lesser actors, the choice of cases clearly demonstrated that the left strongly influenced the selection of topics. Russell Tribunal veterans such as Dedijer, Basso, Schwartz, Dellinger, and Morikawa all played a significant role as panelists. Not surprisingly, numerous tribunal verdicts were not accompanied by a recorded vote, implying either unanimity of viewpoint or a predetermined outcome. The growth of the Internet enhanced the development of tribunals, since activists from around the globe were more easily able to organize on behalf of common concerns.

Framework

In early 1970, the Bertrand Russell Peace Foundation considered the organization of a follow-up tribunal to evaluate American involvement in Cambodia and Laos. Members from Stockholm and Roskilde were to be invited again, along with replacements for those who had died. Specifically recommended was M.I.T. linguistics professor Noam Chomsky. The rationale for another tribunal that the United States had expanded the war, and that the previous sessions were finally becoming "widely respected and publicized in Europe and America."[1] This proposal never came to fruition, but a loose framework for a Russell II series of tribunals was established because of the efforts of the BRPF, Basso, and Dedijer—and with the support of Russell's widow, Edith, and Ken Coates. Basso, although not personally close to Bertrand Russell, had enjoyed the latter's regard for his competence and, unlike Schoenman, he was affable and courteous. Basso became the prime mover in the tribunal process. Three Russell II hearings soon ensued on repression in Latin America, freedom of opinion in West Germany, and the condition of American Indians.[2]

The Latin American tribunal had four annual sessions during 1973–76, alternating between Brussels and Rome. Basso presided, and this process then led him to envision an ongoing tribunal structure based on a radical interpretation of existing international law plus the Universal Declaration of the Rights of Peoples. Drawn up at an Algiers meeting in July 1976, this revolutionary document recognized a right of self-determination—by force if necessary. It also assured those struggling on the basis of such a right that their cause was legitimate. Basso was instrumental in the production of this declaration, and he also founded that year the Lelio Basso International Foundation for the Rights and Liberation of Peoples, headquartered in Bologna. Basso died in 1978, but he surely provided the impetus for the creation in June 1979 of the Permanent People's Tribunal. These two organizations now operate out of Rome.

Basso was a wealthy Italian lawyer and parliamentarian who was part of a counterelite of leftist intellectuals. The Soviet Union was included in his list of legal clients, but he was an independent socialist rather than a formal communist. Basso's use of the term "people's" (especially in reference to "people's tribunals") surely had some communist connotations, which was recognized by Basso as a possible public relations defect, but he adopted the word "people's" rather than "citizens'" because he considered the latter to be too "bourgeois." Basso was an effective organizer, a man of charm, charisma, and generosity who attracted supporters as much through the force of personality as through ideological commitment.[3]

The Permanent People's Tribunal (PPT) is based on the proposition that there must be "people's courts for the dispossessed," for "marginalized voices," which can expose injustices not addressed by governments or the United Nations. International human rights laws are interpreted by the PPT as superseding sovereignty, and "sentences" are passed against violators even though there is no enforcement mechanism. In the words of one of its members: "While the two Russell tribunals were simply tribunals of opinion, occasional expressions of a fraction of the Western intelligentsia, by conferring on the Tribunal a permanent character and by providing it with an instrument of reference, the Universal Declaration of the Rights of Peoples, the Lelio Basso Foundation aims at contributing to the creation of a transnational humanitarian order." According to Richard Falk, the PPT can thus "relate positively to the energy of decolonization" and it has a moral authority that was lacking in the Russell Tribunal, even though the latter included many panelists with political stature.[4]

The PPT is firmly based on radical leftist ideology, and considers the causes of problems, in addition to evidence of crimes. Basso affirmed a need "to fight the origins of the diverse forms of oppression which are necessary to the survival of the capitalist system," and his colleagues tend to accept the bullet more than the ballot as a means of exercising self-determination. In terms of procedure, PPT supporters replace Dewey's liberal pragmatism with an ends-oriented system in which even lawyers are encouraged to be "engaged" in the cause against defined "evils."[5]

Despite such potential for bias, the PPT has developed a roster of assenting panelists who receive only expense money for their endeavors. At least seven panelists are required for each tribunal. There is also an institutional home, and a common set of guidelines that includes the rights of the accused to be represented and to submit documentation. Basically, potential plaintiffs approach the PPT with requests to organize tribunals. These are often nongovernmental organizations (NGOs), that agree to cover the costs involved. The PPT selects the tribunal topics from among those submitted, and by the turn of the twenty-first century had already conducted twenty-seven hearings. Many other tribunals are established outside of the PPT framework, but their procedures are similar and they frequently have panelists who also serve the PPT.

Group Rights

There have been tribunals about the rights of women, asylum seekers, psychiatric patients, and indigenous peoples. All of these groups are deemed to be "oppressed," and in need of "liberation." In March 1976, over two thousand women from forty countries gathered in Brussels to demand a radical restructuring of "patriarchal societies." This non-PPT session evolved from an August 1974 feminist camp in Denmark and was timed to coincide with the U.N.-declared International Women's Year. Gloria Steinem sent a rather hyperbolic letter of support proclaiming: "But not even the echo of Nuremberg and of American atrocities in Vietnam that are brought by this tribunal can equal the suffering now being experienced by human beings simply because they were born female."[6] Simone de

Beauvoir agreed to deliver the keynote address, but the date of the tribunal was shifted from November to March and she was unable to participate. Instead, she sent the following greeting: "I salute the Tribunal as being the start of a radical decolonization of women."[7]

The Brussels tribunal aimed at counteracting what it viewed as the "token integration" of the International Women's Year and was critical of existing legal norms developed by "patrimonial" states, since "all man-made forms of women's oppression" were seen as crimes. Topics included forced motherhood, persecution of nonvirgins and unmarried mothers, sexist medical practices, compulsory heterosexuality, violence against women, and sexual "objectification" of women. Considerable attention was paid to gay rights, and a large lesbian demonstration was held. A German rock group called the Flying Lesbians provided the entertainment.[8]

The tribunal represented an early effort to address some emerging women's issues, but did so in a manner that undercut overtures to public opinion. Crimes against women were covered at length, but not the means of combating them. Personal testimony of victims took center stage, but the findings of experts were rarely presented. Witnesses were not cross-examined, and there really was no jury since everyone present was considered a judge. Particularly counterproductive was the controversy over male media representatives. Many women objected to the presence of men and charged editors with "sexist insensitivity" for assigning them to the conference in the first place. How could there be cooperation with males, they asked, while "patriarchy" was being condemned? The tribunal then expelled male reporters after the first half-hour of the hearings. They were initially permitted to attend press conferences, but even this right was soon taken away.[9]

A tribunal on women's rights, convened in Tokyo in December 2000, was much more focused. It dealt specifically with the role of the Japanese military in sexual slavery during World War II. A meeting two years earlier of NGO representatives from seven Asian countries had called for such a session because Japan was unwilling to assume responsibility for the transgressions of its state agents. The impetus for the tribunal came especially from Korea, a former Japanese colony whose women had suffered considerably during Japan's World War II occupation. North Korea took the lead, linking an apology and compensation to the renewal of diplomatic relations then being negotiated. Japan, since 1995, had been willing to provide some financial reparations out of a "civilian fund" based on donations, but it balked at paying out of government coffers, since this would be tantamount to acknowledging official responsibility. Japan was also stone-walling on the issue of an apology.

The urgency of a tribunal was later made apparent when the Japanese High Court decided just prior to the first session that the government was under no obligation to pay damages to eighty Filipino brothel workers, even though the Japanese military had violated international law. The tribunal then sought to encourage effective Japanese judicial action and to press for the release and declassification of relevant Allied documents. It examined the legal responsibility of Japan, specific Japanese citizens, and of states that may have a duty to investigate and punish the perpetrators. The tribunal decided to assign individual guilt not only to former Japanese military leaders, but also to the late Emperor Hirohito for acts of enslavement, torture, murder, and crimes against humanity committed by his subordinates. While the Korean media offered extensive coverage of the tribunal, those in Japan generally avoided the topic.[10]

An interesting human rights angle was the subject of a 1994 London tribunal on immigration rights and asylum. British practices were accentuated, and the main concerns were detention pending the adjudication of cases and a law under which women marrying British citizens must live with them for at least one year. The tribunal raised the salient point that some of these women were being abused, but it realized that permitting them to leave their spouses could trigger procedures for their repatriation.[11] In the planning stage is a tribunal in Berlin on psychiatric malpractice, in which the World Psychiatric Association's policies will be examined in regard to patient rights consonant with the Universal Declaration of Human Rights. The Bertrand Russell Peace Foundation is playing a major organizing role.[12]

The rights of indigenous peoples have been promoted by several tribunals. A 1977 Geneva conference on discrimination against indigenous peoples in the western hemisphere set the stage. Then the Dutch-based Workgroup Indian Project and the BRPF cooperated in the organization of a November 1980 Russell II tribunal in Rotterdam on American Indians. More than one hundred indigenous representatives attended, and panelists considered evidence pertaining to forty-seven cases. Fourteen were accepted for inclusion, and a fourteen hundred-page report was prepared.[13]

Testimony was heard on charges of genocide and "ethnocide" (cultural genocide that does not include physical extermination), and cases ranged from the United States and Canada to Bolivia, Guatemala, El Salvador, and Chile. The Canadian cases, related to Ontario and Quebec, were directed at influencing an upcoming November 1981 conference on Indian rights under the Canadian constitution. Two tantalizing themes raised at Rotterdam were criticisms of Christian missionaries "because of their obvious complicity in the genocidal process carried out against Indigenous Peoples," and of South American governments for resettling white Rhodesian emigrants in areas previously considered the domain of indigenous peoples, especially in Bolivia. The tribunal panel determined that there had been violations of international law pertaining to genocide and ethnocide, and of U.S. law in reference to cases specifically within Washington's jurisdiction.[14]

Indigenous peoples in Brazil's Amazonia were the topic at a Paris tribunal in 1990. Genocide was charged, but the panel recognized Brazilian authority in the Amazonia region and made no demand for self-determination.[15] In 1993, a tribunal in Hawaii claimed that the 1959 statehood plebiscite was invalid, as were U.S. land laws. Its verdict condemned the overthrow of the Hawaiian monarchy in 1893 (the tribunal marked its centennial) and found the United States (which refused to send a representative) guilty of genocide. At a Denver tribunal in 1997, timed to correspond with an expanded (adding Russia as an eighth country represented) G–7 summit, the effects of environmental devastation on indigenous rights were examined in reference to an oil pipeline in Burma, logging on Indian land in British Columbia, radioactive waste disposal in Colorado, and other issues.[16] Basically, indigenous peoples were portrayed as more attuned to ecology than were more modernized nationality groups. That same year, a tribunal sponsored by the Council of Canadians Against APEC took place in Vancouver during an APEC (Asia-Pacific Economic Cooperation) summit, with the aim of encouraging Prime Minister Jean Chretien and Foreign Minister Lloyd Axworthy to press human rights concerns. Indigenous rights were emphasized and aboriginal prayers, songs, and greetings both opened and closed the gathering. Some specialized sessions had jurors and issued judgments, but no overall verdict was issued by this "People's Summit."[17]

Under the Boot

Internal political repression, which often is related to the rights of indigenous peoples, is a frequent target of tribunals. In 1972, Lelio Basso met some Brazilians in Chile who were anxious to have a tribunal on their country's practices. This led to 1973 hearings in Brussels under the auspices of the Russell II tribunal and, while still in session, Salvador Allende's Chilean government was overthrown. His widow then requested that the tribunal add Chile to its agenda, and the following three hearings in Rome and Brussels therefore expanded their coverage to Chile plus Uruguay and

Bolivia. Lelio Basso served as president; Vladimir Dedijer and the Colombian novelist Gabriel Garcia Marquez as vice presidents; and former Dominican president Juan Bosch, Greek Socialist leader Andreas Papandreou, the American pediatrician Benjamin Spock, and the French mathematician Laurent Schwartz were members of the panel. The emphasis was on U.S. human rights violations in the four countries covered, and the verdict was that crimes against humanity had been committed in all of them.[18]

The Permanent People's Tribunal conducted two similar hearings on Latin America. The first was precipitated by the July 1982 complaint of the Guatemalan Human Rights Commission, which asked for a tribunal to hear its case prior to Pope John Paul II's visit. The January 1983 Madrid session was then chaired by Harvard biologist and Nobel laureate George Wald. Harvard theology professor Harvey Cox served as a judge. The Guatemalan government ignored an invitation to President Efrain Rios Montt, which asked him to send representatives.

Much of the testimony dealt with the treatment of indigenous Indians who were subjected to alleged genocide. The verdict condemned all Guatemalan governments since 1954 for war crimes, crimes against humanity and genocide. The United States also was found guilty because of its involvement in Guatemalan affairs. Indian violence was considered justified as a necessary response to oppression. The verdict, along with a letter on political repression in Guatemala, was forwarded to the Pope. On March 3, Guatemala executed six guerrillas despite the Pope's appeal for clemency. In his welcoming speech on arrival four days later, he decried "inequalities" and "abuses." Addressing an audience of Guatemalan Indian peasants, the Pope told them "to organize associations for the defense of your rights and the realization of your projects." On August 8, Rios Montt was overthrown in a military coup.[19]

In April 1991, the Permanent People's Tribunal held hearings in Bogota on crimes against humanity in Latin America. They followed a series of preliminary sessions in Colombia, Uruguay, Argentina, Paraguay, Brazil, Peru, Guatemala, and Honduras. A lack of adequate security had prevented such sessions in El Salvador and Haiti. Bolivia, too, had forbidden a session, but evidence pertaining to events there was presented at the Colombia preliminary session. The verdict condemned the 1989 U.S. invasion of Panama and demanded the payment of an indemnity to victims, the termination of U.S. military missions in Latin America, and the closure of CIA stations there. It also found the United States guilty of crimes against humanity for counterinsurgency actions, military intervention, and military aid. Most unusual was the finding that the Peruvian

Maoist guerrilla group Sendero Luminoso was adjudged guilty of crimes against humanity.[20] This ran counter to the refusals of the Russell Tribunal on Vietnam, and the PPT tribunal on Guatemala, to accept the concept of moral equivalence.

Highly instructive was the PPT's 1980 Antwerp tribunal on the Philippines, because it applied concepts presented in the 1976 Algiers declaration related to self-determination. George Wald presided, and Richard Falk and Harvey Cox were among the panelists. The "collective rights of peoples" were emphasized, and groups engaged in armed struggle against the government of Ferdinand Marcos were legitimized. The Bangsa-Moro people of the southern Philippines were deemed to be distinct from Filipinos and to have a history of independence. Their military confrontation with the Philippines was thus portrayed as a "condition of belligerency" between legitimate political authorities rather than as an internal "insurgency." The Bangsa-Moro Army, an arm of the Moro National Liberation Front, was therefore depicted as having legal status. So, too, was the New People's Army, affiliated with the National Democratic Front of the Philippines. It was seen as Filipino ethnically (there were no separatist territorial claims), but was considered to have taken over the mantel of legitimacy from the Marcos regime because of the latter's descent into illegitimacy. This was due, it was alleged, to fraudulent elections, the imposition of martial law, neocolonial dominance by the United States, and economic subservience to the dictates of the World Bank, International Monetary Fund, and specific large corporations.

The verdict was an endorsement of armed struggle by the two antigovernment armies. Filipino and American officials had been invited to participate in the tribunal but did not respond. Afterward, President Marcos's office prepared a written refutation of the charges—pointing out that the movements tapped as legitimate could not be considered representative of the people, since they had never been endorsed through election.[21] Copies of the tribunal transcript circulated widely in the Philippines. From the perspective of Richard Falk, this was the PPT's "most successful" tribunal because of its implementation of the Algiers declaration, its legitimization of anti–Marcos forces, and its influence on the February 1986 "people's power" revolution, which overthrew the Filipino president.[22]

Other PPT tribunals on political repression have dealt with Western Sahara (Brussels, 1979); Argentina (Geneva, 1980); Eritrea (Milan, 1980); the Philippines (Antwerp, 1980); Afghanistan (Stockholm, 1981 and Paris 1982); East Timor (Lisbon, 1981); El Salvador (Mexico City, 1981); Zaire (Rotterdam, 1982); Puerto Rico (Barcelona, 1989); Tibet (Strasbourg,

1992); and the former Yugoslavia (Rome and Barcelona, 1995). These tribunals stressed physical human rights violations, such as torture, and included findings of genocide (which under international law must be ethnic) in cases such as those involving East Timor and El Salvador.

Sometimes, cases of political repression are publicized in conjunction with the foreign visits of national leaders. In November 1977, President Suharto of Indonesia was scheduled to attend a meeting of APEC in Vancouver, Canada. Less than two weeks before his arrival, pointedly on the anniversary of killings six years earlier in Dili, East Timor, a tribunal comprised of Canadians initiated hearings on his alleged war crimes, crimes against humanity, and genocide.[23] Similarly, Colombian President Andres Pastrana's May 1999 visit to Canada was preceded by a tribunal convened by the Canadian Council of Churches on killings and disappearances of civilians in May 1998. Genocide was not charged, but the Colombian government was found guilty of war crimes and crimes against humanity for abetting right-wing paramilitary forces and failure to prosecute the perpetrators of nonjudicial killings. The tribunal called on Prime Minister Jean Chretien to investigate the matter, and also asserted that Canadian law authorized the prosecution of Colombian government officials. Note, however, that Pastrana (in contrast to Suharto) was not personally charged nor found guilty of committing crimes.[24]

Following the collapse of the Soviet Union, there has been a decline in the number of tribunals dealing with political repression, especially in conjunction with an American role. Instead, the United States is accused of economic exploitation concomitant with the spread of "global capitalism" and the growing influence of the World Bank and International Monetary Fund.

Also apparent has been the Eurocentric nature of tribunals. Although abuses may be considered on a world scale, the venues are mainly European and are not regionally related to the location of the crimes under investigation. The panels are similarly dominated by European and American academicians. The infrastructure and cost factors help explain this phenomenon, but it appears that tribunals are still largely the preserve of well-meaning Western intellectuals.

Anatolian Tragedy

In 1915 and 1916, during the course of World War I, Turks engaged in extensive human rights abuses toward their Armenian minority. British pressure on Turkey then led to an Ottoman court's consideration, in April

1919, of Turkish war crimes against Armenians. Two officials were tried and convicted, including the lieutenant governor of a district where deportations and atrocities had taken place. He was sentenced to death and hanged, but the process of trying other perpetrators collapsed as the Ottoman Empire disintegrated.[25]

In April 1984 a PPT tribunal in Paris set out to reassess what had come to be called the "Armenian genocide." Memories of the Holocaust and of Hitler's reputed remark, "Who remembers the Armenians?," aroused a need to attribute responsibility for acts committed many years ago. So, too, did Armenian terrorist attacks on Turkish diplomats.

The tribunal dealt with the problem of contemporary relevance and concluded that there was an imperative to act, especially because the injustice had not been addressed for so long. Turkey had prevented its discussion before the United Nations Commission on Human Rights, and other countries had permitted a Turkish cover-up. This Turkish attitude of denial was deemed the provocation for assaults by Armenian militants.

The tribunal also had to cope with the ex post facto application of international law, since the Genocide Convention was written in 1948 and only came into force in 1951. Even the term "genocide" did not exist in 1915 and 1916. The tribunal noted, however, that the nature of Turkish conduct toward the Armenians was condemned by international law then existent. In addition, the Genocide Convention included a recognition "that at all periods of history genocide has inflicted great losses on humanity." This was interpreted as germane to earlier incidences retroactively. Also, the fact that Turkey had ratified the Genocide Convention in July 1950 precluded any argument that a nonratifying state was exempt from the Convention's strictures. Going further, the tribunal maintained that Turkey bore responsibility for compensating the victims of the genocide, even though the individual perpetrators were themselves dead. Reparations were in order despite the passage of time, although it was not clear to whom payments were to be made.[26]

The Armenia tribunal had thirteen jurors, at least six of whom were lawyers. International law expert Richard Falk was on the panel, as was PPT veteran George Wald. The impetus for the hearings came from human rights activists in France, West Germany, and the United States. Kurdish filmmaker Yilmaz Guney angered his government by presenting a statement acknowledging that genocide had been carried out against the Armenians. Turkey did not respond to an invitation to attend officially, but did submit a report on the Armenian issue that was published as part of the tribunal's record. In addition, the progovernment testimony of Professor Ataou of Ankara University was included in the tribunal's evidence. It had been given before a Paris criminal court that January.[27] Most previous international citizens' tribunals had failed to address adequately the absence of the defendant state.

The PPT tribunal on Armenia contributed to an upsurge of interest in the Armenian issue and was often cited as a factor in decisions to recognize the events of 1915 and 1916 as genocide. In 1985, the United Nations Commission on Human Rights made such a judgment, as did the European parliament in 1987. Israel, Russia, Canada, and France later arrived at similar conclusions.[28]

Acts of External Aggression

The original Russell Tribunal accumulated considerable evidence on legally questionable American military practices in Vietnam, but it did not undermine Washington's continuing effort or develop meaningful links to the U.S. war resisters' movement. It also did not manage to organize hearings on American soil, but the panelist Dave Dellinger (spurred by the 1968 My Lai killings) forged ahead with a plan to have American veterans serve as witnesses before a new forum. He participated in a coordinating committee that included Noam Chomsky, Julius Lester, and Benjamin Spock—with much of the preparatory work done by the antiwar activists Tod Ensign and Jeremy Rifkin. Their efforts led to 1970 public testimony by veterans in eleven U.S. cities, plus Toronto, Canada. In the words of the organizers, "We have attempted to shift the focus of veterans from concern for personal guilt to an analysis of institutional responsibility." The aim was to gather evidence that could be used to request a Congressional inquiry into what was viewed as "official and de facto policies of genocide."[29]

As an institution, Congress was partly responsible, constitutionally, for violations of international law. Predictably, it rejected a formal investigation, but Congressman Ron Dellums (a black representative from California) did arrange for unauthorized ad hoc hearings. Twenty-one antiwar members of the House of Representatives then assembled in Washington from April 26 through 29, 1971, for what they called the Citizens' Commission of Inquiry. The Department of Defense was uncooperative, refusing to permit testimony by military personnel and indicating that it would only assist formal standing committees designated by Congress. Dellums expressed the rather unrealistic hope that his hearings would spark the Armed Services Committee to take action.[30] Government officials, generals, and members of the National Security Council were invited to attend—but did not do so.

Dellums set the tone by declaring, "We have to deal with the racism, militarism, and sexism in this country and how that gets extended to our foreign policies abroad. It is not enough to lay blame on a given individual." Sociological analysis was more prevalent than international law during the questioning of Vietnam veterans by House members. Racial factors were highlighted as Dellums and Shirley Chisholm charged that there was pervasive racism in the United States and that it was being applied to Southeast Asia in a manner that made Asians appear to be less than human. Bella Abzug described U.S. policy as being "essentially to wipe out the people in Vietnam," while Major Gordon Livingston (a surgeon) testified on the alleged dehumanization of Vietnamese. Dellums then queried: "What is the effect of the racist practices visited upon the Vietnamese between the race relations between black and white Americans?" Similarly, Parren Mitchell asked Captain Fred Laughlin about how violence against Vietnamese affected his attitude toward "other than white Anglo-Saxon partisans." Representative Patsy Mink, an Asian-American from Hawaii, asked Laughlin about "MGR"—which she said was the "Mere Gook Rule." He replied that he had never heard of this expression, but that many soldiers believed it. Dellums referred to the accused war criminal William Calley as a scapegoat who understood that "you don't have to be black to be treated as a nigger in this society."[31]

The Dellums hearings demonstrated the radicalization of the antiwar and civil rights movements. Members of the House were prepared to break so openly with their government, although it must be recognized that they were all Democrats, whereas President Richard Nixon was a Republican. In any case, the hearings represented a strange amalgam of an international citizens' tribunal and an investigation by legislators. As such, they were part of a broader war resisters' process, in which grassroots pressure from below became fused with efforts from above by elected representatives.

While the Dellums hearings were taking place, a separate international commission of inquiry was already concentrating on the American role in Vietnam. It sent investigators to North Vietnam in May 1971 and then held a five-day session in Oslo in June. The verdict was that the United States had committed genocide in Vietnam, but the names of panel members arriving at this conclusion were not indicated. Richard Falk, in his introduction to the commission's report, explained that the finding of genocide was based on "pacification of entire population groups by active military struggle."[32]

Charges of American aggression against Nicaragua were considered at an October 1984 Brussels tribunal. The Permanent People's Tribunal had become interested in this issue and so had dispatched three investigators to Nicaragua in August 1983. They did not seek evidence from the U.S.-supported Contras. In April 1984, Nicaragua registered a complaint with the International Court of Justice, which made a temporary ruling in May to consider hearing the case. The tribunal then scheduled hearings in October to influence the Court's final decision on its authority in the matter. Whether the tribunal in fact affected the Court's deliberations is not really known, but the November 24 decision asserted the Court's authority to adjudicate the case.

The tribunal heard eleven witnesses, including two Americans, backing Nicaragua's charges. The U.S. government did not send a representative, so Francis Boyle, an American professor of international law, took it on himself to defend the official position. Boyle was actually pro-Sandinista, but he did his best to demonstrate the tribunal's fairness. Richard Falk, who was on the jury along with fellow American George Wald, made a presentation about Nuremberg and the issue of accountability under international law. The fifteen-member panel found that the United States was guilty of aggression and illegal intervention.[33]

Whereas the Nicaragua tribunal was organized carefully in terms of procedure and attention to the provisions of international law, the non-PPT tribunal on the U.S. invasion of Panama was not. In January 1990, a month after the intervention, former Attorney-General Ramsey Clark traveled to Panama on a fact-finding mission and immediately established an Independent Commission of Inquiry to investigate further. Evidence was then gathered by commission staffers and human rights groups, and the commission engaged in a public relations campaign to publicize "the truth" about the invasion. In April, over two thousand people assembled at Town Hall in New York to participate in what was more a rally than a tribunal. The United States was not accused of specific crimes, no vote was recorded, and international law did not serve as the basis for most accusations about American illegalities. The event featured individuals who were really speakers, not witnesses, since they were not questioned nor cross-examined.[34]

The twenty-six member commission, which included Clark and the novelist Graham Greene, concluded that the United States intended to overthrow the Panamanian government and renegotiate the 1977 Panama Canal treaties. The United States additionally was found to have planned, in contravention of treaties, to keep the Southern Command in Panama as a forward power base in Latin America. Research, rather than evidence presented at Town Hall, played an important role in arriving at these determinations. Olga Mejia, president of the National Human Rights Commission of Panama, told the gathering that the United States had committed "genocide" and compared it to Nazi killings at Lidice, Czechoslovakia. Such accusations did not appear in the commission statement. The book prepared by the commission included a contribution by the renegade CIA case officer Philip Agee, who argued that revelation of U.S. actions in Panama was a means of forestalling an American invasion of Cuba. There is, however, no indication that Agee spoke before the Commission. After the April meeting, the Commission continued to collect information on the U.S. role in Panama.[35]

American intervention in the Gulf War in 1990 and 1991 led Ramsey Clark to establish yet another commission of inquiry. He had been the first westerner permitted by Iraq to view the damage in the southern city of Basra. His commission produced a May 1991 "initial complaint" against President George Bush, Secretary of Defense Richard Cheney, Commander of Allied Forces in the Gulf Norman Schwarzkopf, and other Americans deemed responsible for wartime acts against Iraq. Witnesses then testified at several U.S. locations and there was then a February 29, 1992 hearing in New York, called the International War Crimes Tribunal. The panel of twenty-two (including six Americans) did not feature any luminaries, and media attention was limited because Clark's public image had been tarnished by his sympathy for Iran's Islamic republic during the 1980s. This was somewhat ironic, since he was now coming to the defense of Iraq, which had been Iran's bitter adversary in an eight-year war.

The tribunal charged the United States with nineteen counts related to crimes against peace, war crimes, crimes against humanity, and violations of the U.N. Charter and the U.S. Constitution—but not with genocide. The U.S. government, and individuals specifically accused, did not provide testimony nor submit evidence. The first charge obliquely recognized Iraqi aggression against Kuwait, but interpreted it as an American-inspired provocation aimed at justifying subsequent U.S. intervention. The second charge sought to undercut U.N. legal authorization of American actions by claiming that the favorable Security Council vote was achieved through bribery and the dispensation of military and economic benefits.

Several charges were based on the bombing of civilian targets, and of Iraqi soldiers who were "seeking to surrender and in disorganized individual flight, often unarmed and far away from combat zones." It was alleged that American forces used prohibited weapons (such as cluster and fragmentation bombs, and napalm), and that attacks were made on suspected Iraqi nuclear and chemical weapons sites, even though Iraq did not introduce such weapons into combat. Acknowledging that there was no loss of life as a consequence of the leakage of lethal materials, the explanation was that the United States knew in advance that "the release of dangerous forces from such installations" was possible. It turned out, however, that these materials were not in fact present at the sites bombed.

Another charge was that the American invasion of Panama in December 1989 had been illegal. It was related to the Iraqi situation by the argument that more Panamanians were killed by the United States than Kuwaitis by Iraq. Legally, a crime is not usually absolved by resorting to such an exercise in comparative guilt. Security Council support for American efforts was challenged on the ground that Chapter VI Charter provisions on the peaceful settlement of disputes should have been applied, rather than Chapter VII provisions on aggression and threat to international peace and security.

Four of the charges arose from American actions after the war. The United States was castigated for encouraging rebellion by Shiite Arabs and Kurds, using embargoes to restrict the delivery of food and medicine to the Iraqi people, violating Iraqi sovereignty via military operations, and advocating the payment of reparations by Iraq, which would produce its impoverishment. It was further claimed that most of the damage to Kuwait was caused by the United States, not Iraq, and that reparations "are a neocolonial means of expropriating Iraq's oil, natural resources, and human labor."[36]

Clark's tribunal produced a finding of guilty on all nineteen charges. No breakdown of the vote was presented. It recommended "the immediate revocation of all embargoes, sanctions and penalties against Iraq because they constitute a continuing crime against humanity." Going into concerns far beyond the legal issues at hand, the tribunal called for the prevention of future U.S. aggression against Libya, Cuba, Haiti, North Korea, Pakistan, and the Palestinian people. It concluded with a demand for a complete overhaul of the U.N. structure: "The Members urge that the power of the United Nations Security Council, which was blatantly manipulated by the U.S. to authorize illegal military action and sanctions, be vested in the General Assembly, that all permanent members be removed and that the right of veto be eliminated as undemocratic and contrary to the basic principles of the U.N. Charter."[37]

Balancing Act

PPT organizers recognized that their early hearings were strongly anti-American, revealing an evident ideological bias. In order to promote an image of integrity and evenhandedness, they therefore decided that some abuses by Communist-ruled states should be investigated. The place to start was the Soviet Union's military intervention in Afghanistan, since it exhibited many parallels to previous U.S. policies in Vietnam. Thus, a tribunal was assembled in Stockholm in 1981, chaired by Laurent Schwartz, and including Vladimir Dedijer as a panelist. There was later a second session in Paris in 1992. The verdict was that the Soviet Union had failed to adhere to the rules of war pertaining to the treatment of civilians, and had committed numerous human rights violations. Recognize, however, that the verdict was issued only after the Soviet Union no longer existed.

The tribunal found that Moscow had used illegal weapons and had engaged in torture and rape while carrying out aggression and denying the right of self-determination. Also, prisoners of war had been executed. Charges were considered in regard to the introduction of chemical and biological weapons, but the panelists decided that there was insufficient evidence to prove such allegations. Although many of the issues discussed were similar to those raised at the Russell Tribunal, the question of possible genocide was never broached.[38]

At Strasbourg in 1992, the PPT examined China's role in Tibet. Beijing did not participate officially, but pro-Chinese publications provided by the Consulate General in Milan were accepted as evidence. In addition, a representative was appointed by the tribunal to defend China's position. China was accused of illegally occupying Tibet, violating the human rights of its inhabitants, and preventing self-determination. Noteworthy points included in the verdict were that the Tibetan government in exile was representative of the region's people, China was destroying the unity of the Tibetans territorially by incorporating ethnic Tibetan areas into neighboring provinces, and that China was undermining Tibet's ethnic homogeneity through the transfer of its own Han civilians into Tibet. In contrast to the Afghanistan tribunal, the applicability of genocide was considered, but panelists maintained that its existence was not established beyond a reasonable doubt. Cultural transgressions against Tibetans were noted, but it was argued that international law did not recognize any concept of "cultural genocide."[39]

Postcommunist Russia's military involvement in Chechnya was the subject of tribunal sessions during the nineties. The United Nations Commission on Human Rights was not going to investigate an influential member of the Big Five. Even the United States was unwilling to press for the establishment of an International Criminal Tribunal along the lines of those set up by the Security Council for the former Yugoslavia and Rwanda. Amnesty International later stated: "Russia's seat in the UN Security Council must not mean it be allowed to evade scrutiny of its human rights record."[40]

Behind this effort lay a broad coalition comprising the Russian human rights activist Sergei Grigoryants, the former Soviet Foreign Minister Boris Pankin, the former U.S. State Department official Paul Goble, the Nobel Peace laureate and writer Elie Wiesel, the Olof Palme International Center in Sweden, and the Bertrand Russell Peace Foundation. Two days of hearings took place in Stockholm in December 1995, in the same hall that had served the Russell Tribunal in 1967. Russian denial of an exit visa prevented the appearance of a Chechen witness and many documents being forwarded to Stockholm were seized by Russian security agents at a Moscow airport. Nevertheless, the tribunal used the available documentation to conclude that several Russian leaders, including President Boris Yeltsin and Minister of Defense Pavel Grachev, were responsible for violations of international law. Follow-up sessions were held in Moscow (February and April 1996), Prague (May 1996), and in Khassaviurta and Grozny (August 1996).[41]

Another part of the former Soviet Union was investigated at an April and August 1976 PPT-sponsored tribunal on the Chernobyl nuclear disaster in Ukraine. The opening session was timed to commemorate the tenth anniversary of this horrifying event, and tribunal panelists demanded a shutdown of the reactor (eventually completed in December 2000). They also called for the replacement of nuclear energy with renewable energy sources.[42]

Polarization

The last decade of the twentieth century witnessed the development of tribunals focusing on the reputed perils of "global capitalism." The concerns are similar to those raised by demonstrators in Seattle, Washington, and Prague—namely, that the combination of globalization and capitalism is being spread by an exploitative "system" to the detriment of "the people." Basically, the left sees the post–Cold War era as unleashing large corporations and international monetary institutions (portrayed as promoting American interests) on a somewhat defenseless world.

In July 1993, just prior to a G-7 summit of the leading industrial powers in Tokyo, a tribunal heard thirteen witnesses who were critical of structural adjustment programs (SAPs) being forced on aid recipients by the World Bank and International Monetary Fund. These institutions made aid dependent on reforms by the recipient states such as privatization, a salary freeze, reduced government spending, a downsized civil service, and currency devaluation. Opponents of SAPs decried what they viewed as a coercive extension of capitalism designed to secure advantage for American corporations in overseas investment opportunities and cheaper imports of foreign goods.

The Tokyo tribunal did not include any representatives of the accused, since ostensibly they wouldn't want to take part in such a "process of assessment and condemnation." Organizers claimed that they were aware of G-7 positions and that the tribunal would be "sensitive" toward such viewpoints in its indictment. Carrying it out as a judgment, as advocated by the tribunal member Richard Falk, was the responsibility of those directly affected. It was clearly stated that the indictment was not expected to influence G-7 deliberations, so the tribunal's goals were "primarily educative and mobilizing."[43]

The G-7 were to be confronted rather than cajoled, and those dominating the global system were castigated for acting as if they were above the law. Participants declared: "The formation of this tribunal is an expression of the continuing struggle of the peoples of the world to establish effective forms of transnational democracy as a counter to oppressive patterns and practices emanating from the geopolitical centers of power in the North."[44] Proponents acknowledged that the tribunal was one-sided but, "if the industrial states can create the G-7 framework, certainly the NGO community can establish a people's tribunal!"[45]

Coinciding with the November 1997 APEC summit in Vancouver, Canada, was a People's Summit, as well as a more specialized International Tribunal on Workers' Rights. Both supporters and opponents of APEC participated and they were united in pressuring APEC to respond to human rights concerns. The opening speaker at the summit was 1996 corecipient of the Nobel Peace Prize Jose Ramos Horta of East Timor, who lambasted the International Monetary Fund and World Bank for not paying sufficient heed to the negative consequences of development. He told the gathering: "When a group of leaders meet [sic] and ignore the choking clouds of forest fires, the misery of the poor who lost their savings and jobs, indifferent to the armies of peasants and workers expelled from their land, the labor leaders, students and activists imprisoned because of their opinions, then it is courting revolution."[46]

The PPT's May 1998 Brussels tribunal on workers and consumers rights in the garment industry stressed similar themes related to the exploitation of women, low pay, and lengthy working hours. Particularly focused among the groups involved was The Clean Clothes Campaign, representing a coalition of European unions and NGOs. It helped arrange hearings on the policies of seven sportswear manufacturers, at which they were accused of fostering a "globalization of poverty, and a feminization of poverty." Twelve witnesses offered testimony on labor practices, as did a representative of one of the defendants—Swedish retailer H&M. Attempting to counter negative publicity, H&M's representative argued that corporations could not be held responsible for actions by their subcontractors. In documents submitted, Nike made the same point. Both companies affirmed that they had voluntary codes of conduct, but evidence demonstrated that they were not enforceable in courts and were flouted by subcontractors. The tribunal found the seven firms guilty of labor violations.[47] Later that year, a tribunal in New York on Corporate Crimes Against Humanity concentrated on union-busting at sweatshops, consumer deception, and unfair monopolistic practices. It had been preceded by a "We Don't Buy It" march on the day after Thanksgiving, the busiest shopping date of the year.[48]

Safety and environmental conditions produced the 1992 tribunal on the 1984 Bhopal chemical disaster in India. It was held on the spot in Bhopal, and the panel was largely Asian. In January 1994, thirteen doctors went to Bhopal without remuneration other than expenses to treat survivors of the 1984 catastrophe. That year in London, pointedly on the tenth anniversary of the incident, there was a tribunal on industrial hazards and human rights that dealt with Bhopal and other issues related to chemical damage. A charter on workers' rights in conjunction with industrial hazards was recommended (the final version was ratified in 1996) and there was a call for India's prosecution of the former director of Union Carbide, co-owner of the ill-fated Bhopal plant. The findings of the six-member panel were presented during a press conference at the British parliament.[49]

Individual Justice

Recent tribunals have concentrated on broad issues, with little concern being shown for the fate of individuals. A notable exception was a Tokyo tribunal, which sought to save the life of the imprisoned South Korean dissident Kim Dae Jung.[50] The most famous case, however, involves the Philadelphia black radical Mumia Abu-Jamal. In December 1981, Mumia was charged in the killing of police officer Daniel Faulkner. In July 1982, a Common Pleas Court jury of ten whites and two blacks (a third black who had violated sequestration rules had earlier been replaced by a white) found him guilty of first-degree murder and sentenced him to death. In May 1983, trial judge Albert Sabo upheld the verdict and called for execution in the electric chair. Mumia then threatened Sabo, proclaiming: "You have just convicted yourself, and sentenced yourself to death."[51] Since then, the Mumia case has garnered international notoriety revolving around the issues of guilt, due process, and the application of the death penalty.

In 1990, the U.S. Supreme Court refused to order a new trial. The case then reverted to the original court in Philadelphia, where new grounds were cited, but Judge Sabo in 1995 turned down a request for a retrial.[52] An appeal to the Pennsylvania Supreme Court in September 1997 then triggered the establishment of a tribunal to attempt at influencing a favorable decision. Instrumental were the International Concerned Family and Friends of Mumia Abu-Jamal and the Ad Hoc Coalition for a People's International Tribunal for Justice for Mumia Abu-Jamal, groups citing racism and class discrimination as behind an unjust verdict. In a reference to the upcoming December 6 tribunal in Philadelphia, Mumia supporters declared that "the genuine criminals—those who keep an iron boot heel on the necks of the oppressed—will be tried. Unfortunately, they won't actually be sitting in the prisoner's docket [*sic*]. But when those who are tyrannized and downtrodden try their oppressors in absentia, it brings closer the day these capitalist criminals-for-hire stand trial in person, and must answer for their crimes against humanity."[53]

Tribunal coordinator Pam Africa of MOVE, whose headquarters were bombed in 1985 on orders from Philadelphia's first black mayor, Wilson Goode, accused the government of trying "to silence our brother forever." She added: "The conspiracy against Mumia is part of a larger pattern of police brutality, corruption, racism and disparity in sentencing the poor. Only through mobilization of the masses demanding truth and justice for Mumia and all political prisoners will the conspiracy be exposed."[54]

Julia Wright, the daughter of the deceased author Richard Wright, used the occasion of the October 25 "Million Woman March" in Philadelphia to tell Mayor Ed Rendell, "Mr. Mayor, it is an honor for me to present you with this notification of charges for your indictment emanating from the highest authority in the land, the people, the black women of the people, assembled here today in the presence of two million of us." Wright complained that on June 5 she and a delegation including the sons of W. E. B. DuBois and Kwame Nkrumah were denied the opportunity to meet with him to request backing for a new trial. Rendell was not only the mayor, but also had been the district attorney, who in 1982 had decided to seek the death penalty against Mumia. According to Wright, the delegation was told that Rendell was not available and that no one on his staff was able to receive the group on his behalf. Wright averred: "We were left in front of your door, packed like animals, guarded like delinquents—not the delegates of world opinion we were."[55]

The tribunal assembled in Philadelphia on December 6, 1997. Twenty-five panelists from seven countries took part, including Julia Wright, David DuBois, Gamal Nkrumah, Michael Meeropol (the son of Julius and Ethel Rosenberg), Dennis Brutus (the South African poet), and Claude Lanzmann (who had worked with the Paris group during the Russell Tribunal). The "indicted" defendants included Sabo, Rendell, Pennsylvania Governor Tom Ridge, Philadelphia District Attorney Lynne Abraham, and U.S. Attorney-General Janet Reno. They were all charged with contributing to violations of human rights, racial discrimination, and inhumane treatment of Mumia.

Tribunal members listened to testimony not heard in court, regarding the murder and the police's treatment of witnesses, and also considered documents that had been submitted prior to the hearings. Then, apparently by consensus, since no vote was recorded, they concluded: "We find as a fact that those charged are guilty of a criminal conspiracy to deny Mumia Abu-Jamal's human rights and we call for his immediate release, exoneration and compensation." Mumia's conviction was described as "unjust" and his death sentence as "illegal." The tribunal called for the removal from office of all responsible officials and a ban on their assumption of public office in the future. The Secretary-General of the United Nations and the U.N. High Commissioner for Human Rights were asked to appoint special rapporteurs to deal with the Mumia case. The tribunal judgment was then delivered to the High Commissioner on December 10, International Human Rights Day.[56]

The Mumia campaign attracted considerable attention in the United States and even more abroad. This was due to the energy and organizing abilities of his proponents, rather than to the tribunal itself. The tribunal was rarely mentioned, except on some pro-Mumia websites, and it generated scant media interest despite drawing an audience of two thousand. *The Philadelphia Inquirer* and the *Daily News* did not cover the event, although it was in that city, but the black-oriented New York publication *Amsterdam News* ran an article on the subject.[57] The reasons for such obscurity were probably the radicalism and racial focus (especially through

MOVE's leading role) of the pro–Mumia forces, as well as basic American aversion to attacks on the legal system.

The tribunal clearly did not sway the Pennsylvania Supreme Court, which in October 1998 denied Mumia's request for a new trial. It found no basis for the charge that the prosecution had kept blacks off the jury, and determined that Judge Albert Sabo had presided impartially over the Common Pleas Court's hearing on a retrial. The court further affirmed that Sabo did not have to recuse himself from the case just because he had been the judge at the original trial. In fact, it noted that it was usually preferable to have the same judge reconsider a case since he would be familiar with it.[58]

In December 1998, Angela Davis led a delegation to the European Union (EU) parliament in Strasbourg to lobby for a resolution condemning the death penalty. It not only passed on December 17, but referred specifically to Mumia's "unfair trial."[59] The Mumia bandwagon continued with a January 1999 concert in the New Jersey Meadowlands, a February rally at New York's Town Hall, and an April "Millions for Mumia" March (on his birthday) in Philadelphia. The campaign did not impact the U.S. Supreme Court, which decided in October not to reconsider Mumia's appeal for a new trial.[60]

In February 2000, Amnesty International came out in favor of a new trial for Mumia. So did demonstrators in Philadelphia during that year's Republican National Convention. Pro-Mumia activists claimed that evidence had been withheld from the defense and that Philadelphia's courts had a highly prejudiced record in sentencing nonwhites to capital punishment.[61]

Recent pro-Mumia efforts have concentrated on due process and rejection of the death penalty, rather than on alleged innocence. This is a clever tactical move, since broader support can be attracted from white liberals opposed to capital punishment. A paid advertisement in *The New York Times* is instructive in this regard. Signed by hundreds of educators (including Toni Morrison, Cornel West, Frances Fox Piven, Jonathan Kozol, Manning Marable, and Howard Zinn), it states: "AS EDUCATORS, IN PENNSYLVANIA, ACROSS THE UNITED STATES AND THE WORLD, WE STRONGLY OPPOSE THE EXECUTION OF MUMIA ABU-JAMAL. While there are those who believe Mumia is innocent and should be freed now, and others who have no opinion about his innocence, we are all united in viewing Mumia's 1982 trial as a travesty of justice, and affirm that he MUST have a new trial!"[62]

Overall, international citizens' tribunals over the last two decades of the twentieth century have not been highly effective, as they have been too partisan, shrill, anti-American, and leftist. While often raising important issues and presenting critical evidence, their credibility generally has not been accepted by the media or public. Also, luminaries with prestige equal to that of Dewey or Russell are no longer involved. An excellent concept directed at the furtherance of justice has thus been thwarted in its application by poor execution. The time to remedy this unfortunate situation is now!

Chapter XVI

AGENDA FOR REFORM

International citizens' tribunals could be especially relevant and constructive in conjunction with the growing world trends toward the rule of law and participatory democracy. However, the efficacy of such tribunals has been decreasing. The Reichstag fire Commission of Inquiry helped save four innocent defendants. The Dewey Commission contributed to the public exoneration of Trotsky, helped undermine the credibility of the Moscow trials, and highlighted the importance of liberal insistence on due process and judicial objectivity. It could not, however, prevent additional show trials based on falsified charges. The Russell Tribunal presented important evidence of American war crimes, energized the West European and Japanese antiwar movements, but was unsuccessful in galvanizing a war resisters' movement in the United States or in encouraging a military withdrawal from Vietnam. Over the last thirty years of the twentieth century, tribunals came to address many crucial issues, but they did not mobilized public opinion effectively or alter significantly the legal course of justice. Reform of the ways in which tribunals are organized and operated is therefore imperative.

It is still difficult to bring major powers to account under international law. In 1993–94, the U.N. Security Council established an International Criminal Tribunal to deal with the former Yugoslavia and Rwanda. Additional cases may come to include Cambodia, or possibly the Democratic Republic of Congo and Sierra Leone, but it is highly unlikely that the five permanent Security Council members will ever be charged with violations. These members were instrumental in setting up the International Criminal Tribunal in accordance with Article 39 provisions of the U.N. Charter on restoring international peace and security. Had the General

Assembly acted instead on the basis of Article 22 authority regarding the establishment of "subsidiary organs as it deems necessary for the performance of its functions," then the Big Five would not have enjoyed such protection. The new International Criminal Court presents a similar problem, as the Security Council will be able to interfere in cases, or keep some of them out of the court's jurisdiction altogether. States also will be entitled to withhold evidence on the ground of national security. It is obvious that the United States is trying to weaken the court's mandate even further as a condition of ratifying its initial charter.

Ken Coates, chairman of the Bertrand Russell Peace Foundation and a member of the European Union's parliament, has expressed concern about continuing great power dominance of the official tribunal framework. He views the International Criminal Tribunal for the former Yugoslavia as the creation of an "all-dominating center-left," which has "taken a leaf from Bertie's book by organizing its own Tribunals." They are, writes Coates, as one-sided as the Russell Tribunal hearings were alleged to have been, and he has not been able to interest the prosecutor "in certain delinquencies of the alliance." Coates is obviously alluding to the tribunal's unwillingness to consider possible crimes committed by NATO states in their operations against Serbia. He goes on: "Your book may have a topicality that we would all wish it had not."[1]

International citizens' tribunals have a role to play in terms of examining controversial issues in a broader contextual framework than legally established courts. Their panelists are not all lawyers, and they may consider evidence that otherwise could be deemed excludable.[2] Their structure permits considerable leeway in introducing historical, economic, or military material. They are not a substitute for official institutions, but rather, catalysts that can help generate legal action. One way they can do this is to furnish new evidence. The Dewey Commission determined that Trotsky could not have met alleged coconspirators at locations and on specific dates cited in the Moscow court because it confirmed that he was elsewhere on those occasions. Also pertinent is that tribunals don't permit appeals, because their goal is influencing courts or governments, not determining final justice.

Public opinion is the ally of international citizens' tribunals, so tribunal organizers should try to locate hearings in important media centers; maintain open admission for journalists, despite their ideology or gender; and arrange for television coverage that would be more ample were there to be a vigorous defense and the cross-examination of witnesses. Having panelists from many countries is also crucial, as the media tend to cover their own nationals. A fundamental reason why the Reichstag inquiry was so successful in shaping public opinion was that the focus was on Pritt in the British press, Hays in the American, Moro-Giafferi in the French, and Branting in the Swedish. Furthermore, tribunals must be aware of the essentiality of celebrity (Muenzenberg certainly knew how to attract attention by using Einstein's name), media savvy, and self-promotion skills on the part of panelists, because publicity must be used to buttress their findings.

In order to enhance their proficiency, tribunals should have a permanent institutional base, a common set of procedures, and a pool of qualified panelists. Building on the existing Permanent People's Tribunal would therefore make sense, although replacing the term "people's" would surely be helpful. As presently constituted, tribunals have no standardization and panelists are often selected by the same activist group that is pressing (as was the Trotsky defense committee) for a hearing. Using a pool of potential panelists therefore reduces the degree of partisanship. Tribunals must not only be objective but also appear to be so. They will, additionally, have to be more wary of NGOs. Although cooperation may often prove to be beneficial, as in human rights cases, it must be taken into account that NGOs have their own vested institutional interests and sometimes promote governmental interests, as well.

The left (and, more recently, its most radical wing) has been prominent in the organization of tribunals, thereby creating the impression that the process serves ideological ends. There is no logical reason why tribunals cannot be centrist, or even conservative, in their perspective, and it is probable that such greater ideological diversity could only increase public support for hearings. A step in this direction is now being taken by a coalition of anticommunists who are accusing former regimes of genocide, illegal annexation, and crimes against humanity. This group has already prepared statutes, established an institutional structure, and has held sessions on abuses by the former government of Lithuania. Coincidentally, China's speaker of the legislature, Li Peng, was visiting Lithuania in September 2000 while the tribunal was meeting and he cut his visit from two days to two hours, rather than be present while Communist systems were being attacked.[3]

Tribunals are moving toward generalized charges against "the system" or "global capitalism." This may promote public relations, but it is not conducive to the operation of a process with quasi-legal pretensions. Specificity of charges would sharpen their focus because investigations of individuals responsible for human rights violations, labor abuses, or environmental damage would relate tribunals more directly to the formal legal system.

Of utmost importance is the inclusion of a defense. Fairness is important in terms of the public and media images, a point not adequately taken into account by many tribunals that don't place a premium on impartiality. The recent hearings on Japanese sexual slavery did not come to this realization, unfortunately, with organizers maintaining that if the Japanese government had wanted to present a defense, it should have done so before national or international courts.[4]

It has been evident that accused parties shy away from defending themselves before tribunals, but they would be more likely to participate if assured of an open-minded panel that deliberates seriously before rendering findings and permits differences of opinion to be voiced. Hasty and sometimes predetermined judgments do not entice defendants to play their requisite adversarial role. By contrast, divisions among panelists could undermine the tribunal process and forestall a common decision. This was problematic at the 1993 Hawaiian hearings, which were otherwise quite instructive on the underlying issues and successful in attracting media attention.[5]

As was enunciated by several panelists (and by those rejecting invitations) associated with the Dewey and Russell hearings, the term "tribunal" implies a legal forum with judges and a verdict. Many tribunals have, in fact, issued "verdicts," despite claims that they were purely investigatory bodies. Such practices contribute to a kangaroo court atmosphere, so it would have been preferable had such bodies retained the label "commissions of inquiry." It is probably too late to turn back the clock in this regard, but at least "panelists" (not "judges") should "investigate" (not "indict") countries, organizations, and individuals in order to arrive at "findings" (not "verdicts"). Presumptuous usage of legal terminology has proven to be divisive and counterproductive.

Tribunal proponents fear moral equivalence. This then leads them to bar evidence against one side in a conflictive situation. Staughton Lynd presciently warned about such a Stalinist approach to ethics, and asserted that "an action defined as a 'crime' remains criminal no matter who commits it." He disagreed with the exclusion of testimony about Dresden, Hiroshima, and Nagasaki at the Nuremberg hearings.[6] Tribunal organizers are concerned that such evidence would tend to equate crimes, or have an exculpatory effect in regard to the side charged, but these concerns are surely outweighed by exhibitions of strident censorship, accompanied by moral cowardice. The involvement of an active defense should help alleviate this problem.

The three major tribunals covered in this study had panels that arrived at decisions. More recently, there have been hearings at which all in attendance have carried out this function in accordance with the theory that a small group should not be permitted to act on behalf of everyone.[7] Such a distorted interpretation of participatory democracy predictably generates findings by acclamation achieved without due deliberation. A mass populist psychology has clearly gained hold. This is certainly not a constructive antidote to the deficiencies of appointed panels, regardless of their intellectual elitism.

International citizens' tribunals should separate public relations from investigations. Activist groups, such as the Trotsky defense committee or the Bertrand Russell Peace Foundation, are surely entitled to champion their causes, but they should be distinctly compartmentalized from the hearings themselves. Their role may be propagandistic or educational, but tribunal panelists should, to the contrary, demonstrate discretion and avoid public comment prior to or during the inquiry sessions.

It is herein recommended that international citizens' tribunals should have the following features:

1. A PERMANENT INSTITUTIONAL STRUCTURE AND POOL OF PANELISTS. APPROXIMATELY HALF SHOULD BE LAWYERS, BUT THERE SHOULD ALSO BE EXPERTS ON HISTORY, BUSINESS, ECONOMICS, MILITARY AFFAIRS, AND OTHER RELEVANT FIELDS. The Permanent People's Tribunal already operates on this basis, with the selection of panelists related to the subject at hand. The Reichstag fire Commission of Inquiry was appropriately made up exclusively of lawyers. The Dewey Commission had limited legal credentials. It therefore failed to delve into juridical aspects of the show trials. The Russell Tribunal was balanced in terms of the expertise of its members, but ideological shrillness undercut its potential influence on public opinion.

2. THE COMPOSITION OF PANELS SHOULD BE TRULY INTERNATIONAL, WITH MEMBERS FROM NUMEROUS COUNTRIES AND ATTENTION PAID TO ADEQUATE REPRESENTATION FROM AREAS OTHER THAN WESTERN EUROPE AND THE UNITED STATES. The Reichstag fire Commission of Inquiry dealt with a European issue, and its members represented a cross-section of the Continent's liberal high profile intelligentsia. The Dewey Commission had little impact on European opinion because of

its lack of Europeans with stature. The Russell Tribunal was able to affect the Japanese left because two Japanese were included as panelists, but the American members were too radical to sway their more mainstream countrymen.

3. PANELISTS SHOULD BE OF DIVERSE VIEWPOINT, WITH NO IDEOLOGICAL LITMUS TEST APPLIED TO THEIR APPOINTMENT. The fire trial Commission of Inquiry leaned over backward and effectively maintained credibility by not including Communists (although this could be construed as a reverse ideological litmus test). The Dewey Commission surely represented a range of thought. The Russell Tribunal clearly was too stacked with pro-NLF ideological partisans.

4. THE SCHEDULING OF HEARINGS SHOULD BE TIMED TOWARD MAXIMUM IMPACT ON CASES BEFORE NATIONAL OR INTERNATIONAL COURTS, OR DECISIONS BEING MADE BY GOVERNMENTAL, CORPORATE, OR ORGANIZATIONAL BODIES. The fire trial Commission of Inquiry astutely held its countertrial just before the Leipzig court convened. The Dewey Commission was reactive to the first Moscow show trial, and did not manage to have its hearings in Mexico City until after the second show trial. It did, however, have some influence over the international media reaction to the third show trial. The Russell Tribunal attempted to coordinate action with David Mitchell's defense team in the United States, but was unable to change the course of American justice.

5. ALL HEARINGS SHOULD INCLUDE REPRESENTATION OF THE DEFENDANTS OR THE COUNTRY BEING INVESTIGATED, AND SUCH COUNSEL SHOULD BE ASSIGNED IF THE DEFENDANTS OR COUNTRY CHOOSE NOT TO PARTICIPATE NOR TO APPOINT THEIR OWN REPRESENTATIVES. All three tribunals studied were deficient in this regard, thus giving the impression that they were biased rhetorical exercises, rather than impartial confrontations. If there is no representation, then grounds for indictment, rather than final judgments, should be announced —with the panelists, in effect, serving as a nonofficial grand jury.

6. ALL WITNESSES SHOULD BE SUBJECTED TO CROSS-EXAMINATION. This did not take place at the Reichstag fire

Commission of Inquiry or at the Russell Tribunal. There was some cross-examination of Trotsky by the Dewey Commission, but the time allotted was insufficient and the questioning was not sufficiently probing.

7. CHARGES SHOULD BE SPECIFIC, LEGALLY BASED, AND DEVOID OF BIASED IDEOLOGICAL JARGON. There should not be broad references to "global capitalism" or "imperialism," and any reference to genocide should be consistent, in terms of usage, with the 1948 Genocide Convention.

8. FINDINGS SHOULD BE DETERMINED BY PANELISTS, NOT BY PREPARATORY COMMITTEES OR ATTENDEES. ADEQUATE TIME SHOULD BE ALLOTTED TO PERMIT PANELISTS TO DELIBERATE AND TO PREPARE CAREFULLY CRAFTED FINDINGS. The 1976 Brussels tribunal on women's rights contravened the first proviso. As for the second, the Reichstag fire trial Commission of Inquiry dealt with a time constraint effectively by issuing a preliminary finding just prior to the opening of the Leipzig trial, and then its final judgment after the conclusion of court testimony. The Dewey Commission examined evidence for many months before reaching a final verdict. The Russell Tribunal was rushed in its deliberations because some members were anxious to go home.

9. THE VOTE ON ALL FINDINGS SHOULD BE MADE PUBLIC, AND PANELISTS VOTING IN OPPOSITION TO THE MAJORITY ON ANY POINT SHOULD BE ENCOURAGED TO PRESENT WRITTEN MINORITY OPINIONS. The findings of the Reichstag fire trial and the Dewey Commission were arrived at through consensus and no vote was recorded. The Russell Tribunal did record votes, but not the names of those supporting or opposing each item in the verdict. Minority reports were not issued by any of the tribunals, but Beals certainly had his say publicly after the Dewey Commission hearings in Mexico.

10. THE PERMANENT INSTITUTIONAL STRUCTURE SHOULD SERVE AS A CLEARINGHOUSE AFTER THE HEARINGS TO DISTRIBUTE TRANSCRIPTS AND TO SERVE AS A RESEARCH DEPOSITORY FOR ALL DOCUMENTS COLLECTED DURING THE INVESTIGATION. Additionally, new technology, such as the Internet,

should make such transcripts and documents easily available to everyone, eliminating the need to travel to archives.

If such guidelines for reform are followed, polarizing ideology will be reduced and the moral and legal influence of the international citizens' tribunals enhanced. Such self-purification should thus contribute to more salutary action, and perhaps the above recommendations would evolve into methodological "Ten Commandments."

Unfortunately, the first three tribunals under review became progressively weaker in their influence. Recent sessions have failed to reverse this deleterious trend, mainly as a consequence of their rhetorical excess and marginalization of democratic techniques of jurisprudence. The radical tribunal advocates have much to offer in terms of a relevant theoretical framework based on global participation by citizens and an institutional infrastructure geared toward permanence. These attributes, however, must be amalgamated with the pragmatic liberal emphasis on the primacy of procedure demonstrated at the Reichstag fire trial and Moscow show trial tribunals in order to transform a currently debilitated and partisan process into one that is vigorous and impartial. Focusing on ideological ends has proven counterproductive. Therefore, public opinion for the advancement of human rights should be mobilized on the basis of transparent operational commonality rather than doctrinal disparity.

Notes

Chapter 1

1. Ogden Nash poem cited in memo from Joseph Califano to Lyndon Johnson, January 12, 1967 (White House Central Files, box 339, name file [Russell], LBJL).

2. Walter Lippmann, *The Phantom Public* (New York: Harcourt, Brace, 1925), pp. 55, 69–70, and 197.

3. Henry Kissinger, *Diplomacy* (New York: Simon and Schuster, 1994), pp. 232, 235, and 247 and Gary Jonathan Bass, *Staying the Hand of Vengeance* (Princeton, NJ: Princeton University Press, 2000), chapters 3 and 4.

4. Walter Lippmann, *Public Opinion* (New York: Macmillan, 1947), pp. 31 and 408. This book was first published in 1922.

5. Genocide was mentioned at Nuremberg, but was not included in the charges against the defendants and was not an operative legal concept. For a discussion of the evolution of the genocide concept and its application at trials, see Arthur Jay Klinghoffer, *The International Dimension of Genocide in Rwanda* (London: Macmillan, 1998).

6. John Duffett, ed., *Against the Crime of Silence* (New York: Simon and Schuster, 1970), p. 33; Frank Browning and Dorothy Forman, eds., *The Wasted Nations* (New York: Harper and Row, 1972), pp. vii–viii; and Ebbe Reich, *Ekstra Bladet,* November 22, 1967.

7. Duffett, p. 650.

8. Russell in Duffett, p. 4 and Sartre in Duffett, p. 44.

9. Bertrand Russell, *War Crimes in Vietnam* (London: Allen & Unwin, 1967), p. 125.

10. Richard Falk is the most prominent legal theorist of international citizens' tribunals. See The International People's Tribunal, *The People vs. Global Capital* (New York: Apex, 1994) and Marlene Dixon, ed., *On Trial: Rea-*

gan's War Against Nicaragua (San Francisco: Synthesis, 1985), p. 20. See also James Crawford, "Negotiating Global Security Threats in a World of Nations," *American Behavioral Scientist,* Vol. 38, No. 6 (May 1995)–available in EBSCO.

11. Lelio Basso, "Inaugural Discourse," in William Jerman, ed., *Repression in Latin America* (Nottingham: Spokesman Books, 1975), pp. 4–5.

12. Harvey Cox, "Foreword," in Dixon, pp. ii–iii.

13. "The 1997 People's Summit on APEC," http://www.vcn.bc.ca/summit/popindex.htm; Permanent People's Tribunal, *A Crime of Silence: The Armenian Genocide* (London: Zed, 1985), p. 242; and Gunnar Myrdal in Browning and Forman, pp. vii–viii.

14. Guenther Lewy, *America in Vietnam* (Oxford: Oxford University Press, 1978), pp. 224–25; Basso in Jerman, p. 5; and Bill Bowring, "Socialism, Liberation Struggles and the Law," http:// members.netscapeonline.co.uk/suzyboyce1/files/book1/3_9.htm

15. The International People's Tribunal, p. 4, and interview with Richard Falk, March 6, 2001.

16. Sally Engle Merry, "Resistance and the Cultural Power of the Law," *Law and Society Review,* Vol. 29, No. 1 (1995)—available in EBSCO.

17. Duffett, pp. 15 and 43; Russell autobiography, p. 215; and Jean-Paul Sartre, "Imperialist Morality," *New Left Review.* no. 41 (January–February 1967): 10. For an excellent analysis of truth commissions, see Priscilla Hayner, *Unspeakable Truths: Confronting State Terror and Atrocity* (New York: Routledge, 2001), especially pp. 14, 16, 23, and 239.

18. Basso in Jerman, p. 9.

19. Priscilla Hayner maintains that truth commissions examining past wrongs should be evaluated, in part, on the basis of their later impact. See Hayner, p. 252. International citizens' tribunals, by contrast, seek to have a more immediate impact because they hope to stop injustices while they are still taking place. Of course, this is a difficult task, since organizing a tribunal is time consuming.

20. Bertrand Russell, *The Autobiography of Bertrand Russell,* Vol. III, 1944–1967 (London: Allen and Unwin, 1969), p. 216; Russell, *War Crimes in Vietnam,* p. 126; and *National Guardian,* December 3, 1966.

21. Falk interview.

22. In French, with no author cited (10.5/384, BRA), and Russell, *War Crimes in Vietnam,* p. 127.

23. The International People's Tribunal, pp. 5 and 8.

24. Duffett, p. 6; Russell, *War Crimes in Vietnam,* p. 127; and The International People's Tribunal, p. 1.

25. Duffett, pp. 32 and 315.

26. Diana Russell and Nicole Van de Ven, eds., *Crimes Against Women: Proceedings of the International Tribunal* (Millbrae, CA: Les Femmes, 1976), p. 240 and The International People's Tribunal, p. 123.

27. Xenia Zeldin, "John Dewey's Role in the 1937 Trotsky Commission," *Public Affairs Quarterly,* Vol. 5, No. 4 (October 1991): 393.

28. Mumia Abu-Jamal is an African-American radical convicted in the 1981 slaying of a Philadelphia police officer, and sentenced to death. Appeals have held up the carrying out of this sentence.

29. http://www.grisnet.it/filb, p. 10. This passage appears in a commentary supporting a tribunal investigating sweatshop labor practices.

30. The International People's Tribunal, p. 124.

31. The Citizens Commission of Inquiry, *The Dellums Committee Hearings on War Crimes in Vietnam* (New York: Vintage, 1972), p. 335.

Chapter 2

1. See Franz Borkenau, *World Communism* (Ann Arbor: University of Michigan Press, 1962), pp. 380–81.

2. *Inprecorr,* March 9, 1933, p. 264.

3. Stephen Koch, *Double Lives* (New York: Free Press, 1994), p. 49 and Douglas Reed, *The Burning of the Reichstag* (London: Victor Gollancz, 1934), p. 20. Reichstag President and Prussian Minister of the Interior, Hermann Goering, estimated that four thousand to five thousand Communists were rounded up that night. The official government statement about the fire portrayed it as the "most outrageous act yet committed by Bolshevism in Germany" and cited Goering as calling for "utmost discipline" and for special measures to prevent further acts. See *The Times,* March 1, 1933.

4. Hitler came in second in the March 1932 presidential balloting, and Thaelmann third. See Frederick Schuman, *The Nazi Dictatorship* (New York: Knopf, 1935), p. 156.

5. *Deutsche Allgemeine Zeitung* as cited in *Manchester Guardian Weekly,* September 1, 1933, and Gordon Craig, *Germany: 1866–1945* (New York: Oxford University Press, 1978), pp. 144–50.

6. *Inprecorr,* March 17, 1933, p. 310, and April 7, 1933, p. 358.

7. Fritz Tobias, *The Reichstag Fire* (New York: G. P. Putnam's Sons, 1964), pp. 47–49.

8. Arthur Koestler, *The Invisible Writing* (New York: Macmillan, 1954), p. 201. The German newspaper *Deutsche Allgemeine Zeitung* maintained that it was incomprehensible that a Communist would have been stupid enough to set the fire. Cited in *The Times,* March 1, 1933.

9. Gunther Nollau, *International Communism and World Revolution* (New York: Praeger, 1961), pp. 143–44 and 162, and Edward H. Carr, *The Twilight of Comintern, 1930–1935* (London: Macmillan, 1982), p. 88.

10. Review by Herman Veenhof of Martin Schouten, *Marinus van der Lubbe, een biografie* (Amsterdam: Uitg. De Bezige Bij, 1999), *Nederlands Dagblad,* http://chip.nd.nl/htm/rec/recm17.htm, and Martin Meijer, "De tien

minuten van Marinus van der Lubbe," *NRC Handelsblad,* November 1998, http://www.nrc.nl/W2/Profiel/IDFA-1998/Profiel/lubbe.html

11. *Manchester Guardian,* April 26 and 27, 1933.

12. William Shirer, *The Rise and Fall of the Third Reich* (Greenwich, CT: Fawcett, 1959), p. 271, and Craig, p. 574. Precedent for the decree had been set by Bismarck with his 1878 "Socialist Law."

13. *The Brown Book of the Hitler Terror* (New York: Knopf, 1933), p. 284.

14. *The New York Times,* March 30, 1933.

15. Ben Fowkes, *Communism in Germany Under the Weimar Republic* (London: Macmillan, 1984), p. 171.

16. Carr, p. 87. On March 2, Hitler blamed the fire on the "Bolsheviks" and criticized the Soviet system. This was not typical of his comments during this period. Note that a similar episode, in reverse, had taken place in February 1928 when the Soviet Union indicted five Germans in the Shakhty affair—accused of economic "wrecking." Two were released within a fortnight. The German ambassador Count Ulrich von Brockdorff-Rantzau insisted on visiting the three jailed Germans, and was given permission to do so. On July 7, after a trial attended by the ambassador, two of the Germans were acquitted. The third was sentenced to one year's imprisonment, but was immediately released. Eleven of the fifty Soviet fellow defendants were sentenced to death. See Louis Fischer, *Russia's Road From Peace to War* (New York: Harper and Row, 1969), pp. 184–85.

17. Robert C. Tucker, *Stalin in Power* (New York: W. W. Norton, 1990), p. 234 and Carr, p. 95. Earlier that month, Germany had announced the deferral of a credit repayment owed by the Soviets. See Gerhard Weinberg, *The Foreign Policy of Hitler's Germany* (Chicago: University of Chicago Press, 1970).

18. Ruth Fischer, *Stalin and German Communism* (Cambridge, MA: Harvard University Press, 1948), p. 534.

19. *Dimitroff's Letters From Prison* (London: Victor Gollancz, 1935), p. 33.

20. David Dallin, *Soviet Espionage* (New Haven, CT: Yale University Press, 1955), p. 121.

21. In the spring of 1933, it was not yet clear that a public show trial would actually take place. On March 19, *The Spectator* speculated on the fate of van der Lubbe and even considered the possibility that he had been secretly executed.

22. *Manchester Guardian* Weekly, December 22, 1933; Reed, p. 336; and *The New York Times,* August 1, 1933.

23. *Brown Book,* pp. 102–103; *Inprecorr,* June 9, 1933, p. 545; and *The New York Times,* September 26, 1933.

24. *Dimitroff's Letters From Prison,* p. 59.

Chapter 3

1. *The Reichstag Fire Trial* (New York: Howard Fertig, 1969), p. 32.
2. Arthur Koestler, *The Invisible Writing* (New York: Macmillan, 1954), p. 194.
3. Jorgen Schleimann, "The Organization Man: Willi Munzenberg," *Survey,* Vol. 55 (April 1965): 69.
4. Schleimann, p. 68; Ruth Fischer, *Stalin and German Communism* (Cambridge, MA: Harvard University Press, 1948), p. 611; Richard G. Powers, *Not Without Honor: The History of American Anti-Communism* (New Haven, CT: Yale University Press, 1998), p. 120; and David Caute, *The Fellow-Travellers* (New York: Macmillan, 1973), p. 132. The Amsterdam rally was outwardly sponsored by French author Romain Rolland.
5. Stephen Koch, *Double Lives* (New York: Free Press, 1994), p. 62, and Koestler, p. 198.
6. Fritz Tobias, *The Reichstag Fire* (New York: G. P. Putnam's Sons, 1964), p. 103. Even *The New York Times* accepted the genuineness of the document. See the issue of July 16, 1933.
7. This organization was sometimes called the World Committee for the Victims of Hitler Fascism or the World Committee for the Relief of the Victims of German Fascism.
8. Babette Gross, *Willi Munzenberg: A Political Biography* (East Lansing: Michigan State University Press, 1974), p. 263, and information provided by Anson Rabinbach based on his examination of Comintern documents.
9. Christopher Andrew and Harold James, "Willi Munzenberg, the Reichstag Fire and the Conversion of Innocents," in David Charters and Maurice Tugwell, eds., *Deception Operations* (London: Brassey's, 1990), p. 30, and *Manchester Guardian Weekly,* July 7, 1933. Gustav Regler, who helped write the "Brown Book," said of Muenzenberg: "He believed that one had to outdo a cynical liar in cynicism." See Schleimann, p. 69.
10. Christopher Andrew and Oleg Gordievsky, *KGB: The Inside Story* (New York: HarperCollins, 1990), pp. 187–88, and Ronald Clark, *Einstein: The Life and Times* (New York: World Publishing, 1971), p. 494.
11. *The Brown Book of the Hitler Terror* (New York: Knopf, 1933), p. 52 and "Statement by the Presidium of the Communist Reichstag Fraction," March 21, 1933 in *Inprecorr,* April 7, 1933, p. 358. Note that the *Second Brown Book of the Hitler Terror* was published in April 1934, after the Reichstag fire trial. The English edition was issued in London by Bodley Head. See also "Who Burnt the Reichstag?," in *History Today* (August 1960): 522. The "Brown Book's" deemphasis on Hitler's possible culpability may have been an effort to drive a wedge between him and Goering or part of a Soviet strategy to maintain normal state relations with Germany.
12. Gross, p. 252.
13. Andrew and Gordievsky, p. 190, and *Manchester Guardian Weekly,* July 7, 1933.

14. *The Times,* August 17, 1933, and *Keesing's,* August 4, 1933, p. 916.

15. *Keesing's,* August 24, 1933; Tobias, p. 126; and Arthur Garfield Hays, *City Lawyer* (New York: Simon and Schuster, 1942), p. 344.

16. Arthur Garfield Hays, "The Burning of the German Reichstag," *The Nation,* November 22, 1933, p. 586; Hays, *City Lawyer,* p. 344; *The New York Times,* September 3, 1933; and D. N. Pritt, *The Autobiography of D. N. Pritt: From Right to Left* (London: Lawrence and Wishart, 1965), p. 53.

17. Pritt, p. 54.

18. Two other commissioners had participated in the September meeting: Francesco Nitti (Italian) and Johannes Huber (Swiss). Commission member George Branting, a Socialist deputy, was the son of former Swedish Prime Minister Hjalmar Branting. Valdemar Hvidt's National Association Against Unemployment was not backed by the Denmark's communists and was later strongly criticized by them when some association members expressed support for the policies of the Portuguese strongman Antonio Salazar.

19. Pritt, pp. 38–39 and 42, and Gross, pp. 255–56. In 1934, Pritt became chairman of the Society for Cultural Relations, a British-Soviet people's organization. He later wrote positively about the Moscow show trials, and represented the Soviet Union in a legal case.

20. Patricia Strauss, *Cripps: Advocate Extraordinary* (New York: Duell, Sloan, and Pearce, 1942), p. 97, and Gross, p. 255.

21. *The New York Times,* September 15, 16, 17, and 19, 1933.

22. Tobias, p. 125; Hays, *City Lawyer,* p. 349; Pritt, p. 59; *The New York Times,* September 14, 1933; and *The New Statesman and Nation,* September 23, 1933, p. 343. Tobias asserts that the alleged Storm Trooper was really an imposter.

23. *The Reichstag Fire Trial,* p. 34, and Tobias, p. 126.

24. *Keesing's,* September 11–12, 1933, p. 946; *Manchester Guardian Weekly,* September 15, 1933,; and *The New York Times,* September 12, 1933.

25. Pritt, p. 54.

26. *The Reichstag Fire Trial,* p. 37; Gross, pp. 257–58; and Pritt, p. 60.

27. *The New York Times,* September 21, 1933.

28. *The New Statesman and Nation,* September 23, 1933, p. 343; *The Spectator,* September 15 and 22, 1933; and editorial in *The New York Times,* September 23, 1933.

29. *Inprecorr,* September 22, 1933, p. 906.

30. *Inprecorr,* September 22, 1933, p. 912, and *The Times,* September 16, 1933. Also published in Germany in September 1933 was Adolf Ehrt's *Communism in Germany,* which claimed that the Communists had set the fire.

31. Peter Bell, *Chamberlain, Germany and Japan, 1933–4* (London: Macmillan, 1996), pp. 11–12.

32. *The New York Times,* April 2, 5, 9, and 15, 1933.

33. *The New York Times,* May 12 and 14, 1933.

34. Strauss, pp. 100–02.

35. *The Reichstag Fire Trial,* p. 36.

36. *Manchester Guardian Weekly,* July 14 and September 15, 1933; Tobias, p. 218; and August 24 letter to Rolland in *Dimitroff's Letters From Prison* (London: Victor Gollancz, 1935), p. 157. Torgler's wife, Margaret, complained that her husband was unable to select his own counsel.

37. *Dimitroff's Letters,* p. 40.

38. *Dimitroff's Letters,* pp. 53–54 and 62–63.

39. *The New York Times,* June 23 and September 17, 1933 and *Manchester Guardian Weekly,* September 15, 1933. There was an attempt to secure the services of D. N. Pritt as assistant counsel for Torgler. This was before Pritt was selected to chair the countertrial. Philip Seuffert was appointed by the Supreme Court to represent van der Lubbe.

40. William and Martha Dodd, eds, *Ambassador Dodd's Diary, 1933–1938* (New York: Harcourt, Brace, 1941), p. 21, and *The New York Times,* June 27, September 6, and September 14, 1933. Other Philadelphia lawyers, members of the Lawyers' Committee of Philadelphia for the Defense of German Political Prisoners, also tried to enter the fray. See *The New York Times,* July 15, 1933.

41. Hays, *City Lawyer,* pp. 283 and 339–43; Hays, "The Burning," p. 587; and *The New York Times,* August 17, 20, and 27, 1933. Hays refers to Levinson as Edward Levenson, but this is probably incorrect. See *City Lawyer,* p. 339.

42. Tobias, pp. 121–22; *The Reichstag Fire Trial,* p. 87; *Inprecorr,* August 25, 1933, pp. 306–307, and September 1, 1933, p. 826; and *The New York Times,* August 24, 1933.

43. *The New York Times,* September 8, 1933; *The New Statesman and Nation,* September 2, 1933; *The Reichstag Fire Trial,* p. 102; and Gross, p. 257.

Chapter 4

1. Frederick Schuman, *The Nazi Dictatorship* (New York: Knopf, 1935), p. 331, and *The New York Times,* September 23 and 24, 1937. A verdict of innocent could improve Germany's image by demonstrating respect for judicial independence, but it could also undercut the Nazi claim that Communists were conspiring against their government. A *New York Times* editorial on September 23 alluded to serious impairment of the "moral foundations" of the Nazi regime, should there be a verdict of innocent.

2. *Neueste Nachrichten* cited in *The New York Times,* September 29, 1933 and *The New York Times,* September 8, 1933. While the trial was in progress there was a ceremony in front of the courthouse in which ten thousand lawyers gave the Nazi salute and pledged to follow the Fuehrer. See Ingo Muller, *Hitler's Justice: The Courts of the Third Reich* (Cambridge, MA: Harvard University Press, 1991), p. 283.

3. *Inprecorr,* October 27, 1933, p. 1038, and Douglas Reed, *The Burning of the Reichstag* (London: Victor Gollancz, 1934), p. 122. Otto Katz labeled the

"Brown Book" the "sixth defendant." See Fritz Tobias, *The Reichstag Fire* (New York: G. P. Putnam's Sons, 1964), p. 131.

4. *Manchester Guardian Weekly,* November 17, 1933, and *The New Statesman and Nation,* October 14, 1933.

5. Arthur Garfield Hays in *The Nation,* September 22, 1933. The judges at Leipzig may have felt that they were under the gun, since three Supreme Court judges had recently been pressured to resign. See *The New Statesman and Nation,* October 14, 1933.

6. Arthur Garfield Hays, *City Lawyer* (New York: Simon and Schuster, 1942), p. 353.

7. Reed, p. 9; *The New York Times,* September 26, 1933; and John Gunther, "The Reichstag Fire Still Burns," *The Nation,* December 13, 1933.

8. See Edward H. Carr, *The Twilight of Comintern, 1930–1935* (London: Macmillan, 1982), p. 102, and *The New York Times,* September 26, 1933.

9. A. J. P. Taylor, "Who Burnt the Reichstag?," *History Today* (August 1960): 518; *The New York Times,* September 29, 1933; and review by Herman Veenhof of Martin Schouten, *Marinus van der Lubbe, een biografie* (Amsterdam: Uitg. De Bezige Bij, 1999), *Nederlands Dagblad,* http://chip.nd.nl/htm/rec/recm17.htm.

10. Walther Hofer, Edouard Calic, Karl Stephan, and Friedrich Zipfel, *Der Reichstagsbrand,* Vol. I (Berlin: Arani Verlags-GmbH, 1972); Vol. II (Munich: K.G. Saur Verlag KG, 1978), and Hofer, et al., *Der Reichstagsbrand: eine wissenschaftliche Documentation* (Freiburg: Ahriman-Verlag, 1992). See also Tobias, especially p. 72. Many noncommunist European newspapers blamed the Nazis for the Reichstag fire. There also was a confession by a former Storm Trooper, and a posthumous one by another Storm Trooper. In addition, there were claims that Hitler had the Nazi perpetrators killed in June 1934. Later, at Nuremberg, after World War II, several Nazi witnesses blamed Goering and Nazi propaganda chief Joseph Goebbels for the fire. See *The New York Times,* March 2, 1933; January 14, 1936; March 19, 1946; and April 26, 1946; *The Times,* March 1, 3, 5, and 7, 1933; Koestler, p. 201; and William Shirer, *The Rise and Fall of the Third Reich* (Greenwich, CT: Fawcett, 1959), p. 269.

11. H .R. Trevor-Roper, *New York Review of Books,* April 2, 1964; Veenhof review; and Meijer.

12. *The New York Times,* September 24, 1933; *The Reichstag Fire Trial* (New York: Howard Fertig, 1969), p. 58; and *Dimitroff's Letters From Prison* (London: Victor Gollancz, 1935), p. 77. In 1948, Dimitrov implied that the Communists did carry out the cathedral bombing. See Koestler, p. 202. Note that Dimitrov had been sentenced to death by Bulgaria, so it therefore provided no assistance to him in Leipzig. In fact, the Bulgarian embassy in Berlin cooperated with Germany during the preliminary investigation of Dimitrov and even asked for the extradition of all three Bulgarians who had

earlier sentences imposed on them for acts in their home country. See *Inprecorr,* October 10, 1933, p. 1021.

13. *Dimitroff's Letters,* p. 82. According to *The New York Times* of October 19, 1933, Dimitrov did receive information contained in the "Brown Book" from Teichert—but not the book itself.

14. D. N. Pritt, *The Autobiography of D. N. Pritt: From Right to Left* (London: Lawrence and Wishart, 1965), p. 67, and *Dimitroff's Letters,* p. 77. The pro-Nazi newspaper *Volkische Beobachter* called on the court to increase its control over Dimitrov. See *The Times,* November 2, 1933.

15. Reed, p. 287.

16. Martha Dodd, *My Years in Germany* (London: Victor Gollancz, 1939), pp. 54–55. Torgler was manacled for five months while in prison and this experience appeared to have taken its toll. *The New York Times* on September 26, 1933 referred to "the lines of suffering" in Torgler's face.

17. Babette Gross, *Willi Munzenberg: A Political Biography* (East Lansing: Michigan State University Press, 1974), p. 253.

18. *The New York Times,* October 13, 1936, and Pritt, p. 79.

19. *The New York Times,* September 2, 4, and 26, 1933.

20. Koestler, p. 198; *The Reichstag Fire Trial,* p. 2; and *The New York Times,* October 21, 1933.

21. *The New York Times,* October 21, 1933. Another line of analysis is provided by Arthur Koestler, who saw Helldorf as representative of the German master race in confrontation with the underclass, as represented by van der Lubbe, a drifter and alleged homosexual. See Koestler, pp. 196–97.

22. *The New York Times,* November 5, 1933.

23. *The New York Times,* September 23, 1933; *Manchester Guardian Weekly,* September 29, 1933; and Carr, p. 99.

24. Reed, pp. 231–32, and *The New York Times,* December 14, 1933.

25. *The New York Times,* September 28, 1933.

26. Alan Bullock, *Hitler and Stalin: Parallel Lives* (London: HarperCollins, 1991), p. 480; Fritz Morstein Marx, *Government in the Third Reich,* second edition (New York: McGraw-Hill, 1937), p. 76; and *Dimitroff's Letters,* p. 123.

27. *The New York Times,* November 12, 1933.

28. See *The Times,* December 6, 1933.

29. *Dimitroff's Letters,* p. 159 and *The New York Times,* December 14, 1933. According to Arthur Garfield Hays, Werner revealed to him that evidence cleared Dimitrov and Torgler of setting the fire. See *The New York Times,* September 26, 1933.

30. See Werner's comments in *The New York Times,* November 19, 1933. *Neueste Nachrichten* stated on September 24 in regard to Dimitrov: "It is immaterial what role he played in the Reichstag fire. This much has been proven, that Dimitrov is a moral incendiary of gigantic proportions."

31. *The Reichstag Fire Trial,* p. 43; Taylor, p. 518; and *The Times,* December 16, 1933.

32. Reed, pp. 266–67, and Tobias, p. 282.

33. Pritt, p. 63, and *The Times,* December 15, 1933.

34. Tobias, p. 252.

35. *Dimitroff's Letters,* pp. 122–23.

36. Reed, pp. 311 and 321; Hays, pp. 384–85, and Muller, p. 34.

37. Reed, p. 325, and *Dimitroff's Letters,* p. 125.

38. *The New York Times,* December 13 and 18, 1933; Tobias, pp. 252–53; *Boersen Zeitung,* December 17, 1933; *Volkische Beobachter,* December 17, 1933; and *The Times,* December 16, 1933.

39. Dodd, p. 57 and Pritt, p. 71.

40. *The New York Times,* September 23, 1933.

41. *The Times,* November 6, 1933, and Reed, pp. 232–33.

42. *The Times,* December 14, 1933, and *The New York Times,* September 24 and December 22, 1933.

43. *The New York Times,* October 5, 1933; *Inprecorr,* October 10, 1933, p. 1021; and Pritt, p. 72.

44. *Manchester Guardian Weekly,* November 24, 1933.

45. *The Reichstag Fire Trial,* p. 243; *Inprecorr,* December 22, 1933, p. 1266; and Pritt, pp. 72–73. Hays did not attend, and possibly was not invited. See Tobias, p. 131.

46. *The New York Times,* November 12 and 18, 1933.

47. *The New York Times,* December 18 and 20, 1933.

48. *The New York Times,* October 25, 28, 29, and November 3, 1933.

49. *The New York Times,* September 23, 1933, and *The Times,* September 25, 1933.

50. Hays, p. 351.

51. Arthur Garfield Hays, "The Burning of the German Reichstag," *The Nation,* November 22, 1933; Hays, *City Lawyer,* p. 357; *The New York Times,* September 24, 1933; and *The Times,* October 6, 1933.

52. *The New York Times,* September 25 and 26, October 6, and November 30, 1933. Sack later commented that Hays had been fair during the trial but critical. See *The New York Times,* February 28, 1934.

53. *The New York Times,* October 8, 1933, and *The Times,* September 21 and 25, 1933.

54. *The New York Times,* October 15, 1933; Tobias, p. 129; Hays, "The Burning," p. 587; and Hays, *City Lawyer,* p. 279.

55. *The New York Times,* November 8, 1933, and *Fair Lawn and Paramus Clarion,* December 15, 1933.

56. *New York City Herald Tribune,* November 12, 1933, and *New York City American,* November 13, 1933.

57. Hays, *City Lawyer,* p. 386.

58. Tobias, p. 268.

59. Taylor, p. 518; Tobias, p. 269; Pritt, pp. 73–74; and notes for Hays speech, March 7, 1934, AGHP 33/5.

60. Muller, p. 33.

61. *The New York Times,* October 6, 1933. The president of the court, Wilhelm Buenger, acknowledged that a great amount of time was spent on refuting "Brown Book" and countertrial charges. See *Inprecorr,* December 29, 1933, p. 1300.

62. Stephen Koch, *Double Lives* (New York: Free Press, 1994), pp. 113–16, and Ruth Fischer, *Stalin and German Communism* (Cambridge, MA: Harvard University Press, 1948), p. 309.

63. For criticisms of the "deal" theory, see Gunther Nollau, *International Communism and World Revolution* (New York: Praeger, 1961), p. 144; Koestler, p. 203; and David Caute, "Assignment in Utopia," *The New Republic,* May 30, 1994.

64. Robert C. Tucker, *Stalin in Power* (New York: W. W. Norton, 1990), pp. 236–37 and 255, and Carr, p. 99. Radek may have had secret contacts with Dirksen in October 1933. See Koch, p. 54.

65. Koch, pp. 114–15.

Chapter 5

1. *Keesing's,* December 27, 1933, p. 1067, and *The New York Times,* December 24, 1933.

2. *The New Statesman and Nation,* December 30, 1933 and *The New York Times,* December 24, 1933 and December 27, 1933 (citing the *Daily Telegraph* and *The Times*). George Bernard Shaw said that the countertrial had looked "silly," since the verdict turned out to be fair. See *The New York Times,* December 24, 1933. The Nazi organ *Volkische Beobachter* declared that Germany would "draw the necessary consequences" from the verdict and "quickly put an end to conditions which are calculated to impair the success of the Nazi revolution." See *Keesing's,* December 27, 1933.

3. D. N. Pritt, *The Autobiography of D. N. Pritt: From Right to Left* (London: Lawrence and Wishart, 1965), p. 74.

4. *The New York Times,* November 5, 1933. See also William and Martha Dodd, eds., *Ambassador Dodd's Diary, 1933–1938* (New York: Harcourt, Brace, p. 65; Martha Dodd, *My Years in Germany* (London: Victor Gollancz, 1939), pp. 56–58; and *The Spectator,* December 22, 1933.

5. *Manchester Guardian Weekly,* December 22, 1933.

6. *Inprecorr,* February 9, 1934, p. 209.

7. *The New York Times,* December 24, 1933.

8. Stephen Koch, *Double Lives* (New York: Free Press, 1994), p. 123, and Alan Sheridan, *Andre Gide: A Life in the Present* (Cambridge, MA: Harvard University Press, 1999), pp. 462–63. Malraux claimed that he had met with Joseph Goebbels, but this is unlikely. Gide later served as honorary chairman of the January 31, 1934, protest rally in Paris, where a letter from him was read.

9. *The New York Times,* December 29, 1933, and January 20, 21, 25, and 31, 1934.

10. *Dimitroff's Letters From Prison* (London: Victor Gollancz, 1935), pp. 130–31, and *The New York Times,* February 7 and 11, 1934.

11. *Manchester Guardian Weekly,* January 26, 1934. Photos were taken on January 22 and were published in newspapers ranging from *The New York Times* to the German Nazi organ *Volkische Beobachter.*

12. Pritt, pp. 75–76; *The Times,* January 18, 1934 and editorial, February 21, 1934; and *Manchester Guardian Weekly,* January 26 and February 23, 1934.

13. Peter Bell, *Chamberlain, Germany and Japan, 1933–4* (London: Macmillan, 1996), p. 30.

14. *The New York Times,* January 7 and 25 and March 4, 1934, and *The Times,* February 26, 1934.

15. *Inprecorr,* June 2, 1933, p. 522; *The New York Times,* December 31, 1933 and January 1, 1934; *Dimitroff's Letters,* p. 138; and Edward H. Carr, *The Twilight of Comintern, 1930–1935* (London: Macmillan, 1982), p. 102.

16. Koch, p. 360 and Alexander Dallin and F. I. Firsov, eds., *Dimitrov and Stalin, 1934–1943* (New Haven, CT: Yale University Press, 2000), p. 5.

17. Carr, p. 118 and *Inprecorr,* January 12, 1934, p. 41.

18. *The Reichstag Fire Trial* (New York: Howard Fertig, 1969), p. 269; Gunther Nollau, *International Communism and World Revolution* (New York: Praeger, 1961), p. 144; and *The New York Times,* February 17, 18 and 23, 1934. On February 7, Dimitrov had threatened a hunger strike, but he renounced it once he was granted Soviet citizenship.

19. *Inprecorr,* March 4, 1934, p. 404, and *The Times,* February 21, 1934.

20. *The Times,* February 21 and 24, 1934, and *The New York Times,* February 23, 1934.

21. *The Times,* March 1, 1934 and *The New York Times,* March 1, 1934. On February 23, the Soviet Union made a second request for the release of the Bulgarians. See *The Reichstag Fire Trial,* p. 269.

22. *The Times,* March 2, 1934; *The New York Times,* February 28, 1934; and Carr, p. 124. The Soviet Union released four Germans accused of espionage, plus three other foreign nationals. This act appears to have been part of the scenario regarding the Bulgarians. The latter left behind more than $1,000 in personal property, which Germany confiscated under a May 26, 1933, law on the seizure of communist property and funds used for subversion. See *The New York Times,* October 10, 1935.

23. Koch, p. 125; Franz Borkenau, *World Communism* (Ann Arbor: University of Michigan Press, 1962), p, 384; and review by Herman Veenhof of Martin Schouten, *Marinus van der Lubbe, een biografie* (Amsterdam: Uitg. De Bezige Bij, 1999), *Nederlands Dagblad,* http://chip.nd/htm/rec/recm17.htm.

24. *The New York Times,* January 26, 1934 and June 13, 1935; *The Times,* March 1, 1934; and *Manchester Guardian Weekly,* March 2, 1934.

25. Frederick Schuman, *The Nazi Dictatorship* (New York: Knopf, 1935), p. 338; Fritz Tobias, *The Reichstag Fire* (New York: G. P. Putnam's Sons, 1964), p. 284; *Manchester Guardian Weekly,* January 12, 1934; Douglas Reed, *The Burning of the Reichstag* (London: Victor Gollancz, 1934), p. 352; and Veenhof review.

26. *The New York Times,* January 18, 1940. The lawyer, Friedrich Roetter, later left Germany for Czechoslovakia.

27. *The Times,* May 14, 1934; *Inprecorr,* February 9, 1934, p. 209; *Manchester Guardian Weekly,* August 3, 1934 and March 27, 1936; Fritz Morsten Marx, *Government in the Third Reich* (New York: McGraw-Hill, 1937), p. 75; Alan Bullock, *Hitler and Stalin Parallel Lives* (London: HarperCollins, 1991), p. 481; and Ingo Muller, *Hitler's Justice: The Courts of the Third Reich* (Cambridge, MA: Harvard University Press, 1991), p. 140. The law on people's courts went into effect on August 1, 1934. Consideration was given to trying Torgler in such a court.

28. *Inprecorr,* May 11, 1934, p. 757, and *Manchester Guardian Weekly,* August 3, 1934. Not surprisingly, the first defendant brought before a people's court on August 1 was a young communist charged with acts preparatory to treason.

29. *Manchester Guardian Weekly,* October 19, 1934.

30. *Manchester Guardian Weekly,* March 23 and October 19, 1934. See also a letter from Isidor Englander to Arthur Garfield Hays, January 26, 1935, AGHP 3/8. In 1937, two British members of Parliament were denied permission to visit Thaelmann in prison. See *Manchester Guardian Weekly,* November 19, 1937.

31. *Inprecorr,* February 2, 1934, p. 154.

32. *Dimitroff's Letters,* pp. 149–50.

33. *The New York Times,* September 15, 1944 and August 10, 1946.

34. *The New York City Sun,* March 8, 1934.

35. Letter to "dear friend," June 19, 1934 and undated notice, American Committee Against Fascist Oppression in Germany, AGHP 3/4.

36. Hays to Darrow, June 5, 8, and 18, 1934, AGHP 3/4. The American Commission of Inquiry was comprised of Hays, Darrow, Edwin Costigan, Dudley Malone, John Lovejoy Elliott, George Medalic, George Gordon Battle, and Roger Baldwin. It had connections to Lord Marley's British branch of the Committee for the Relief of Victims of German Fascism.

37. Hays to Luther, June 23, 1934; Koelble to Hays, June 28, 1934; and Louis Gibarti to Hays, June 30, 1934, AGHP 3/4. There also was concern that Koelble had been disorderly and was expelled from a Congressional hearing before the Dickstein Committee. Giberti represented the American Committee Against Fascist Oppression in Germany, and was a secretary to Lord Marley's committee.

38. "Why the American Inquiry Commission?," 1934, AGHP 3/4, and *The New York Times,* September 3, 1934.

39. Jorgen Schleimann, "The Organization Man: The Life and Work of Willi Muenzenberg," *Survey* (April 1965): 78 and Gibarti to Hays, July 25, 1934, AGHP 3/4. Muenzenberg's lecture tour took him to New York, Washington, Boston, Chicago, Detroit, and Cleveland. Hays was invited to the New York reception for Muenzenberg, but it is unclear if he attended.

40. C. A. Hathaway, editor of *The Daily Worker,* to Hays, December 19, 1936, and Hays's notes, AGHP 3/5. On the tenth anniversary of the verdict, Hays participated in a New York commemorative ceremony led by Communist Party General-Secretary Earl Browder. See *The New York Times,* December 23, 1943.

Chapter 6

1. Boris Nicolaevsky, *Power and the Soviet Elite* (New York: Praeger, 1965), pp. 40–41; and Amy Knight, *Who Killed Kirov?* (New York: Hill and Wang, 1999), pp. 202–04 and 207.

2. Knight, pp. 200–01; Leonard Schapiro, *The Communist Party of the Soviet Union* (New York: Random House, 1971), p. 405; and *The Anti-Stalin Campaign and International Communism* (New York: Columbia University Press, 1956), p. 25.

3. Knight, p. 220.

4. Knight, p. 222; *Manchester Guardian Weekly,* January 18, 1935; and Schapiro, p. 406.

5. *The Times,* December 13, 1933.

6. Isaac Deutscher, *The Prophet Outcast* (New York: Oxford University Press, 1963), pp. 15–16.

7. Trygve Lie, *Oslo-Moskva-London* (Oslo: Norsk Forlag, 1968), pp. 64–65.

8. Deutscher, p. 188 and Dmitri Volkogonov, *Trotsky: The Eternal Revolutionary* (New York: Free Press, 1996), p. 331. Increased participation by the Soviet Union in European affairs probably paid dividends in the form of other states rejecting Trotsky's requests to relocate.

9. *Manchester Guardian Weekly,* April 20, 1934. That same year, there were efforts by American Trotskyists to secure his asylum in the United States. See Alain Dugrand, *Trotsky in Mexico* (Manchester: Carcanet, 1992), p. 16.

10. *Trotsky's Diary in Exile* (Cambridge, MA: Harvard University Press, 1976), pp. 125, 136, and 154, and Lie, pp. 65–67.

11. Deutscher, pp. 324–25 and 330.

12. *Manchester Guardian Weekly,* August 21, 1936.

13. *The Nation,* July 4, 1936; Lie, pp. 71–72; and *The New York Times,* June 16, 1936.

14. *The New York Times,* August 9 and 15, 1936.

15. Deutscher, p. 330; Alan Wald, "Memories of the John Dewey Commission: Forty Years Later," *Antioch Review,* no. 35 (Fall 1977): 440; and George Dykhuizen, *The Life and Mind of John Dewey* (Carbondale: South-

ern Illinois University Press, 1973), p. 281. In an unusual twist, Vyshinsky was the person who was given Trotsky's apartment when the latter was exiled to Kazakhstan. See Volkogonov, p. 372.

16. Frederick Schuman, "Leon Trotsky: Martyr or Renegade?," *Southern Review,* vol. III (1937–38), p. 66, and Vadim Rogovin, *1937: Stalin's Year of Terror* (Oak Park, MI: Mehring Books, 1998), pp. 37–38.

17. D. N. Pritt, *The Autobiography of D. N. Pritt: From Right to Left* (London: Lawrence and Wishart, 1965), pp. 111–12, and Rogovin, pp. 37–38.

18. Volkogonov, pp. 335–36 and 370–71.

19. David Large, *Between Two Fires: Europe's Path in the 1930s* (New York: W. W. Norton, 1990), p. 284; *The New York Times,* August 20, 1936; Rogovin, pp. 154–55; and Joseph Nedava, *Trotsky and the Jews* (Philadelphia: The Jewish Publication Society of America, 1972), pp. 184–85. Many Jews were reluctant to reach the same conclusion as Trotsky since they viewed the Soviet Union as a bulwark against Nazism. Nahum Goldmann, the Jewish Agency representative at the League of Nations, declared that no nation had less antisemitism than the Soviet Union. See *The New York Times,* August 9, 1936.

20. Trotsky notes, January 31, 1937 JDP 102/10/9.

21. *The New York Times,* August 16, 1936 and *Manchester Guardian Weekly,* August 21, 1936. In the United States, Soviet operatives clipped articles to gauge American reaction to Trotsky's critique of the Moscow trial and the Soviet embassy put out a press release justifying the trial. See Volkogonov, p. 390.

22. Albert Glotzer, *Trotsky: Memoir and Critique* (Buffalo, NY: Prometheus, 1989), p. 238; Rogovin, p. 85; and *The New York Times,* August 30, 1936.

23. Deutscher, p. 326, and Lie, pp. 73–74.

24. *The New York Times,* August 16, 21, and 29, 1936.

25. Deutscher, p. 336; Preliminary Commission of Inquiry, *The Case of Leon Trotsky* (New York: Merit, 1937), pp. ix and 66; and *The New York Times,* August 30, 1936.

26. Rogovin, p. 46, and Yngvar Ustvedt, *Verdensrevolusjonen paa Hoenefoss: en beretning om Leo Trotskijs opphold i Norge* (Oslo: Gyldendalnorskforlag, 1974), p. 234.

27. *The New York Times,* August 31 and September 1 and 4, 1936; *Newsweek,* September 5, 1936, p. 66; and Trotsky notes, January 31, 1937. Note also that Sweden and Denmark backed Norway against the Soviet Union on the expulsion issue. Norway's ruling Labor Party was noncommittal on whether the Moscow trial served justice, but was supportive of Trotsky's right to asylum. See Ustvedt, pp. 129 and 154.

28. Lie, pp. 71–72; Rogovin, p. 47; and Deutscher, pp. 336–37.

29. *The Nation,* October 10, 1936, and Deutscher, p. 294.

30. Ustvedt, p. 132.

31. Lie, p. 72, and *Manchester Guardian Weekly,* August 28, 1936.

32. Deutscher, pp. 339–40; Ustvedt, pp. 234–35; and Lie, pp. 72–73. Victor Serge, a Russian expelled from the Soviet communist party in 1928 for his pro-Trotsky stance, advised from his exile in France: "The legal position seems absolutely clear to me. The refugee must refrain from any political activity within the country which offers him hospitality, but he keeps full liberty to express his views on whatever happens in his own country of origin and elsewhere in the world." See letter from Serge to Trotsky, August 30, 1936, in D. J. Cotterill, ed., *The Serge-Trotsky Papers* (London: Pluto Press, 1994), p. 96.

33. Lie, pp. 73 and 75–76; Jean van Heijenoort, *With Trotsky in Exile* (Cambridge, MA: Harvard University Press, 1978), p. 89; and *The New York Times,* September 1, 1936.

34. *Newsweek,* September 5, 1936, p. 66; *The Case of Leon Trotsky,* p. 37; and Heijenoort, pp. 90–91.

35. Trotsky to Dewey, July 15, 1938, JDP 102/11/5 and Lie, p. 74. Lie may have desired public friction with the Soviet Union in order to improve his party's chances in the upcoming October parliamentary election. Labor had an image of being too close to the Soviet Union, which Lie hoped to rectify. It turned out that the Trotsky flap did not have a major impact, as Labor secured a plurality but not a majority. See Lie, pp. 69 and 74, and *The New York Times,* November 27, 1936. In reference to Trotsky's internal exile in Hurum, *The New York Times* on November 15, 1936, pondered whether Hurum would become his Elba or his St. Helena.

36. Pavel and Anatoli Sudoplatov, *Special Tasks* (Boston: Little, Brown, 1994), p. 82 and Christopher Andrew and Vasili Mitrokhin, *The Sword and the Shield* (New York: Basic Books,, 1999), p. 71. The "Red Book" drew a comparison between the Leipzig and Moscow trials. See Rogovin, p. 55. Some of Trotsky's papers had been stolen in August from the Paris office of Menshevik exile Boris Nicolaevsky. They had been given to him for safekeeping by Lev Sedov. See Nicolaevsky, p. 8.

37. Deutscher, pp. 343–44 and 350, and Heijenoort, pp. 90–91.

38. Lie, p. 77; Deutscher, p. 351; and *The New York Times,* December 7 and 8, 1936. Trotsky had lived in New York prior to the February revolution of 1917 and had many supporters in the United States.

39. Deutscher, p. 350, and Lie, pp. 76–77.

40. Lie, p. 77. It is unlikely that Norway decided to expel Trotsky because the Soviet Union decided to purchase more Norwegian herring. For such a claim, see Bertram Wolfe, *The Fabulous Life of Diego Rivera* (New York: Stein and Day, 1963), p. 237.

41. Rogovin, p. 131; Lie, p. 78; and *The New York Times,* December 8 and 30, 1936. Serge later wrote to Trotsky that he had secured a Belgian transit visa for him in early December. This was apparently to be used en route to France to visit his son. See Serge to Trotsky, January 10, 1937, in Cotterill, p. 99.

42. Lie, p. 78; Deutscher, p. 351; and *The New York Times,* January 10, 1937.
43. Trotsky notes, January 31, 1937.

Chapter 7

1. *The New York Times,* December 14, 1936.
2. Alain Dugrand, *Trotsky in Mexico* (Manchester: Carcanet, 1992), p. 16; Alan Wald, *James T. Farrell: The Revolutionary Socialist Years* (New York: New York University Press, 1978), p. 65; Isaac Deutscher, *The Prophet Outcast* (New York: Oxford University Press, 1963), pp. 356–57; and *Time,* January 25, 1937, p. 16.
3. Later that year, there was a purge of Jewish leaders in the Jewish autonomous region of Birobidjan. They were accused of being Japanese spies. See *Manchester Guardian Weekly,* November 5, 1937.
4. Letter from Dudley Collard, *The New Statesman and Nation,* February 6, 1937; Peter Deli, "The Image of the Russian Purges in the Daily Herald and the New Statesman," *Journal of Contemporary History,* Vol. 20, No. 2 (April 1985): 273; Trotsky supplemental statement on Malraux, January 1937, JDP 102/10/10; and *The New York Times,* February 17, 1937. After the show trial, Victor Serge was involved in a campaign to publicize Soviet political prisoners, and he asked Trotsky to provide available photos of them. See David Cotterill, ed., *The Serge-Trotsky Papers* (London: Pluto Press, 1994), p. 106.
5. *The New York Times,* January 10 and 24, 1937 and February 1, 1937; Preliminary Commission of Inquiry, *The Case of Leon Trotsky* (New York: Merit, 1937), p. x; Dmitri Volkogonov, *Trotsky: The Eternal Revolutionary* (New York: Free Press, 1996), pp. 372 and 386; and Deutscher, pp. 361–62.
6. Patrick Marnham, *Dreaming With His Eyes Open: A Life of Diego Rivera* (New York: Knopf, 1998), pp. 275–78; and Robert Warth, *Leon Trotsky* (Boston: Twayne Publishers, 1977), p. 172.
7. *The New York Times,* November 8, 1936. Cardenas, by admitting Trotsky, could have been trying to show the United States that he wasn't pro-Soviet, but this explanation is very questionable; the U.S. government was not pleased with Cardenas's decision, since it did not want Trotsky living so close to the American border. See Donald Herman, *The Comintern in Mexico* (Washington, DC: Public Affairs Press, 1974), p. 130.
8. M. S. Venkataramani, "Leon Trotsky's Adventure in American Radical Politics, 1935–7," *International Review of Social History* Part 1, Vol. IX (1964): 13 and *The New York Times,* December 19, 1936.
9. Herman, p. 63, and Joe Ashby, *Organized Labor and the Mexican Revolution Under Lazaro Cardenas* (Chapel Hill: University of North Carolina Press, 1963), p. 35.
10. *The New York Times,* November 19, 1936; Herman, p. 110; and Friedrich

Schuler, *Mexico Between Hitler and Roosevelt* (Albuquerque: University of New Mexico Press, 1988), pp. 57 and 60.

11. *The New York Times,* January 14, 1937.

12. *Inprecorr,* February 13, 1937, p. 192.

13. Herman, p. 109, and *Daily Worker,* December 17, 1936.

14. Herman, p. 132, and Ashby, pp. 40–41.

15. Ashby, pp. 11 and 19, and Robert E. Scott, *Mexican Government in Transition* (Urbana: University of Illinois Press, 1959), p. 130. During the early 1930s, while serving as Minister of National Development, Mugica had tried to make a deal for the import of Soviet technology, but it fell through when Mexico couldn't provide acceptable goods in return. See Schuler, p. 55.

16. Louis Adamic, *My America* (New York: Harper and Brothers, 1938), p. 85; New York hearings, July 26–27, 1937, Albert Glotzer Collection, Morris Library, Southern Illinois University, p. 113; Wald, p. 63; and Christopher Phelps, *Young Sidney Hook* (Ithaca, NY: Cornell University Press, 1997), pp. 142 and 152.

17. "Dear Friend" proclamation of the Provisional American Committee for the Defense of Leon Trotsky, October 22, 1936, CDS 07805, and "Declaration of Purposes by the American Committee for the Defense of Leon Trotsky," March 1, 1937, in Jo Ann Boydston, ed., *John Dewey: The Later Works, 1925–1953,* Vol. 11: 1935–1937 (Carbondale: Southern Illinois University Press, 1987), pp. 304–305.

18. Mauritz Hallgren, "Why I Resigned from the Trotsky Defense Committee" (New York: International Publishers, 1937), pp. 13–14 and *The New York Times,* January 10 and February 8, 1937.

19. Adamic, p. 85.

20. Phelps, p. 152 and Dewey to Hook, November 16, 1936, H-DC 143/1/4.

21. Author Mary McCarthy had said that Trotsky deserved a hearing, but claims that the committee had then listed her name without permission. See Sidney Hook, *Out of Step* (New York: Harper and Row, 1987), p. 533.

22. Dewey to Hook, March 12, 1937, H-DC 143/1/5; Hook, *Out of Step,* p. 226; Dewey to Hays, March 30, 1937, CDS 08772; and Adamic, p. 83.

23. Joseph Nedava, *Trotsky and the Jews* (Philadelphia: The Jewish Publication Society of America, 1972), pp. 186–87. When Trotsky died, Wise referred to his "heart of vindictiveness against the Jewish people" and described him as a "wayward son of his people."

24. Adamic, pp. 82–85, and Phelps, p. 154.

25. Gary Bullert, *The Politics of John Dewey* (Buffalo, NY: Prometheus, 1983), p. 134; Eugene Lyons, *The Red Decade* (New Rochelle, NY: Arlington House, 1970), p. 252; and David Dallin, *Soviet Espionage* (New Haven, CT: Yale University Press, 1955), p. 407.

26. *The Sunday Referee,* April 23, 1933; Phelps, p. 154; and Deutscher, p. 369.

27. Jean van Heijenoort, *With Trotsky in Exile* (Cambridge, MA: Harvard University Press, 1978), p. 143, and Deutscher, p. 368.

28. *The New York Times,* February 6, 1937.
29. Neal Wood, *Communism and British Intellectuals* (London: Victor Gollancz, 1959), p. 42; *The New Statesman and Nation,* January 30, 1937; and John Diggins, *Up From Communism* (New York: Harper and Row, 1975), p. 179. A letter to the British publication *The New Statesman and Nation,* September 12, 1936, commented that the August 1936 show trial had raised doubts about the Soviet system, as it showed that there were "desperate malcontents" and that force was the only way to effect a change in power.
30. Venkataramani, pp. 1, 4, and 11; Daniel Aaron, *Writers on the Left* (New York: Octagon, 1961), p. 447; *The New York Times,* February 15, 1937; Frank Warren, *The Socialist Party in the 1930's* (Bloomington: Indiana University Press, 1974), pp. 142–43; and W. A. Swanberg, *Norman Thomas: The Last Idealist* (New York: Charles Scribner's Sons, 1976), p. 218.
31. Kenneth Murphy, *Retreat From the Finland Station* (New York: Free Press, 1992), p. 115; Vadim Rogovin, *1937: Stalin's Year of Terror* (Oak Park, MI: Mehring Books, 1998), p. 306; Deutscher, pp. 366–67; Harvey Klehr, *The Heyday of American Communism* (New York: Basic Books, 1984), p. 364; and George Novack, *Pragmatism vs. Marxism* (New York: Pathfinder Press, 1975), p. 277.
32. Louis Budenz, *Men Without Faces* (New York: Harper and Brothers, 1950), p. 227; Aaron, p. 447; and Corliss Lamont, "Faith in the Soviet Union," *Soviet Russia Today,* Vol. 6, No. 6 (August 1937): 6. Lamont had taken some courses from Dewey at Columbia. See Hook, *Out of Step,* p. 237.
33. Bullert, p. 135; "Correspondence," *Southern Review,* Vol. III 1937–38, p. 199; Hook, *Out of Step,* p. 231; and Dewey to Bruce Bliven, May 26, 1937, H-DC 143/1/5.
34. *New Masses,* February 16, 1937; Phelps,, p. 154; Wald, pp. 59–60 and 67; Irving Howe and Lewis Coser, *The American Communist Party* (New York: Praeger, 1962), pp. 300–01; Richard G. Powers, *Not Without Honor: The History of American Anti-communism* (New Haven, CT: Yale University Press, 1998), p. 143; Lyons, p. 253; Klehr, p. 360; and *Soviet Russia Today,* March 1937. Suzanne La Follette condemned *The Nation* for condoning the January 1937 show trial while claiming impartiality. It was a "naive and disingenuous" attitude and was at variance with the magazine's approach toward German courts. See letter to editor of February 13, 1937.
35. Mauritz Hallgren, *The Tragic Fallacy* (New York: Knopf, 1937).
36. *The New York Times,* February 5, 1937, and Hallgren, "Why I Resigned."
37. *The New York Times,* February 6 and 8, 1937, and Novack to Dewey, February 15, 1937, CDS 08838. In November 1937, Hallgren attended a Carnegie Hall celebration of the twentieth anniversary of the Bolshevik revolution. See Lyons, p. 259.
38. "The Leon Trotsky Inquiry," in Boydston, p. 640; Wald, pp. 130–31; and *The New York Times,* December 27, 1936 and February 1, 1937.
39. *The New York Times,* February 1, 3, 4, 6, 10, and 11, 1937.

40. Hook, *Out of Step,* pp. 225–26; Phelps, p. 151; Novack to Trotsky, February 15, 1937, CDS 08838; Trotsky to Novack, March 9, 1937, CDS 08842; Deutscher, p. 372; Diggins, p. 180; and Novack to Trotsky, March 22, 1937, CDS 08839.

41. Novack to Trotsky, February 15, 1937; Hook, *Out of Step,* pp. 68 and 227; Wald, p. 68; and Kluger to Wolfe, February 27, 1937, CDS 08804.

42. Felix Morrow to Edward Ross, January 15, 1937, CDS 09168, and Stolberg speech at Mecca Temple, New York, May 9, 1937, Dewey VFM 98, Morris Library, Southern Illinois University.

43. Morrow to Ross, January 15, 1937; Novack to Trotsky, March 22, 1937; and *New Masses,* April 20, 1937, p. 28.

44. Hook, *Out of Step,* pp. 463–65, and Phelps, p. 153.

45. Novack to Trotsky, March 22, 1937.

46. Beard to Novack, September 26, 1936 and Beard to Thomas, March 27, 1937 in Harold Kirker and Burleigh Taylor Wilkins, "Beard, Becker and the Trotsky Inquiry," *American Quarterly,* Vol. XIII, No. 4 (Winter 1961): 518; Beard to Novack, March 19, 1937, JDP 102/10/10, and Beard to Dewey, March 22, 1937, CDS 08769.

47. Novack to Trotsky, March 22, 1937. Dewey invited Waldo Frank to join the subcommission going to Mexico. He replied that he was unavailable, but was willing to be a member of the full commission. Frank commented that Dewey's leadership assured a nonpartisan investigation. Note that Dewey was anxious to include Frank in order to illustrate that the commission was not anti-Soviet. See Dewey to Frank, March 22, 1937, CDS 07830 and Frank to Dewey, March 24, 1937, CDS 08770. For more on Frank's potential involvement, see Alan Trachtenberg, ed., *Memoirs of Waldo Frank* (Amherst: University of Massachusetts Press, 1973), p. 192, and Klehr, p. 361.

48. Hays to American Committee for the Defense of Leon Trotsky, March 29, 1937, AGHP 4/4.

49. Pritt to Hays, July 5, 1937, AGHP 4/4.

50. Dewey to Hays, March 30, 1937, CDS 08772, and Dewey and Finerty to Brodsky, March 30, 1937, CDS 08771.

51. Novack to Trotsky, March 22, 1937, and Novack to Ross, March 31, 1937, CDS 09173.

52. Hays to Pritt, June 1, 1937, and Pritt to Hays, June 15, 1937, AGHP 4/4.

53. Volkogonov, pp. 387–88; *The Case of Leon Trotsky,* p. 594; and *The New York Times,* April 4 and May 8, 1937.

54. Novack to Friend, March 22, 1937, CDS 08843.

55. Hook, *Out of Step,* pp. 227–28; Novack to Trotsky, March 22, 1937; Novack to Ross, March 22, 1937, CDS 09166; and Dewey to Ross, February 19, 1937, CDS 19170.

Chapter 8

1. James Farrell, "Dewey in Mexico," in Sidney Hook, ed., *John Dewey: Philosopher of Science and Freedom* (New York: Barnes and Noble, 1950), p. 357, and Alan Wald, *The New York Intellectuals* (Chapel Hill: University of North Carolina Press, 1987), p. 137.
2. Dewey statement of April 10, 1937, JDP 102/10/11.
3. *John Dewey's Impressions of Soviet Russia and the Revolutionary World* (New York: Teachers College of Columbia University, 1964), p. 111.
4. Gary Bullert, *The Politics of John Dewey* (Buffalo, NY: Prometheus, 1983), pp. 127–32; Agnes Meyer, "Significance of the Trotsky Trial: Interview With John Dewey," *International Conciliation,* no. 337 (1938): 50; and petition to Troyanovsky, January 18, 1935, AGHP 3/5.
5. Alain Dugrand, *Trotsky in Mexico* (Manchester: Carcanet, 1992), p. 25; Wald, p. 121; and George Novack, *Pragmatism vs. Marxism* (New York: Pathfinder Press, 1975), p. 13. The difference between Trotsky and Dewey may be summed up as Trotsky emphasizing justice and "the liberation of mankind," and Dewey stressing democracy and "self-realization." See Xenia Zeldin, "John Dewey's Role on the 1937 Trotsky Commission," *Public Affairs Quarterly,* Vol. 5, No. 4 (October 1991): 392–93.
6. Christopher Phelps, *Young Sidney Hook* (Ithaca, NY: Cornell University Press, 1997), pp. 156 and 159; Bullert, p. 135; John Dewey and Horace Kallen, "Statement of the American Committee for the Defense of Leon Trotsky," February 17, 1937 in Jo Ann Boydston, ed., *John Dewey: The Later Works, 1925–1953, Vol. 11: 1935–1937* (Carbondale: Illinois University Press, 1987), p. 598; and Sidney Hook, *Out of Step* (New York: Harper and Row, 1987), pp. 216–17.
7. Zeldin, p. 393; Bullert, p. 135; Meyer, pp. 53 and 55; *The New York Times,* April 7, 1937; and James Farrell, "Memories of John Dewey," November 5, 1965, Tape 13, JDP 102/81.
8. John Dewey, "Democracy is Radical," *Common Sense,* No. 6 (January 1937): 10–11, in Boydston, p. 298; and John Dewey, *Human Nature and Conduct* (New York: Modern Library, 1922), pp. 223, 229 and 236–37.
9. John Dewey, "Means and Ends," *New International,* No. 4 (August 1938), in Jo Ann Boydston, ed., *John Dewey: The Later Works, 1925–1953, Vol. 13: 1938–1939* (Carbondale: Southern Illinois University Press, 1991), p. 352.
10. Zeldin, pp. 388–89 and 392–93, and "Memories of John Dewey."
11. Alan Wald, "Memories of the John Dewey Commission: Forty Years Later," *Antioch Review,* No. 35 (Fall 1977); 443. See also Wald, *The New York Intellectuals,* p. 133. Soviet intelligence may have had an agent within Trotsky's entourage, a secretary named Maria de la Sierra. See Pavel and Anatoli Sudoplatov, *Special Tasks* (Boston: Little, Brown, 1994), p. 69.
12. Suzanne La Follette speech at Mecca Temple, New York, May 9, 1937;

Bertram Wolfe to Arthur and Rosemary Mizener, April 16, 1937, CDS 07855; Dewey VFM 98, JDP; and Farrell, "Dewey in Mexico," p. 361.

13. *The Nation,* May 1, 1937, and Selden Rodman, "Trotsky in the Kremlin: An Interview," *Common Sense,* No. 6 (December 1937) in Boydston, Vol. 13, p. 395. In a letter from Mexico to Roberta Lowitz Grant, whom he later married in 1946, Dewey revealed in reference to a fellow panel member: "I never cared much for Stolberg, but he has brains if he uses them, + doesn't try to get by on his own clever facility." Letter of April 4, 1937, JDP 102/10/11.

14. Carleton Beals, "The Fewer Outsiders the Better," *The Saturday Evening Post,* June 12, 1937, pp. 74 and 76.

15. Preliminary Commission of Inquiry, *The Case of Leon Trotsky,* (New York: Merit, 1937), pp. xxxv and 6.

16. Alan Spitzer, "John Dewey, the Trial of Leon Trotsky and the Search for Historical Truth," *History and Theory,* Vol. XXIX, No. 1 (1990): 21; Beals, p. 76; Wald, "Memories of the John Dewey Commission," p. 450; *The New York Times,* April 6 and 13, 1937; Dewey to Hook, August 14, 1937, H-DC 143/1/5; Wald, *The New York Intellectuals,* p. 138; and *Manchester Guardian Weekly,* November 5, 1937.

17. Kingsley Martin in *The New Statesman and Nation,* April 10, 1937.

18. Stolberg speech at Mecca Temple, New York, May 9, 1937; *The New York Times,* April 5, 1937; and Dewey VFM 98.

19. Farrell, "Memories of John Dewey."

20. Dewey to Roberta Lowitz Grant, April 6 and 18, 1937, JDP 102/10/11.

21. Wald, "Memories of the John Dewey Commission," p. 451.

22. Albert Glotzer, *Trotsky: Memoir and Critique* (Buffalo, NY: Prometheus, 1989), p. 267; John Britton, *Carleton Beals: A Radical Journalist in Latin America* (Albuquerque: University of New Mexico Press, 1987), pp. 166–68; and "Correspondence," *Southern Review,* Vol. III (1937–38): 203–205.

23. "Correspondence," p. 204; Beals, p. 77; La Follette, May 9, 1937; Britton, p. 172; and *The Case of Leon Trotsky,* p. 67.

24. La Follette, May 9, 1937; Beals, pp. 74 and 77; Wolfe to the Mizeners, April 16, 1937; and Rodman, p. 395.

25. Beals, pp. 76–77; *The Case of Leon Trotsky,* p. 52; Britton, p. 171; and *The New York Times,* April 11, 1937.

26. Beals, p. 76; *New Masses,* April 27, 1937, p. 7; and Britton, pp. 171–72.

27. *The Case of Leon Trotsky,* pp. xxxv and 412–15; Robert Warth, *Leon Trotsky* (Boston: Twayne Publishers, 1977), p. 174; *Brooklyn Eagle,* April 19, 1937; La Follette, May 9, 1937; Beals statement, April 22, 1937, JDP 102/10/11; and Beals, "The Fewer Outsiders," p. 78.

28. *Brooklyn Eagle,* April 19, 1937; Beals, pp. 77–78; Dewey to "To whom it may concern," April 19, 1937, CDS 07854; Dewey to Roberta Lowitz Grant, undated, JDP 102/10/10; La Follette, May 9, 1937; *New Masses,*

April 27, 1937, p. 10; and John Dewey, "In Defense of the Mexican Hearings," *Common Sense,* No. 7 (1938), in Boydston, Vol. 13, p. 347.

29. *The Case of Leon Trotsky,* pp. 416–17; *Brooklyn Eagle,* April 19, 1937; and *The New York Times,* April 18 and 19, 1937.

30. Beals, p. 78; and *The New York Times,* April 19 and 24, 1937.

31. "Correspondence," pp. 204 and 206–207; *The Case of Leon Trotsky,* p. 67; and Beals to Calverton, April 11, 1938 in Britton, p. 184. At the time of Beals's remark about Trotsky, he was angered that Trotsky had secured his removal as a contributing editor to *Modern Monthly.* The editor, Victor Calverton, had asked Trotsky to write an article for his publication and Trotsky had responded that he would if Beals was sacked. Calverton complied. See Britton, pp. 182–83. In regard to other members of the subcommission, Beals considered La Follette and Stolberg to be committed Trotskyists. He maintained that he appreciated Dewey's honesty but not his judgment. See Beals's statement, April 22, 1937; "Correspondence," p. 206; Beals to Calverton, May 22, 1937 in Britton, p. 181; and Beals, "The Fewer Outsiders," pp. 22–24 and 78.

32. *The New York Times,* April 18 and May 26, 1937; Beals, p. 78; and Phelps, p. 161. Pearl Kluger maintained that Beals was directly or indirectly under Soviet influence. See letter to Harold Robert Isaacs, April 15, 1937, CDS 08806.

33. Dewey to Roberta Lowitz Grant, undated, JDP 102/10/10; Glotzer, p. 267; and Dewey to Hook, June 14, 1937, H-DC 143/1/5.

34. *St. Louis Star-Times,* April 21, 1937, and Dewey to Alex Gumberg, May 12, 1937, JDP 102/10/11.

35. *The New York Times,* May 8 and 10, 1937.

36. Novack to Friend, March 22, 1937, and *The New York Times,* April 13, 1937.

37. Britton, pp. 184–85.

38. Dewey to Hook, June 12 and 14, 1937, H-DC 143/1/5; and La Follette to Dewey, June 15 and 26 1937, JDP 102/11/1. Beals remained a mysterious figure on the political left. His activities generated an investigation by the Federal Bureau of Investigation, which determined that he had been affiliated with front organizations, had never been a member of the Communist Party, and was not a threat to American security. See Britton, p. 208.

39. *The New York Times,* April 16, 1937.

Chapter 9

1. La Follette to Commission members, July 19, 1937, JDP 102/11/2 and "Correspondence," *Southern Review,* Vol. III (1937–38):204.

2. Dewey to Roberta Lowitz Grant, June 18, 1937, CDS 06655.

3. Isaac Deutscher, *The Prophet Outcast* (New York: Oxford University Press, 1963), p. 382. Robert Conquest, a leading authority on the Soviet purges,

later wrote that the Dewey Commission had been "most judicious and meticulous," but that facts it uncovered "went unheard among large sections of well-informed people." See *The Great Terror: The Reassessment* (London: Hutchinson, 1990), p. 465.

4. Max Radin, "The Moscow Trials: A Legal View," *Foreign Affairs*, Vol. 16, No. 1 (October 1937): 76.

5. Albert Glotzer, *Trotsky: Memoir and Critique* (Buffalo, NY: Prometheus, 1989), p. 269, and Dewey to Roberta Lowitz Grant, April 7, 1937, JDP 102/10/11. *The New York Times* had a second correspondent at the hearings, Lorine Pruett, who was impressed by Trotsky. See her April 17 article. The most negative account by *The New York Times* appeared on April 5, without a byline. It predicted that the hearings would probably be a "whitewashing" of Trotsky. Note that the chief *New York Times* correspondent covering the Moscow trials, Walter Duranty, was sympathetic to the Soviet position. Pearl Kluger happily greeted his replacement in 1938. See Kluger to Joe Harrison, March 14, 1938, CDS 08827.

6. *The New York Times*, April 23, and May 10, 1937, and *The Washington Post, April 23, 1937*.

7. Eugene Lyons, *The Red Decade* (New Rochelle, NY: Arlington House, 1970), pp. 327 and 336, and *The New Republic*, January 12, 1938.

8. Daniel Aaron, *Writers on the Left* (New York: Octagon, 1961), pp. 358–59 and 443; Frank Warren, *The Socialist Party in the 1930's* (Bloomington: Indiana University Press, 1974), p. 145; and *The New Republic*, May 12, 1937. Solow wrote that Frank had told him that he did not believe in Trotsky's guilt, nor in Stalin's. See Solow to Dewey, June 2, 1937, JDP 102/11/1.

9. *Time*, May 17, 1937. p. 20.

10. Sidney Hook, *Out of Step* (New York: Harper and Row, 1987), p. 232; Gary Bullert, *The Politics of John Dewey* (Buffalo, NY: Prometheus, 1983), p. 136; and Aaron, p. 338.

11. Dewey to Cowley, June 2, 1937, H-DC 143/1/5.

12. Cowley to Dewey, June 4, 1937, H-DC 143/1/5.

13. "The Leon Trotsky Inquiry," in Jo Ann Boydston, ed., *John Dewey: The Later Works, 1925–1953*, Vol. II: 1935–1937 (Carbondale: Southern Illinois University Press, 1987), p. 646; Gumberg to Dewey, May 11, 1937 and Dewey to Gumberg, May 12, 1937, JDP 102/10/11.

14. *The Washington Post*, December 19, 1937, and Agnes Meyer, "Significance of the Trotsky Trial: Interview with John Dewey," *International Conciliation*, No. 337 (1938): 55–59.

15. Kluger to Trotsky, October 1, 1937, CDS 08810; La Follette, July 19, 1937; and Dewey to Barnes, May 8, 1937, CDS 04372.

16. Dewey to Hook, August 14, 1937, H-DC 143/1/5, and Novack to Dewey and all commission members, April 28, 1937, CDS 04379. La Follette wrote to Trotsky that the committee was pressuring the commission, and

the commission would possibly have to dissociate itself. See letter of May 18, 1937, CDS 08789.

17. Glotzer, p. 258; *The New York Times,* June 11, 1937; M. S. Venkataramani, "Leon Trotsky's Adventure in American Radical Politics, 1935–7," *International Review of Social History,* Vol. IX (1964): 24–25; and Kluger to Dewey, October 1, 1937.

18. *Not Guilty* (New York: Monad Press, 1972), p. 7; Frank Demby to La Follette, July 18, 1937, JDP 102/11/2; and La Follette to Dewey, July 28, 1937, JDP 102/11/2. Many Europeans who wanted to assist research efforts by the commission were intimidated once their names became public. See Earl Balch to Dewey, June 22, 1937, JDP 102/11/1.

19. *Not Guilty,* p. 396, and New York hearings, Albert Glotzer Collection, 153/1/4, Morris Library, Southern Illinois University. One of the witnesses in New York feared retaliation against relatives in the Soviet Union, so he was permitted to go through the transcript of his session to determine what testimony could safely be made public. See La Follette to Dewey, July 28, 1937.

20. "The Leon Trotsky Inquiry," p. 647; Kluger to Trotsky, October 1, 1937; Solow to Dewey, June 16, 1937, JDP 102/11/1; Deutscher, p. 393; and Peter Deli, "The Image of the Russian Purges in The Daily Herald and The New Statesman," *Journal of Contemporary History,* Vol. 20, No. 2 (April 1985): 277. *The Times Literary Supplement,* a British publication, favorably reviewed *The Case of Leon Trotsky* on November 13, 1937. It cited Dewey's fairness and impartiality at the hearings, and Trotsky's successful rebuttal of Moscow show trial testimony. Edmund Wilson later wrote in the December 11 issue of *The Nation:* "The report of the Trotsky Commission is a remarkably interesting document which makes one realize the inadequacy, if not frivolity, of the newspaper accounts of the Mexican hearings."

21. Deutscher, p. 436.

22. *Not Guilty,* pp. xvii, 21, 361, and 394 and "The Leon Trotsky Inquiry," p. 648.

23. Sidney Hook, "Corliss Lamont: 'Friend of the G.P.U.'," *Modern Monthly,* Vol. X, No. 11 (March 1938): 5, and *The New York Times,* December 14 and 15, 1937. *The New York Times* coverage of the debate devoted more space to Dewey than to Lamont.

24. Hook, *Out of Step,* p. 238, and press release on radio address, December 13, 1937 in Boydston, p. 328.

25. Dewey to Barnes, December 22, 1937, CDS 04391 and *The Nation,* December 11 and 25, 1937 and July 30, 1938.

26. *The New York Times,* December 14, 1937; Trotsky to Dewey, July 15, 1938, JDP 102/11/5; and *Manchester Guardian Weekly,* November 5, 1937. Trotsky predicted that Stalin would fall from power but would not be replaced by "bourgeois democracy."

27. *The New York Times,* December 16, 1937.

28. George Novack, *Pragmatism vs. Marxism* (New York: Pathfinder Press, 1975), p. 278.

29. Christopher Andrew and Vasili Mitrokhin, *The Sword and the Shield* (New York: Basic Books, 1999), pp. 75–76, and Pavel and Anatoli Sudoplatov, *Special Tasks* (Boston: Little, Brown, 1994), p. 82.

30. *The New York Times,* March 3, 1938.

31. See David Clay Lodge, *Europe's Path in the 1930's* (New York: W. W. Norton, 1990), p. 315. In a March 14, 1938 letter to Joe Hansen, Pearl Kluger claimed that the more negative press reaction to charges made at the third show trial was the result of the commission's findings. See CDS 08827.

32. Hook, *Out of Step,* p. 238; Lamont to Dewey, March 5, 1938 and Dewey to Lamont, March 5, 1938, JDP 102/11/5; Lamont to Dewey, May 3, 1938, CDS 06717; and Dewey to Frank Trager, November 16, 1939, CDS 06092. Also in 1939, Dewey helped establish the Committee for Cultural Freedom—an effort to confront totalitarianism.

33. Andrew and Mitrokhin, p. 76; Dmitri Volkogonov, *Trotsky: The Eternal Revolutionary* (New York: Free Press, 1996), p. 401; Paolo Spriano, *Stalin and the European Communists* (London: Verso, 1985), p. 61; and Deutscher, pp. 422–24.

34. *Manchester Guardian Weekly,* April 30, 1937; Sudoplatov, p. 67; and Deutscher, p. 508. For a full account of the Trotsky assassination plot, see Isaac Don Levine, *The Mind of an Assassin* (New York: New American Library, 1959).

35. Spriano, p. 56.

36. Farrell to Dewey, May 13, 1937, JDP 102/10/11.

37. *The New Republic,* April 8, 1936 as presented in Henry Dan Piper, ed., *Think Back on Us . . . : A Contemporary Chronicle of the 1930's by Malcolm Cowley* (Carbondale: Southern Illinois University Press, 1967), pp. 111–12.

Chapter 10

1. Arnold Toynbee, "A Man Who Stood His Ground," http://www.home-users.prestel.co.uk/littleton/br7005at.htm.

2. Robert Scheer, "Lord Russell," *Ramparts,* Vol. 5, No. 11 (May 1967): 19, and Horace Thayer, "Two Theories of Truth: Relation Between Theories of Dewey and Russell," *The Journal of Philosophy,* Vol. XLIV, No. 19 (September 11, 1947): 516–17.

3. Paul Johnson, *Intellectuals* (New York: Harper and Row, 1988), pp. 205–206, and 1948 letter to Dr. Marseille, published in *The New Leader,* October 23, 1967, p. 35. Russell wrote in regard to communists: "We hate them because we fear them and they threaten us." See Bertrand Russell, "The Springs of Human Action," March 1952 in Reo Christenson, and

Robert McWilliams, eds., *Voice of the People* (New York: McGraw-Hill, 1962), p. 79.

4. Scheer, p. 20 and Alan Ryan, *Bertrand Russell: A Political Life* (New York: Hill and Wang, 1988), pp. 188–89, 197, and 199.

5. Caroline Moorehead, *Bertrand Russell: A Life* (New York: Viking, 1993), pp. 516 and 520.

6. Ralph Miliband TV interview with Russell, "War and Peace," TWW, 1966, Morris Library, Southern Illinois University, Tape 930 and Russell, "The Springs of Human Action," p. 79.

7. Erich Fromm, "Prophets and Priests," in Ralph Schoenman, ed., *Bertrand Russell: Philosopher of the Century* (Boston: Little, Brown, 1967), p. 79.

8. Moorehead, p. 521 and Russell letter to Lyndon Johnson, February 9, 1965, White House Central File, Box 339, Name File (Russell), LBJL.

9. Russell to Wilson, February 9, 1965 and Wilson to Russell, February 16, 1965, BRA 9.53/320.

10. Home Secretary Frank Soskice to Russell, August 31 and September 20, 1965 BRA 10.12/378; Wilson's office to Russell, September 1, 1965 and Russell press release, September 2, 1965, BRA 9.53/320 (UK); and Ralph Schoenman to scientist and peace activist Joseph Needham, October 12, 1965, BRA 10.12/378.

11. Undated report on Schoenman's meetings with NLF representatives, BRA 10.5/375.

12. As argued by political theorist and Russell biographer Alan Ryan, Russell's political views–often enunciated by Schoenman—came to be influenced by Schoenman. This generated intellectually weak and contradictory positions, and the issuing of questionable facts based on unreliable sources. For Ryan: "Read in the mass, the products of what one might call 'the Schoenman years' are alarming; the proportion of abuse to argument is very high." See Ryan, p. 174.

13. Ronald Clark, *The Life of Bertrand Russell* (New York: Knopf, 1975), p. 623.

14. M. S. Arnoni editorial, written September 4, 1965, *Minority of One,* October 1965; Clark, p. 624; and "UN Secondo Tribunale Per I Crimini Di Guerra?," *Il Paese Oggi,* March 1966, BRA C66.02a. Another advocate of a tribunal was Robin Blackburn of *The New Left Review.* See Ken Coates's letter to authors, September 15, 1999.

15. David Horowitz, *Radical Son* (New York: Free Press, 1997), pp. 146–48.

16. Russell letters of June 16, 1966, BRA 10.1/371.

17. John V. Crangle, "Legal Theories of the Nuremberg and Stockholm–Roskilde Tribunals," *Proceedings of the South Carolina Historical Association* (Columbia, 1990):64; John Duffett, ed., *Against the Crime of Silence* (New York: Simon and Schuster, 1970), p. 4; *New Left Notes,* August 24, 1966, p. 17; and Russell letter to *The Daily Telegraph,* September 30, 1966.

18. Horowitz, p. 48; Clark, pp. 625–26; and Peter Weiss, "Vietnam," *Dagens Nyheter,* August 2, 1966.

19. *New Left Notes,* p. 17; *Dawn* (Karachi), June 9, 1966; and Miliband interview.

20. *Minority of One,* September 1966. Schoenman referred to American leaders as "Hitlers." See Horowitz, pp. 146–47.

21. Ralph Schoenman, "Report From North Vietnam," April 11, 1966, http:www.homeusers.prestel.co.uk/littleton/br67wcvd.htm, p. 1; Russell to Ho, undated 1966, and November 1966 document on visit by Schoenman and Stetler, BRA 10.5/375.

22. Moorehead, p. 522; *Dawn* (Karachi), June 9, 1966; and Bertrand Russell, *War Crimes in Vietnam* (London: Allen and Unwin, 1967), chapter 10.

23. Moorehead, p. 523; report on Schoenman's November 2, 1966 meeting with NLF in Phnom Penh and Russell to Nguyen Huu Tho, July 20, 1966, BRA 10.5/375. An August 10, 1966 letter from Stetler to Peter Weiss suggests that American POWs in Vietnam should testify in the presence of a tribunal member. See BRA 10.1/371.

24. Russell to Ho, July 20, 1966.

25. Russell to Ho, July 20, 1966.

26. Russell to Nguyen Van Sao, October 25, 1966, BRA 10.5/375.

27. Clark, p. 646 and Schoenman to Peter Lorentzon, December 7, 1965, BRA 9.53/320 (Sweden). Although sympathetic to the Chinese position on wars of national liberation, Schoenman was admonished by Prime Minister Zhou Enlai for crude and insulting behavior during a visit to Beijing. See Moorehead, p. 533.

28. Ryan, p. 205 and *The Spectator,* July 21, 1966.

29. Russell to Kosygin, September 19, 1966, and December 16, 1966, and undated response prepared on behalf of Kosygin, BRA 9.54/320.

30. Moorehead, pp. 529 and 534 and Ralph Schoenman, "Bertrand Russell and the Peace Movement," in George Nakhnikian, ed., *Bertrand Russell's Philosophy* (London: Duckworth, 1974), p. 250.

31. Russell review of Isaac Deutscher's *The Prophet Armed, The Observer,* March 21, 1954.

32. Telephone interview with David Horowitz, May 18, 1999; Scheer, pp. 22–23; *The New York Times,* May 2, 1967; and Ken Coates's letter to authors, March 31, 2000. Although Schoenman was attracted to Trotskyism, he did not belong to any Trotskyist political party and, according to Coates, "was kept at arm's length."

33. Miliband interview; Charles DeBenedetti, *An American Ordeal: The Antiwar Movement of the Vietnam Era* (Syracuse, NY: Syracuse University Press, 1990), p. 158; and *World Outlook,* October 14, 1966, p. 27.

34. Russell to Simone de Beauvoir, September 3, 1966, BRA 9.70/340 (1966).

35. Nancy Zaroulis and Gerald Sullivan, *Who Spoke Up?: American Protests Against the War in Vietnam 1963–1975* (New York: Holt, Rinehart, and Winston, 1984), p. 225, and *The New York Times,* September 16, 1965, March 17, 1966 and March 21, 1967. Mark Lane was a link between the

Mitchell case and Russell. Lane and Russell had earlier been in contact in regard to Lane's attacks on the Warren Commission report on the Kennedy assassination.

36. "Joint Declaration on the Mitchell Case," September 12, 1966, BRA C66.25; Russell to Weiss and Russell to Isaac Deutscher, September 3, 1966, BRA 9.38/315; and Russell cable to Mitchell, February 23, 1967, BRA 9.70/340 (1967).

37. Russell to Nguyen Van Hieu, January 25, 1966 and Russell to Ho Chi Minh, January 25, 1966, BRA 10.5/3.75.

38. Schoenman to Pham Van Dong, March 3, 1966, BRA 10.5/375 and Schoenman to Gunther Anders, April 7, 1967, BRA 10.2/371.

39. Interview with Jean-Paul Sartre, "Crimes in Vietnam?," *Liberation,* vol. XI, no. 10 (January 1967):17.

Chapter 11

1. John Duffett, ed., *Against the Crime of Silence* (New York: Simon and Schuster, 1970), p. 15.

2. Bertrand Russell Peace Foundation, "Postscript: To the Conscience of Mankind," September 1966, BRA C66.24; Russell to Alexander von Winthofen, September 8, 1966, BRA 10.10/377; Russell to Ali Kasuri, March 1, 1967, BRA 10.1/371; and "Rules," November 1966, BRA 10.15/384.

3. Russell to Dedijer, June 16 and August 18, 1966, BRA 10.1/371 and Vladimir Dedijer, "Crimes in Vietnam?," *Liberation,* Vol. XI, No. 10 (January 1967): 18.

4. Simone de Beauvoir, *All Said and Done* (New York: Paragon House, 1993), pp. 339–40; Deirdre Bair, *Simone de Beauvoir: A Biography* (New York: Summit, 1990), p. 520; and Claude Francis and Fernande Gontier, *Simone de Beauvoir: A Life, a Love Story* (New York: St. Martin's, 1987), p. 321.

5. Weiss to Schoenman, September 14, 1966, BRA 10.1/371.

6. Carmichael to Russell, July 15, 1966, BRA 10.1/371, and *The Washington Post,* August 14, 1966.

7. Tynan to Russell, November 7, 1966; Mumford to Russell, August 16, 1966; Russell to Mumford, October 21, 1966; and Miller to Russell, November 2, 1966, BRA 10.3/372. Mumford thought that the tribunal members were too leftist and that conservatives and clergymen should be appointed.

8. Stone to Russell, March 11, 1967; Marcuse to Russell, February 24, 1967; and Russell to Marcuse, March 10, 1967, BRA 10.3/372.

9. Sartre to Russell, April 14, 1967; Russell to tribunal members, April 18, 1967; and Russell to Hernandez, April 18, 1967, BRA 10.2/371.

10. *Le Figaro* as cited in Walt Rostow memo to Lyndon Johnson, May 5, 1967,

National Security File, box 27, file 16 and Ronald Clark, *The Life of Bertrand Russell* (New York: Knopf, 1975), p. 624.

11. Telephone interview with David Horowitz, May 18, 1999 and Deutscher to Russell, June 18, 1966, BRA 10.1/371.

12. Mumford to Russell, August 16, 1966 and Anders to Russell, September 27, 1966, BRA 10.1/371. Anders's letter refers to Russell's letters of September 15 and 22.

13. Russell interview, *The Toronto Star,* October 21, 1966; "Postscript;" and Russell to Weiss, September 22, 1966, disc supplied by Nicholas Griffin, BRA 10.1/371.

14. Anders to Russell, March 8, 1967, BRA 10.2/371; and Anders to tribunal members, January 18, 1967, BRA and Russell to Anders, October 21, 1966, BRA 10.1/371. Dave Dellinger, an American antiwar activist who became a tribunal member, compared American attitudes toward Vietnam to those of Germans in the 1930s who at first had little "criminality of intent" but who believed in supporting state goals. See "Report From the Tribunal," *Liberation,* Vol. XII, No. 2 (April 1967): 7.

15. David Horowitz, *Radical Son* (New York: Free Press, 1997), p. 148, and *Newsweek,* May 15, 1967, pp. 44 and 60. Russell did not invite Jackson to be a tribunal member because the retired judge no longer endorsed the Nuremberg precedent. Haika Grossman, who had commanded the Jewish resistance in the Bialystok Ghetto, was considered as a tribunal member, but did not serve, as there was a dispute over the lateness of the attempted appointment. Also, three Israeli judges from the 1961 trial of Adolf Eichmann were invited as tribunal observers. See Sartre report, April 11, 1967, BRA 10.2/371.

16. *The New York Times,* March 12, 1967, and *Newsweek,* September 12, 1966, p. 2. Note that the charge of genocide investigated by the Russell Tribunal was based on the post-Nuremberg Genocide Convention of 1948.

17. Deutscher to Russell, September 22, 1966 and Russell to Deutscher, September 30, 1966, BRA 10.1/371.

18. Mumford to Russell, August 16, 1966, BRA 10.3/372.

19. Russell to Johnson, August 25, 1966, White House Central File, Name File (Russell), Box 339, LBJL; Duffett, pp. 18–20; *National Guardian,* September 17, 1966; and "Postscript."

20. Leonard Marks to Bill Moyers, August 25, 1966, Confidential File, Name file, Box 150, LBJL. Marks was director of the United States Information Agency; Moyers was Johnson's chief of staff.

21. Telephone conversation between Johnson and U.N. Ambassador Arthur Goldberg, December 31, 1966, Recordings and Transcripts, Tape F6612.04, PNO 3, LBJL.

22. Nancy Zaroulis and Gerald Sullivan, *Who Spoke Up?: American Protests Against the War in Vietnam 1963–1975* (New York: Holt, Rinehart, and Winston, 1984), p. 66, and Sidney Lens, *Unrepentant Radical* (Boston: Beacon Press, 1980), p. 310. Dave Dellinger was to be a participant in the first

American mission to North Vietnam, but family considerations led him to forgo the trip. He then participated in another investigatory mission in October 1966. Interview with Dave Dellinger, June 15, 2000 and "North Vietnam: Executive Report," in Dave Dellinger, *Revolutionary Nonviolence* (Indianapolis: Bobbs-Merrill, 1970), p. 53.

23. Lynd interview in James Finn, *Protest: Pacifism and Politics* (New York: Random House, 1967), pp. 225 and 242–43.

24. Finn, p. 225.

25. Staughton Lynd, "The War Crimes Tribunal: A Dissent," *Liberation*. Vol. XII, Nos. 9–10 (December 1967–January 1968): 76; Lynd to Russell, January 13, 1867, BRA 10.3/372; Horowitz, *Radical Son,* p. 149; and Caroline Moorehead, *Bertrand Russell: A Life (*New York: Viking, 1993), p. 524. Note that Lynd's close friend Dave Dellinger, who was the editor of *Liberation,* agreed to be a tribunal member and that Lynd encouraged Carl Oglesby to serve as well, because the tribunal wanted some participation from Students for a Democratic Society. Telephone interview with Carl Oglesby, April 25, 2000.

26. Lynd, "The War Crimes Tribunal," p. 77, and Schoenman to Lynd, February 15 and March 16, 1967, BRA 10.3/372.

27. Wicken to Russell, October 19, 1966; Schoenman to Wicken, October 26, 1966; Russell to Nyerere (not sent), October 27, 1966; and Wicken to Schoenman, November 1, 1966, BRA 9.53/320 (Tanzania). One African leader, former Ghanaian president Kwame Nkrumah, did not withdraw his BRPF sponsorship.

28. Nyerere press release, November 14, 1966; Russell to Nyerere, November 10 and 25, 1966; Nyerere to Russell, November 17, 1966; and Schoenman to Wicken, December 8, 1966, BRA 9.53/320 (Tanzania).

29. Anders to Russell, September 10, 1966, BRA 10.1/371.

30. Russell to de Beauvoir, September 15, 1966; Deutscher to Russell, September 22, 1966; Russell to Deutscher, October 5, 1966, BRA 10.1/371; and disc from Griffin.

31. Russell to Deutscher, September 30, 1966 and early October undated Russell–Deutscher correspondence, BRA 10.1/371.

32. Bertrand Russell, *War Crimes in Vietnam* (London: Allen & Unwin, 1967), p. 126; agenda, BRA 10.3/372; transcript, BRA 10.15/384; rules, BRA 10.5/374; and Samuel Rosenwein, "International War Crimes Tribunal: Stockholm Session," *The National Lawyers Guild Practitioner,* Vol. 26, No. 4 (Fall 1967): 142.

33. Rosenwein, p. 142; transcript; and H. A. DeWeerd, "Lord Russell's War Crimes Tribunal," RAND Corporation, P-3561,March 1967, p. 10.

34. Lelio Basso, "Inaugural Discourse," in William Jerman, ed., *Repression in Latin America* (Nottingham: Spokesman Books, 1975), p. 3; *Evening Standard,* November 16, 1966; *Daily Mirror,* November 17, 1966; and Bertrand Russell, *The Autobiography of Bertrand Russell,* Vol. III, 1944–1967 (Lon-

don: Allen and Unwin, 1969), pp. 215–16. Marti had written: "He who witnesses a crime in silence, commits it." When Russell departed, Schoenman presided over the remainder of the conference.

35. David Horowitz, "The Final Passion," 1977, http://www.homeusers.prestel.co.uk/littleton/br7005dh.htm, p. 4, and Bernard Levin, *The New York Times Magazine,* February 19, 1967, p. 24.

36. Russell to Dedijer, February 14, 1967; Schoenman to Sartre, December 31, 1966; and Schoenman to Dedijer, January 6, 1967, BRA 10.1/371; Russell to tribunal members, April 26, 1967, BRA 10.2/371; and de Beauvoir, pp. 340–41.

37. Claude Cadart to Schoenman, December 19, 1966, BRA 10.5/374 and Dedijer in *Peace News,* November 25, 1966.

38. Schoenman to Dellinger, December 23, 1966, BRA 10.1/371; Schoenman to Russell Stetler, April 12, 1967; and Chris Farley memorandum, March 15, 1967, BRA 10.3/372. Donnell Boardman, who had agreed to serve on an investigating team but then changed his mind, sent a letter to Russell attacking Schoenman. Boardman had sought U.S. State Department approval for his mission to North Vietnam; his failure to receive it may have influenced his decision not to go. See Boardman to Russell, March 19, 1967 and Russell to Kathleen Lonsdale, April 14, 1967, BRA 10.3/372. Farley had been suspicious of Boardman from the start, and didn't want him to go to Vietnam. He described Boardman as "the wooliest sort of liberal who will doubtless create difficulties for us when he goes back to the States." See March 15 Farley memorandum.

39. Stokely Carmichael also pressed for a tribunal session in the United States, but he realized that visas would probably be denied to foreign tribunal members. He therefore suggested that members visit the United States for ostensible speaking engagements, and then announce the tribunal once they were in the United States with valid visas. See Russell to Anders, February 28, 1967, BRA 10.1/371.

40. Horowitz, "The Final Passion," pp. 1–2.

41. Clark, p. 627 and Sartre report, April 11, 1967, BRA 10.2/371.

42. On Russell's intention to hold the first session in Paris, see Russell to Jean-Marie Vincent, July 7, 1966, BRA 10.5/374. See also Russell to de Gaulle, November 15, 1966, BRA 9.44/320 (France).

43. *The Times,* March 25, 1967.

44. *The New York Times,* March 23 and 26, April 12, 18, and 23, 1967 and cable AmEmb Paris to SecSt, April 12, 1967, NSF Country File France, Paris 15970, document 41, box 173, LBJL.

45. *The New York Times,* January 12 and April 21, 1967, and statement by French tribunal committee, undated, BRA 10.15/384.

46. Annie Cohen-Solal, *Sartre: A Life* (New York: Pantheon, 1987), p. 456 and Duffett, pp. 27–28. De Gaulle's letter to Sartre was followed by a rejection issued by the prefect of police. See de Beauvoir, p. 341.

47. *The Washington Post,* August 14, 1966, and cable from "Chip" Bohlen
    AmEmb to SecSt, December 29, 1966, NSF, Country File France, Paris
    9736, document 9, box 173, LBJL.
48. Russell to Roy Jenkins, November 25, 1966; Russell to Wilson, February
    4, 1967; and Wilson to Russell, March 14, 1967, BRA 9.53/320 (UK); and
    Duffett, pp. 20–21.
49. Russell to Wilson, March 27, 1967 and Wilson to Russell, April 17, 1967,
    BRA 9.53/320. Russell wrote to Wilson again, citing a newspaper article
    that referred to a Home Office decision that there would not be "a blanket
    exclusion of a whole category of people (e.g., those connected with the
    Russell Tribunal)." Russell asserted that a tribunal in Britain would there-
    fore be possible. Wilson replied that no such intention had been suggested
    to the Home Office, and that the March 14 letter refusing visas to North
    Vietnamese witnesses was still valid. See Russell to Wilson, May 30, 1967
    and Wilson to Russell, June 14, 1967, BRA 9.53/320 (UK).
50. Deutscher to Russell, February 14, 1967, BRA 10.1/371, and *The New
    York Times,* May 2, 1967.
51. Russell to Hans-Peter Tschudi, November 25, 1966, and Office of the
    Chancellor of the Confederation to Russell, February 27, 1967, BRA
    9.53/320; and Deirdre Griswold to Ellen Brun, from British to Danish
    committees, April 11, 1967, BRA 10.10/377.
52. *The New York Times,* March 30, 1967.
53. Ken Coates's letter to authors, September 15, 1999.

Chapter 12

1. *The New York Times,* May 2, 1967.
2. Schoenman to Dr. Pham Ngoc Thach, Minister of Health of North Vietnam, September 27, 1967, BRA 10.6/375.
3. On May 23, Baldwin was kept in custody for ninety minutes on arrival at
   London's airport. The Home Office issued the instruction as it claimed that
   his visit was related to the tribunal, and therefore didn't want to permit his
   entry. This decision was quickly reversed once Baldwin was able to
   demonstrate that he was to there meet with his publisher. See *The New
   York Times,* June 4, 1967.
4. Dave Dellinger, *From Yale to Jail* (New York: Pantheon, 1993), p. 244;
   interview with Julius Lester, March 15, 2000; and interview with Dave
   Dellinger, June 15, 2000.
5. *Ekstra Bladet,* November 18, 1967, and Jean-Paul Sartre, Imperialist Morality," *New Left Review,* No. 41 (January–February 1967): 5–6 and 9.
6. Samuel Rosenwein, "International War Crimes Tribunal: Stockholm Session," *The National Lawyers Guild Practitioner,* Vol. 27, No. 1 (Winter
   1968): 29; Robert Scheer, Lord Russell," *Ramparts,* Vol. 5, No. 11 (May
   1967): 21–22; and "Interview with Jean-Paul Sartre: Crimes in Vietnam?,"

Liberation, Vol. XI, No. 10 (January 1967): 15. Note that the application of international law to Vietnam was dependent to some degree on whether North and South Vietnam constituted two separate states. See Guenther Lewy, *America in Vietnam* (Oxford: Oxford University Press, 1978), p. 225.

7. *The New York Times,* May 3, 1967.

8. Sartre, "Imperialist Morality," p. 5, and *Expressen,* May 6, 1967.

9. Bertrand Russell, *War Crimes in Vietnam* (London: Allen & Unwin, 1967), p. 127; *Svenska Dagbladet,* April 28, 1967; and Sunday Telegraph, April 30, 1967.

10. Russell to Basso, July 5, 1966, BRA 10.1/371; e-mail from Julius Lester, May 11, 1999; and *The New York Times,* April 11, 1967.

11. *The New York Times,* February 16 and 20, 1967.

12. *Le Monde,* May 7–8, 1967.

13. *The New York Times,* May 8 and 11, 1967; Edward Sherman, "Bertrand Russell and the Peace Movement," in George Nakhnikian, ed., *Bertrand Russell's Philosophy* (London: Duckworth, 1974), p. 262; and Hanoi, VNA International Service in English, May 10, 1967 (FBIS 91/67).

14. Tariq Ali, *New Statesman,* May 12, 1967.

15. *The New York Times,* May 6, 1967.

16. Simone de Beauvoir, *All Said and Done* (New York: Paragon House, 1993), p. 345; Russell to Ho Chi Minh, March 25, 1967, BRA 10.6/375; and *Le Monde,* May 5, 1967.

17. John Duffett, ed., *Against the Crime of Silence* (New York: Simon and Schuster, 1970), pp. 25–26; *The Times,* May 4, 1967; and *Le Monde,* May 5 and 6, 1967.

18. De Beauvoir, p. 346; *Svenska Dagbladet,* May 3, 1967; George Bronfen to Russell, April 11, 1967, BRA 10.3/372; *Gens Nyheter,* May 7, 1967; and *Le Monde,* May 9 and 11, 1967. One of the Americans, Texas media owner Gordon McLendon, held a press conference on returning to New York at which he was critical of evidence presented at Stockholm. See Dave Dellinger, *Revolutionary Nonviolence* (Indianapolis: Bobbs-Merrill, 1970), p. 84.

19. Ken Coates's letter to authors, September 15, 1999 and de Beauvoir, p. 341.

20. De Beauvoir, pp. 341 and 344–45.

21. *Expressen,* April 28, 1967, and Geoffrey Sinclair, *Tribune,* May 1967. Dedijer, as a legalist, maintained that war crimes were a possibility that had to be addressed by the tribunal. See *Newsweek,* May 8, 1967, p. 54. The flap over Erlander's message to Russell will be addressed in Chapter XIII. Note that Sartre and Dedijer were upset that they had never been informed about its contents.

22. Sinclair; de Beauvoir, p. 344; and telephone interview with Carl Oglesby, April 25, 2000.

23. Caroline Moorehead, *Bertrand Russell: A Life* (New York: Viking, 1993), p. 527; Schoenman to Pham, September 27, 1967; and Scheer, p. 22.

24. Ken Coates's letter to authors, May 3, 2000. Coates indicates that Schoenman and Dedijer reconciled some years later as Dedijer helped arrange sponsorship for a conference to honor Russell's centenary.

25. Moorehead, p. 526; Coates letter, September 15, 1999; Russell to Dedijer, May 14, 1967, BRA 10.2/371; Oglesby interview; Dellinger interview; and Ronald Clark, *The Life of Bertrand Russell* (New York: Knopf, 1975), p. 627. Coates describes Schoenman as "governed by impulse" and "quite intolerant in his manner." He was also "intellectually open" and Coates "admired him for his courage, but not for his judgment." Ken Coates's letter to authors, March 31, 2000.

26. Deutscher to Russell, May 22, 1967 and Schoenman to Anders, May 11, 1967, BRA 10.2/371; and Tariq Ali, *New Statesman,* May 12, 1967, p. 641.

27. Moorehead, p. 527; Deutscher to Russell, May 22, 1967; Anders to Schoenman, May 11, 1967, BRA 10.2/371; and Julius Lester, *Revolutionary Notes* (New York: Richard W. Baron, 1969), pp. 9–20.

28. Anders to Schoenman, May 11, 1967.

29. Lester, *Revolutionary Notes,* pp. 18–19.

30. Lester, *Revolutionary Notes,* pp. 12–14, and Carl Oglesby, "Vietnam: This is Guernica," *The Nation,* June 5, 1967, pp. 715 and 721.

31. *Newsweek,* May 15, 1967, p. 44.

32. Lester, *Revolutionary Notes,* pp. 16–17, and Lester interview. During his one-month visit to North Vietnam, Lester felt that the Vietnamese still had great affinity for France.

33. Schoenman to Carmichael, May 24, 1967, BRA 10.2/371. Ken Coates, current chairman of the BRPF, has a more cynical interpretation of Schoenman's comments on race: "Ralph was very keen to develop relations with the black activists, and I would not put it past him to tell them what he thought they wanted to hear." Ken Coates's letter to authors, September 29, 1999.

34. Lester, *Revolutionary Notes,* p. 15.

35. Lester, *Revolutionary Notes,* p. 17.

36. Jean-Paul Sartre, "Preface," in Frantz Fanon, *The Wretched of the Earth* (New York: Grove Press, 1968), pp. 13 and 24, and Sartre interview in *Ekstra Bladet,* November 18, 1967.

37. Stockholm Domestic Service in Swedish, May 10, 1967 (FBIS 92/67); *London Bulletin,* No. 2 (September 1967); and Lester, *Revolutionary Notes,* p. 17.

38. http://www.homeusers.prestel.co.uk/littleton/v1119ver.htm.

39. http://www.homeusers.prestel.co.uk/littleton/v1120ver.htm.

40. De Beauvoir, p. 348, and *Gens Nyheter,* May 7, 1967. A generally pro-Soviet group called the International Association of Democratic Lawyers conducted its own investigation in Vietnam, and was therefore somewhat of a competitor with the Russell Tribunal. See Stockholm Domestic Service in Swedish, May 8, 1967 (FBIS 91/67).

41. Moorehead, pp. 528–29; Stockholm Domestic Service in Swedish, May 8, 1967 (FBIS 91/67); and Hanoi VNA International Service in English, May 13, 1967 (FBIS 94/67). North Vietnam issued a book on the Russell tribunal, comparing it to Nuremberg. See Pham Van Bach, "International War Crimes Tribunal," in *US War Crimes in Viet Nam* (Hanoi: Juridical Sciences Institute, 1967), pp. 273–318.

42. *The New York Times,* August 22, 1967; Russell interview, *Aftonbladet,* undated, BRA 9.533/320 (Sweden); Arthur Jay Klinghoffer, *Israel and the Soviet Union* (Boulder, CO: Westview, 1985), pp. 74–75; and *Jewish Observer and Middle East Review,* Vol. XVI, No. 33 (August 19, 1967): 10–12.

43. Rostow to Johnson, May 5, 1967, National Security File, Memos to the President, LBJL 27/16 and Fredrik Logevall, "The Swedish-American Conflict over Vietnam," *Diplomatic History,* Vol. 17, No. 3 (Summer 1993): 430.

44. *Expressen,* May 4, 1967; Stockholm Domestic Service in Swedish, May 8, 1967; and Moscow Domestic Service in Russian, May 10, 1967 (FBIS 92/67).

45. Lester interview.

46. Lester interview.

47. Dellinger, *Revolutionary Nonviolence,* p. 73. After returning home to New Jersey, a print shop partly owned by Dellinger was ransacked and the words "Next time it will be you" were scrawled in red ink that resembled blood. In December 1967 and January 1968, Dellinger received bombs, one of them in the form of a booby-trapped liquor bottle. He suspected U.S. government involvement, and was told by VFW members that some unknown men in suits had attended their meetings recently. Dellinger interview.

48. *Expressen,* May 4, 1967, and Lester interview.

49. Russell Stetler to Stanley Unwin, November 3, 1967, BRA 6.43/70.

50. Flora Lewis, *Sunday Express,* May 14, 1967; C. L. Sulzberger, *The New York Times,* May 12, 1967; Bernard Levin, *The Pendulum Years* (London: Pan Books, 1977), pp. 273–74; and David Horowitz, "The Final Passion," http://www.homeusers.prestel.co.uk/littleton/br7005dh.htm, p. 6.

51. Clark, p. 627, and Sulzberger. The noted cellist Pablo Casals indicated that he did not support the tribunal because its attacks on Johnson were too rash. See *The New York Times,* June 5, 1967.

52. Richard Falk, ed., *The Vietnam War and International Law* (Princeton, NJ: Princeton University Press, 1968), Vol. I, p. 451; Oglesby, "Vietnam: This is Guernica," p. 714; Lester to Schoenman, undated, summer 1967, BRA 9.70/340 (1967); and Lester, *Revolutionary Notes,* p. 12.

53. *The New York Times,* May 7, 1967, and Telford Taylor, *Nuremberg and Vietnam: an American Tragedy* (Chicago: Quadrangle, 1970), p. 99. Note that war crimes could be attributed to the United States even if the war itself was legal.

54. Russell press release, May 21, 1967, BRA 9.70/340; Nancy Zaroulis and Gerald Sullivan, *Who Spoke Up?: American Protests Against the War in Vietnam 1963–1975* (New York: Holt, Rinehart, and Winston, 1984), p. 226; and *The New York Times,* May 16, 17, 18, 21 and 22, 1967.

55. *The New York Times,* May 18, 21, 24, 26, and June 3, 1967.

56. Statement by Sartre, Schwartz, and Dedijer, undated, BRA 10.2/371. Ken Coates advances the "rescue" interpretation in a letter to the authors, September 29, 1999.

57. Clark, p. 628; *Spectator,* November 14, 1967; Russell to Anders, June 16, 1967; Russell to tribunal members, May 4, 1967; Schoenman to Schwartz, September 25, 1967; Schwartz to Russell, June 18, 1967; Schoenman to Anders, May 19, 1967; and Russell to Weiss, June 20, 1967, BRA 10.2/371. Russell complained to Schwartz that the French office had failed to fund Courtland Cox's return to the United States. See letter of October 6, 1967, BRA 10.2/371.

58. *Observer,* May 14, 1967; Schoenman to Hernandez, undated; and Russell to Dedijer, May 14, 1967, BRA 10.2/371. Schoenman wrote to Anders calling for Dedijer's resignation on the ground that he had publicly discussed whether Russell should separate himself from the tribunal. See letter of May 19, 1967, BRA 10.2/371.

59. Russell to Sartre and Schwartz, June 6, 1967; Russell to Anders, June 16, 1967; Farley to Anders, July 28, 1967; Anders to Farley, July 31, 1967; and Farley to Anders, August 7, 1967, BRA 10.2/371.

60. Coates letter, September 15, 1999; Sartre to Russell, May 27, 1967; Russell to Sartre and Schwartz; Deutscher to Schwartz, June 8, 1967; and Deutscher to Russell, August 5, 1967, BRA 10.2/371.

61. Farley to Anders, July 28, 1967 and Russell to Cardenas, August 5, 1967, BRA 10.2/371.

62. Interview with Nicholas Griffin, June 30, 1999.

Chapter 13

1. Schoenman to Erlander, January 1965, BRA p.53/320 (Sweden). Schoenman sent the same letter to Danish Prime Minister Jens Otto Krag. See BRA 9.44/320. Note that Russell had written earlier to Erlander, asking if he would like to associate publicly in Sweden with the BRPF. See letter of February 13, 1964, BRA 9.53/320 (Sweden).

2. Russell to Erlander, November 25, 1966; Erlander to Russell, December 9, 1966, BRA 9.53/320 (Sweden); and Walt Rostow to Johnson, April 25, 1967, National Security File, Rostow, box 12, LBJL.

3. Russell to Erlander, January 4, 1967, BRA 9.53/320 (Sweden); *Svenska Dagbladet,* April 28, 1967; and Rostow to Johnson, April 25, 1967.

4. "Aktuellt," Swedish TV, May 8, 1967; *NSD,* April 29, 1967; and *Dagens Nyheter,* March 18, 1967.

5. Erlander statement, April 24, 1967, BRA 10.18/385; statement by Swedish Committee for Support of the Russell Tribunal, April 25, 1967, BRA 10.18/385; *Newsweek,* May 8, 1967, p. 54; and Russell to Erlander, April 26, 1967, BRA 9.53/320.

6. *NY Dag,* April 28–May 4, 1967; *Expressen,* April 30, 1967; and *Svenska Dagbladet,* April 30, 1967. See also *Glos Pracy* (Warsaw), May 8, 1967 (FBIS 93/67).

7. *NSD,* April 29, 1967; *Dagens Nyheter,* April 28, 1967; Sydsvenska Snall-posten, May 2, 1967; and *Arbetet,* April 29, 1967. Note that Russell and Schoenman favored the defeat of South Vietnam, not a negotiated settlement. See Schoenman to Peter Lorentzon, December 7, 1965, BRA 9.53/320 (Sweden). Erlander told Rostow that he would try to prevent the granting of visas to North Vietnamese. See Rostow to Johnson, April 25, 1967.

8. Rostow to Johnson; Johnson Daily Diary, April 25, 1967, LBJL; Lars-Goran Stenelo, *The International Critic* (Lund: Studentlitteratur, 1984), p. 54; Fredrik Logevall, "The Swedish-American Conflict over Vietnam," *Diplomatic History,* Vol. 17, No. 3 (Summer 1993): 429; *Uppsala Nya Tidning,* May 2, 1967; *The New York Times,* May 9, 1967; and "Aktuellt."

9. *The New York Times,* May 3, 1967. According to *Newsweek,* Johnson sent a note to Erlander asserting that the tribunal could harm bilateral relations. He argued that if de Gaulle could prevent it, so could Erlander. See *Newsweek,* May 15, 1967, p. 12.

10. *Expressen,* April 30, 1967; *Sunday Telegraph,* April 30, 1967; Simone de Beauvoir, *All Said and Done* (New York: Paragon House, 1993), pp. 343–44; and *Tribune,* May 19, 1967.

11. Olof Ruin, *Tage Erlander: Serving the Welfare State, 1946–1969* (Pittsburgh: University of Pittsburgh Press, 1990), p. 286; Stenelo, p. 54; and Logevall, p. 428.

12. Logevall, p. 425; Chris Mosey, *Cruel Awakening* (London: Hurst, 1991), pp. 97–99; Torsten Nilsson, *Ater Vietnam* (Kristianstads: Tidensforlag, 1981), pp. 48–50; and Jussi Hanhimaki, *Scandinavia and the United States* (New York: Twayne, 1997), pp. 131–32.

13. Nils Andren, *Power-Balance and Non-Alignment* (Stockholm: Almqvist and Wiksell, 1967), pp. 168–71.

14. Nilsson, pp. 72–74.

15. Stenelo, pp. 57, 73, and 133; Ruin, pp. 14 and 71; and *The New York Times,* September 25, 1966. In 1966, the voting age was lowered from twenty-one to twenty.

16. Logevall, pp. 444–45. See also Andren, p. 157.

17. *The New York Times,* February 6, 1967.

18. Hanhimaki, pp. 127 and 129–31; Mosey, p. 92; and Kjell Goldmann, "An 'Isolated' Attack Against Sweden and Its World Political Preconditions," *Cooperation and Conflict,* No. 2 (1965): 19.

19. Goldmann, p. 36. In October 1961, Swedish Foreign Minister Bo Osten Unden presented a plan for a nuclear-free zone in the Baltic region. The United States opposed it, and Sweden later opted for its own nuclear development. See Hanhimaki, p. 114. In 1972, while Palme was prime minister, Sweden conducted an underground nuclear test. See Mosey, p. 91.
20. Stenelo, p. 60 and Hanhimaki, pp. 142–43.
21. Logevall, p. 428 and Nilsson, pp. 68 and 75–84.
22. George Herring, ed., *The Secret Diplomacy of the Vietnam War* (Austin: University of Texas Press, 1983), p. 530; Ulf Bjereld, "Critic or Mediator?: Sweden in World Politics, 1945–90," *Journal of Peace Research,* Vol. 32, No. 1 (1995): 31; and Stenelo, pp. 18, 135, and 159.
23. *Svenska Dagbladet,* April 28, 1967; *The New York Times,* April 18, 1967; Cameron to State Department, April 18, 1967 in Herring, p. 681; State Department to American embassy in Stockholm, April 22, 1967 in Herring, pp. 682–83; and Cameron to State Department, April 26, 1967 in Herring, p. 688.
24. *Norskenflammen,* May 2, 1967; *Aftonbladet,* April 25, April 27 and May 2, 1967; *Dagens Nyheter,* April 25, April 28, and May 2, 1967; *Expressen,* April 25, 1967; and *Svenska Dagbladet,* April 26, 1967. The editor of *Var Kyrka,* a backer of the tribunal, commented that it was a "shame" that antitribunal opinion was so strong. Cited in *Svenska Dagbladet,* May 5, 1967.
25. Nilsson and Stockholm Domestic Service in Swedish, May 9, 1967 (FBIS 91/67).
26. Herring, pp. 701 and 852, and *The New York Times,* July 7 and November 7, 1967.
27. Herring, pp. 691–93.
28. Herring, p. 530, and Bjereld, p. 31.
29. Hanhimaki, p. 133; Mosey, p. 102; Ruin, p. 287; Stenelo, p. 145; and Logevall, pp. 432–35. During his visit, Nguyen Tho Chanh met with Foreign Minister Nilsson. Also, early in 1968, the United States was pressuring Sweden to expel American war resisters, many of whom had relocated from Canada. Dave Dellinger went to Stockholm and worked successfully with Palme to thwart this effort. Interview with Dellinger, June 15, 2000.
30. Stenelo, p. 146; Logevall, p. 435; Hanhimaki, p. 141; and Nilsson, p. 129.

Chapter 14

1. Telephone interview with David Horowitz, May 18, 1999.
2. *The New York Times,* November 3, 1967. Schoenman was highly critical of Soviet "revisionism," and of the Communist Party of Bolivia's lack of support for Guevara. See "Bertrand Russell and the Peace Movement," in George Nakhnikian, ed., *Bertrand Russell's Philosophy* (London: Duckworth, 1974), p. 251.
3. On the Japanese media, see Thomas Havens, *Fire Across the Sea: The Viet-*

nam War and Japan, 1965–1975 (Princeton, NJ: Princeton University Press, 1987), p. 37, and Young Kim, "Japan and the Vietnam War," in Gene Hsiao, ed., *The Role of External Powers in the Indochina Crisis* (Edwardsville: Southern Illinois University Press, 1973), p. 164. An argument was presented that American expenditure in Vietnam contributed to black unrest at home. See *The New York Times,* July 29, 1967.

4. *The New York Times,* July 20 and 29, 1967.

5. Havens, pp. 127–28.

6. "Report of the Japanese Commission on the Complicity of Japan," presented at Roskilde, November 1967, http://www2.prestel.co.uk/littleton/v1214jap.htm, p. 1.

7. "Report," pp. 1–4, and Havens, pp. 5, 89–91 and 99–101. Direct U.S. defense expenditures in Japan were $321 million in 1964, $346 million in 1965, $484 million in 1966, and $538 million in 1967. American allies, particularly South Korea, also made military purchases in Japan. See John Clark, "Japanese Foreign Policy and the War in Vietnam, 1964–1969," doctoral dissertation, Sheffield University, 1984, pp. 50–52.

8. Kim, pp. 156–58 and 164, and Clark, pp. 81–82.

9. Hiroshi Fujimato, "Japan and the War in Southeast Asia, 1965–67," in Lloyd Gardner and Ted Gittinger, eds., *International Perspectives on Vietnam* (College Station: Texas A&M University Press, 2000), pp. 177–84; Havens, pp. 131–35; Kim, p. 163; and *The New York Times,* October 29, 1967. Okinawa was returned to Japan in 1972.

10. Helsinki Domestic Service in Finnish, May 10, 1967 (FBIS 92/67); Madeleine Garaudet to Russell, August 16 and September 4, 1967, and Russell to Garaudet, August 26, 1967, BRA 10.5/374; and Dellinger interview.

11. Schoenman to Chriten Amby, November 30, 1966, BRA 9.44/320 (Denmark).

12. Simone de Beauvoir, *All Said and Done* (New York: Paragon House, 1993), p. 352 and "Minutes of the Working Committee," September 20, 1967, BRA 10.5/374. De Beauvoir writes rather delicately that Denmark was selected since "we did not wish to abuse the hospitality of the Swedes."

13. De Beauvoir, p. 352; Nancy Zaroulis and Gerald Sullivan, *Who Spoke Up?: American Protests Against the War in Vietnam 1963–1975* (New York: Holt, Rinehart, and Winston, 1984), pp. 137–39; *Berlingske Tidende,* October 22, 1967; and interview with Ebbe Reich, May 15, 1996.

14. Reich interview, May 15, 1996.

15. *Aktuelt,* November 15, 1967, and *Information,* November 17, 1967.

16. Reich interview.

17. *The New York Times,* November 21, 23, 26, and December 21, 1967. Schoenman was banned from Britain in 1968. See Schoenman, "Bertrand Russell and the Peace Movement," p. 251.

18. De Beauvoir, p. 352, and Reich interview.

19. Russell Stetler's commentary on Roskilde, BRA 10.15/384, p. 9; Reich interview; testimony of David Tuck in Peter Limqueco and Peter Weiss, eds., *Prevent the Crime of Silence* (London: Penguin, 1971), pp. 240–41; and Russell to Ali, undated, and Ali to Russell, November 15, 1967, BRA 9.70/340 (1967). *The New York Times* correspondent did not attend the testimony of former GIs Peter Martinson and David Tuck, and the U.S. media paid little attention to it. See Dave Dellinger, "Report from the International War Crimes Tribunal," in Dellinger, *Revolutionary Nonviolence* (Indianapolis: Bobbs-Merrill, 1970), p. 77.

20. *Le Monde,* November 22, 1967; *Berlingske Tidende,* November 25, 1967; *Facts on File,* 1968, p. 18; and Dellinger interview.

21. Stetler to Carmichael, October 6, 1967, BRA 102/371; Reich interview; de Beauvoir, p. 362; interview with Julius Lester, March 15, 2000; *The New York Times,* December 7, 1967; and *Facts on File,* 1967, p. 564.

22. De Beauvoir, p. 354 and Leo Matarasso, "Report on Genocide in Vietnam," BRA 10.27/385.

23. De Beauvoir, p. 362 and Reich interview. For a discussion of the Holocaust analogy during the Six Day War, see Judith Klinghoffer, *Vietnam, Jews and the Middle East* (London: Macmillan, 1999), Chapter 9. Russell Stetler prepared a memorandum on the genocide issue that accentuated the 1945 Tokyo tribunal. Recognizing that crimes against humanity were considered there, he averred that they qualified as genocide under terms of the later Genocide Convention. Stetler cited the defense argument that Japan had intervened in Vietnam at the invitation of France. It was rejected by American judges at Tokyo, so the United States was hypocritical in trying to claim a South Vietnamese invitation as an extenuating circumstance. See BRA 10.15/384.

24. Preface by Pierre Vidal-Naquet in Permanent People's Tribunal, *A Crime of Silence: The Armenian Genocide* (London: Zed, 1985), p. 5.

25. De Beauvoir, pp. 354 and 358; Reich interview; and telephone interview with Carl Oglesby, April 25, 2000.

26. Richard Falk, who compiled two volumes of materials on the legal aspects of the war, concurred with the genocide decision, stating: "In the Vietnam War the use of bombing tactics and cruel weapons against the civilian population appears to me to establish a *prima facie* case of genocide against the United States." See *The Vietnam War and International Law* (Princeton, NJ: Princeton University Press, 1968), Vol. II, p. 252. Note that the three negative votes on Japan's direct role were at variance with the findings of the 1967 Tokyo tribunal.

27. Hugo Adam Bedau, "Genocide in Vietnam?," in Virginia Held, Sidney Morgenbesser and Thomas Nagel, *Philosophy, Morality, and International Affairs* (New York: Oxford University Press, 1974), p. 7 and de Beauvoir, p. 363. All of the evidence presented at Roskilde was forwarded to U.N. Secretary-General U Thant. See *Berlingske Tidende,* November 26, 1967.

28. John V. Crangle, "Legal Theories of the Nuremberg and Stockholm-Roskilde Tribunals," *Proceedings of the South Carolina Historical Association* (Columbia, SC: 1990): 66 and de Beauvoir, p. 363. When the text of the tribunal sessions was published in the US in 1969 as *Against the Crime of Silence,* there was very little press coverage. See Zaroulis and Sullivan, pp. 352–53. Arthur Garfield Hays pointed out that Americans do not pay much attention to foreign opinion. Foreign lawyers supporting Sacco and Vanzetti were ignored, and generally considered an "impertinence." See *City Lawyer* (New York: Simon and Schuster, 1942), p. 353.

29. *Berlingske Tidende,* December 4, 1967.

30. *Politiken,* February 23, 1968, and *Vestkysten's kronik,* December 30, 1967 and February 5, 1968.

31. Kenneth Miller, *Government and Politics in Denmark* (Boston: Houghton Mifflin, 1968), p. 250, and *The New York Times,* June 26, 1967. A response from two members of the Danish parliament claimed that the ad was not representative of Danish opinion. See *The New York Times,* July 18, 1967.

32. Miller, pp. 89–92, 102, 116, and 259–60.

33. Barbara Haskel, *The Scandinavian Option* (Oslo: Universitetsforlaget, 1976), p. 51; *Jyllands-Postens kronik,* June 23, 1967; and Erling Bjol, "NATO and Denmark," *Cooperation and Conflict,* No. 2 (1968): 93 and 102–03.

34. *The New York Times,* September 28, 1967; *Berlinske Tidende,* October 8, 1967; and *Land og Folk,* October 13, 1967.

35. *The New York Times,* June 23, 1967, and Rusk to ambassador to Denmark May 2, 1967, National Security Files, Denmark, box 168, LBJL.

36. Reich interview, and *Information,* November 9, 1967.

37. K. E. Logstrup, "Statsministeren og Russell-tribunalet," *Informations kronik,* October 5, 1967.

38. Editorial, *Information,* December 2–3, 1967.

39. Ebbe Reich, "Danmark og tribunalet," *Ekstra Bladet,* November 22, 1967; *Politiken,* February 19, 1967; and *Information,* January 10, 1967.

40. *Berlingske Tidende,* November 20, 1967 and *The New York Times,* November 21, 1967.

41. *Berlingske Tidende,* October 8 and November 19, 1967. Before tribunals were held in Stockholm or Roskilde, the Radical newspaper *Politiken* had argued that Johnson was not acting contrary to American opinion and that a mock war crimes tribunal should not be staged to serve a political cause. See *Politiken,* October 29, 1966.

42. Villy Sorensen, "Den ensidige sandhed," *Berlingske Tidende,* November 30, 1967.

43. *Information,* December 2–3, 1967.

44. Reich interview; Miller, pp. 89–92; Bjol, pp. 93 and 103; and *Facts on File,* 1968, p. 48.

45. *The Spokesman-Review,* July 22, 1968; *Post,* August 26, 1968; Russell statement of August 21, 1968, BRA C68.22; and *San Francisco Examiner,*

November 25, 1969. Sartre also opposed the Soviet intervention in Czechoslovakia.

46. Russell to U Thant, December 1 and U Thant to Russell, December 26, 1969, BRA 9.54/320 and Limqueco and Weiss, p. 384.

47. Paul Johnson, *Intellectuals* (New York: Harper and Row, 1988), p. 221; Caroline Moorehead, *Bertrand Russell: A Life* (New York: Viking, 1993), pp. 539–40; *Huddersfield Daily Examiner,* December 9, 1969; and *The Observer,* September 6, 1970. The full text of Russell's memorandum appears in *New Statesman,* September 11, 1970.

48. Ken Coates and Chris Farley, "Ralph Schoenman—A Word of Explanation," June 1970 in Dave Dellinger Papers, Montpelier, Vermont.

49. Lester interview.

50. *Information,* November 20, 1967. The Arab League asked the tribunal to take up the Arab-Israeli issue, and was supported by the pro-Arab Carmichael. Sartre and de Beauvoir were pro-Israeli, leading Russell to decide against having a tribunal session because there was internal division among panelists. See communiqué from Paris secretariat, undated, BRA 10.5/374; Ethel Minor of SNCC to BRPF, June 9, 1967; Pat Jordan response, June 13, 1967, BRA 9.70/340; and interview with Dave Dellinger, June 15, 2000. For an analysis of the split within the left over the Six Day War, see Klinghoffer, especially pp. 162–63 and 167–68.

Chapter 15

1. Bertrand Russell Peace Foundation,"Memorandum on a Possible Third Session of the International War Crimes Tribunal," undated, Dave Dellinger papers, Montpelier, Vermont.

2. Ken Coates's letters to authors, September 15, 1999 and August 8, 2000. The tribunal on freedom of opinion, with Dedijer as president, had three sessions in West Germany during the late seventies. The tribunal on American Indians will be discussed below in the context of indigenous peoples, and the sessions on Latin America will be covered in the section on political repression . Note that there were three Russell II tribunals. Later tribunals organized by Basso and Dedijer were not officially sponsored by the BRPF, in part because it differed with Dedijer over appropriate topics and the procedure for selecting them.

3. Marlene Dixon, ed., *On Trial: Reagan's War on Nicaragua* (San Francisco: Synthesis, 1985), pp. x–xi and interview with Richard Falk, March 6, 2001. The Algiers declaration, symbolically issued on July 4, appears in Permanent People's Tribunal, *Philippines: Repression and Resistance* (Manila: Komite ng Sambayanang Pilipino, 1981), pp. 282–84.

4. http://www.grisnet.T/filb/tribu.eng.html; Permanent People's Tribunal, *A Crime of Silence: The Armenian Genocide* (London: Zed, 1985), p. 241; Dixon, p. xi; and Falk interview.

5. http:www.2facts.com/archive/search/1976111430.asp and Bill Bowring, "Socialism, Liberation Struggle and the Law," http://members.netscape online.co.uk/suzyboyce1/files/book1/3_9.htm.

6. Diana Russell and Nicole Van de Ven, eds., *Crimes Against Women: Proceedings of the International Tribunal* (Millbrae, CA: Les Femmes, 1976), pp. xiii, 218–19, and 239. The Brussels session was preceded by a February 27–29 New York tribunal, at which all present were considered judges, and the aim was "to indict the system."

7. Russell and Van de Ven, pp. xiii and 231.

8. Russell and Van de Ven, pp. xvi, 5, and 218–19.

9. Russell and Van de Ven, pp. xv–xvi, 219, 242, and 264. An attempt to raise funds in advance of the tribunal from American feminists proved unsuccessful, as only $100 was collected. See p. 238.

10. Sihyun Cho, "On the Constitution and the Procedure of the Women's International War Crimes Tribunal on Japan's Military Sexual Slavery in 2000;" http://witness.peacenet.or.kr/symek2000. htm; http:srd.yahoo.com/srst/ 27768279/ japan+sexual+slavery/1/5/http://witness.peacenet.or; http:// www.chosun.com/g_.html; Pyongyang. KCNA in English, December 2, 7, 16 and 17 (FBIS-EAS-2000–1202, 1207, 1216 and 1217)*; World Press Review,* February 2001, p. 28; and *The New York Times,* December 7 and 16, 2000. In September 2000, fifteen female victims of the Japanese military filed a class action lawsuit against Japan in U.S. District Court in New York under the Alien Tort Claims Act. See *The New York Times,* September 16, 2000.

11. "Tribunal Condemns Asylum Practices," *The Ecologist,* Vol. 24, No. 6 (November 1994): 551. The Permanent People's Tribunal also conducted hearings in Berlin in 1994 on the right of asylum.

12. "Do We Need a Russell Tribunal to Defend the Human Rights of Psychiatric Patients?," http://www. fu-berlin.de/wahnsinn/psyerfah/fff/russell_ declaration.htm.

13. *Archive of the Fourth Russell Tribunal on the Rights of the Indians of the Americas* (Zug: Inter Documentation Company, 1986), pp. 1–2. Note that there was a 1992 tribunal in Padua and Venice on "The Conquest of America and International Law."

14. "Declaration of Indigenous Peoples," http://www.cwis.org/fwdp/ International/russell.txt and "Fourth Russell Tribunal: On the Rights of the Indians of the Americas," http://www.sicc.sk.ca/saskindian/a81jan07.htm.

15. http://www.grisnet.it.filb/amazzonit.PDF.

16. Sally Engle Merry, "Resistance and the Cultural Power of the Law," *Law and Society Review,* Vol. 29, No. 1 (1995)—available in EBSCO; http:// nativenet.uthscsa.edu/archive/nl/9308/0306.html; http://nativenet.uth.scsa. edu/archive/9704/0052.html; and *Denver Post,* June 22, 1997.

17. "The 1997 People's Summit on APEC," http://www.vcn.bc.ca/summit/ popindex.htm.

18. *A Crime of Silence,* p. 239; William Jerman, ed., *Repression in Latin America* (Nottingham: Spokesman Books, 1975), pp. 160–63; and http://www. 2facts.com/archive/search/1975057190.asp.

19. Marlene Dixon and Susanne Jonas, eds., *Guatemala: Tyranny on Trial* (San Francisco, CA: Synthesis, 1984), pp. 119, 265–67, 271, and 278, and *Keesing's,* 1983, p. 32430. In December 1982, Ronald Reagan met with Rios Montt in Honduras and indicated that he favored a renewal of U.S. arms deliveries. On January 7, the U.S. State Department announced that arms would be delivered due to the improvement of the human rights situation under the Rios Montt government. See *Keesing's, 1983, p. 31952.*

20. Leslie Wirpsa, "People's Tribunal Fingers U.S. Rights Abuses," *National Catholic Reporter,* May 17, 1991, p. 18.

21. "*Philippines,*" pp. 4, 275–79, and 290–91.

22. Falk interview.

23. The Jungle BBS, October 22, 1997, kerry@jungle.ottawa.on.ca.

24. Nizkor International Human Rights team, May 21, 1999, http://www. derechos.org/nizkor.

25. Gary Jonathan Bass, *Stay the Hand of Vengeance* (Princeton, NJ: Princeton University Press, 2000), pp. 106, 122 and 122–25.

26. *A Crime of Silence,* pp. xii–xiii, 10, 212, 220, and 223.

27. *A Crime of Silence,* pp. xi–xii, xiv, and 243.

28. Turkey retaliated against France economically. See *The New York Times,* January 24, 2001.

29. The Citizens Commission of Inquiry, *The Dellums Committee Hearings on War Crimes in Vietnam* (New York: Vintage, 1972), pp. vii and x–xi.

30. The Citizens Commission of Inquiry, pp. 84, 259, and 332.

31. The Citizens Commission of Inquiry, pp. 18, 23, 55, 243, 281, and 334–35. Congressman Ed Koch of New York agreed with charges of U.S. aggression, but pointed out that the North Vietnamese were as guilty as the Americans of killing South Vietnamese. See p. 77.

32. Frank Browning and Dorothy Forman, eds., *The Wasted Nations: Report of the International Commission of Enquiry into United States Crimes in Indochina, June 20–25, 1971* (New York: Harper and Row, 1972), pp. xv–xvi, 83, 306, and 339.

33. *On Trial,* pp. 18–22, 230, and 239.

34. Independent Commission of Inquiry on the U.S. Invasion of Panama, *The U.S. Invasion of Panama* (Boston: South End Press, 1991), pp. 2–3 and 8.

35. *The U.S. Invasion of Panama,* pp. 17, 19, 21, and 65.

36. The charges appear in http://deoxy.org/wc/warcrim2.htm. For a discussion of Congressional opinion on this matter, see James Ridgeway, ed., *The March to War* (New York: Four Walls Eight Windows, 1991), pp. 188–98.

37. http://deoxy.org/wc/warcrim3.htm.

38. Falk interview; http://www.grisnet.it.filb/afghunit2.PDF; and Permanent People's Tribunal, *Afghanistan People's Tribunal: Sentence.*

39. http://www.grisnet.it.filb/tibetit.PDF, and Permanent People's Tribunal, *Session on Tibet: Verdict.*

40. Letter from Chechen Foreign Minister Ilyas Akhmadov to Madeleine Albright, April 21, 2000 in http://msanews.mynet.net/MSANEWS/200004/20000425.13.html and http://www.neww.org/pipermail/women-in-war-2000–December/000230.html. In 2000, Chechnya filed a suit at the International Court of Justice on alleged Russian genocide. See http://www.rferl.org/welcome/english/releases/chechnya000815.html.

41. http://www.glasnet.ru/ ~ ninis/dbase/english/actions/mtribun.html; http://www.pgs.ca/pages/jna/jna96–2.htm; http://www.palmecenterorg/library/newsletter/1996–01/ne-1996–01–002.html; http://www.amina.com/article/right.html and Coates letter, August 8, 2000. An interesting angle developed by the Chechnya tribunal was the effort to hold Switzerland responsible for failure to uphold the Geneva Conventions on the rules of war.

42. http://www.lightparty.com/Health/Chernobyl/Shutdown/html.

43. The International People's Tribunal, *The People vs. Global Capital* (New York: Apex, 1994), pp. iii, 7, 123, and 125.

44. *The People vs. Global Capital,* pp. 121–22 and 151.

45. *The People vs. Global Capital,* p. 124. The International Monetary Fund and World Bank were the subjects of tribunals in Berlin (1988) and Madrid (1994).

46. http://ichrdd.ca/geninfo E, forumAnnounce.html and "The 1997 People's Summit on APEC," http://www.vcn.bc.ca/summit/popindex.htm.

47. http://www.grisnet.it/filb and http://www.oneworld.org/ips2/may98/16 56 064.html. A tribunal on "Childhood and Minors" in relationship to labor held hearings in Trento, Macerata and Naples in 1995.

48. http://artcon.rutgers.edu/papertiger/nyfma/tribunal/tribmarch.html. In March 2000, a PPT tribunal on Global Corporations and Human Wrongs met in Warwick, England, and accused four corporations of human rights and environmental abuses. Representatives of these corporations were to be invited to a future tribunal to present their rebuttal. See http://www.law.warwick.ac.uk/lawschool/ppt/press.html.

49. http://burn.ucsd.edu/archives/riot-1/1994.Dec/0029.html; http://www.essential.org/monitor/hyper/mm0397.09.html; "Bhopal Tribunal Recommends Charter," *The Ecologist,* Vol. 24, No. 6 (November 1994): SS4; and http://www.corpwatch.org/trac/corner/altvision/charter.html. An International People's Tribunal on Human Rights and the Environment, sponsored by church groups, was held in New York in June 1997.

50. In May 1980, students in Kwangju in Cholla province demonstrated against martial law. A military crackdown then led to approximately two hundred deaths. Opposition leader Kim Dae Jung was accused of fomenting the disturbances, and was charged with sedition. In September, he was sentenced to death. In January 1981 President Chun Doo Hwan commuted the sen-

tence to life imprisonment. In March 1982, it was reduced to twenty years, but was then suspended in December as Kim was permitted to depart for the United States for medical treatment. During his imprisonment, an early 1981 tribunal in Tokyo (which included Dave Dellinger as a panelist) condemned the killings by the military in Kwangju and called for the protection of the imprisoned Kim. For information on these events, see Donald Clark, ed., *The Kwangju Uprising* (Boulder, CO: Westview, 1988); William Gleysteen, *Massive Entanglement, Marginal Influence* (Washington, DC: Brookings, 1999), Chapter 11; *Keesing's,* 1982, p. 31405 and 1983, p. 32129; and interview with Dave Dellinger, June 15, 2000. Kim Dae Jung was elected president of South Korea in 1997.

51. www.mastalk.com and *Philadelphia Inquirer,* May 26, 1983.
52. *Philadelphia Inquirer,* September 16, 1995 and October 5, 1999.
53. Workers World, December 4, 1997, http://www.lol.shareworld.com/Bulletins/ptri.htm.
54. "International Tribunal for Justice," http://www.mumia.org/fns405.html.
55. "One Million Witnesses," http://www.mumia.org/fns405.html.
56. International Tribunal for Justice for Mumia Abu-Jamal, "Findings of Fact and Conclusions of Law," wysiwyg://53/http://www.geocities.com/CapitolHill/4167/tribunal.html; People's International Tribunal for Justice for Mumia Abu-Jamal, "Findings of the Judges," http://www.iacenter.org/Tribunal.htm; "Tribunal Verdict," http://www.mumia.org/fns405.html; and *Amsterdam News,* December 11, 1997.
57. Michael Smerkonish, an attorney and talk show host in Philadelphia, is a major figure in the movement opposed to a new trial for Mumia. His website, www.mastalk.com, includes extensive documentation on the Mumia case—but no mention of the tribunal.
58. www.mastalk.com. Mumia proponents were angered that Justice Ron Castile did not recuse himself from the Pennsylvania Supreme Court's case even though he had once worked in the prosecutor's office when it was filing briefs opposed to a new trial. See http://www.iacenter.org/pressmaj.htm.
59. http://www.iacenter.org/jweuro.htm.
60. *Philadelphia Inquirer,* October 5, 1999. Mumia's attorneys argued that he had been deprived of his right to self-representation during jury selection, prevented from confronting witnesses due to his removal from the courtroom, and excluded from the meeting at which Judge Sabo disqualified a juror.
61. www.j4mumia.org.
62. *The New York Times,* May 7, 2000.

Chapter 16

1. Ken Coates's letter to authors, March 31, 2000. "Bertie" is a reference to Bertrand Russell.

2. See "On the Constitution and the Procedure of the Women's International War Crimes Tribunal on Japan's Military Sexual Slavery in 2000," http://witness.peacenet.or.kr/symek2000.htm.

3. Vilnius International Public Tribunal on the Evaluation of Crimes of Communism, http://ok.w3.1t/cgi-bin/tribunal/En_ Tr_ruling.htm; http:www.time.com/time/asia/asiabuzz/2000/ 09/06/; and http:www.tibet.ca/wtnarchive/2000/9/6_5.html.

4. "On the Constitution."

5. Interview with Richard Falk, March 6, 2001.

6. Staughton Lynd, "The War Crimes Tribunal: A Dissent," *Liberation,* Vol. XII, Nos. 9–10 (December 1967–January 1968): 79.

7. Diana Russell and Nicole Van de Ven, eds., *Crimes Against Women: Proceedings of the International Tribunal* (Millbrae, CA: Les Femmes, 1976), p. 240.

Index

Abendroth, Wolfgang, 124
Abraham, Lynne, 183
Abu-Jamal, Mumia, 9, 181–4
Abzug, Bella, 174
Adamic, Louis, 67, 68
Adenauer, Konrad, 140
Afghanistan, 170, 178
Africa, Pam, 182
Agee, Philip, 176
Ageloff, Sylvia, 99
aggression, 126, 131, 132, 145, 151,
    156, 175, 177
Algeria, 112, 155
Algiers, 6, 164, 170
Ali, Muhammad, 155
Ali, Tariq, 131
Allende, Salvador, 168
Alma-Ata, 54
American Civil Liberties Union, 39
American Committee Against Fascist
    Oppression in Germany, 39, 49
American Federation of Labor, 49
American Friends of the Soviet Union,
    70, 97
American Jewish Congress, 49
American Society for Cultural
    Relations with Russia, 80
Amnesty International, 179, 184
Amsterdam, 20, 154, 199n

Anders, Gunther, 112, 113, 114, 117,
    118, 124, 129, 130, 137
Antwerp, 54, 170
Apple, R. W., 112
Aptheker, Herbert, 116
Arab League, 237n
Argentina, 169, 170
Armenians, 2, 7, 156, 171–3
Arnoni, M. S., 106, 107
Asia-Pacific Economic Cooperation
    (APEC), 168, 171, 180
Asquith, Herbert, 27
Asquith, Margaret, 27
Auschwitz, 112, 114, 120, 130
Australia, 126, 132, 142
Austria, 11, 114
Axworthy, Lloyd, 168
Aybar, Mehmet Ali, 118, 124, 156

Bakker-Nort, Betsy, 22, 23
Balabanova, Angelica, 96
Baldwin, James, 124, 130, 227n
Ball, George, 115
Barcelona, 170, 171
Barnes, Albert, 95
Basso, Lelio, 5, 7, 118, 124, 137, 155,
    162, 163–4, 168, 169
    see also Lelio Basso International
    Foundation

Baunsgaard, Hilmar, 160
Beals, Carleton, 76, 79, 82, 84–9, 91, 96, 100, 193, 217n
Beard, Charles, 74
Becker, Carl, 74
Belfrage, Leif, 146
Belgium, 22, 54, 60
Ben-Gurion, David, 140
Bergery, Gaston, 23, 25
Bergstrom, Richard Hichens, 145
Berlin, 12, 13, 14, 15, 20, 23, 24, 26, 32, 34, 36, 44, 45, 46, 47, 167
Berlin, Treaty of, 16
Berman, Julian, 57
Bernhard, George, 23
Bertrand Russell Peace Foundation (BRPF), 104, 108, 111, 153, 155, 161, 163, 164, 167, 179, 188, 191
    and Paris group, 119, 128–9, 136–7, 152, 154, 183
    and Russell Tribunal, 106, 107, 115, 116–17, 118, 119, 120, 136–7, 149
Bhopal, 181
biological weapons, 178
Birnbaum, Norman, 105, 106
Bismarck, Otto von, 12
Bliven, Bruce, 70
Block, Harry, 87
"Blue House," 81, 82, 92, 99
Boardman, Donnell, 226n
Boas, Franz, 67
Bogota, 169
Bolivia, 149, 167, 168, 169
Bolshevism, 11, 15, 21, 31, 34, 53, 80, 93, 100, 198n
    see also Communist Party of the Soviet Union
Borchers, Johannes, 39
Borodin, Mikhail, 86
Bosch, Juan, 169
Boyle, Francis, 175
Brandt, Willy, 143
Branting, George, 22, 25, 29, 189, 200n

Branting, Hjalmar, 200n
Brazil, 168, 169
Breitscheid, Rudolf, 23
Brest-Litovsk, Treaty of, 85
Breton, Andre, 69
Brezhnev, Leonid, 161
Britton, John, 88
Brockdorff-Rantzau, Ulrich von, 198
Brodsky, Joseph, 75, 76, 83
Bronfen, George, 127
Browder, Earl, 69, 208n
"Brown Book," 20–1, 23, 34, 25, 26, 31, 33, 35, 37, 40, 41, 199n, 202n, 203n, 205n
Brown, Earl, 135, 136
Brussels, 153, 164, 165, 166, 168, 170, 175, 181, 193
Brutus, Dennis, 183
Buchenwald, 48
Budenz, Louis, 68
Buenger, Wilhelm, 29, 32, 33, 34, 36, 39, 52, 205n
Bukharin, Nikolai, 98
Bulgaria, 11, 13, 45, 46, 202n
    see also Georgi Dimitrov, Blagoj Popov, and Vassily Tanev
Burma, 144, 168
Bush, George, 176

Cadart, Claude, 119
Califano, Joseph, 1
Calley, William, 174
Calverton, Victor, 217n
Cambodia, 121, 132, 163, 187
Cameron, James, 77
Cameron, Turner, Jr., 133, 141, 145
Canada, 131, 167, 171, 173, 180
Cardenas, Lazaro, 63–6, 87, 124, 137, 211n
Carmichael, Stokely, 109, 112, 124, 125, 130, 155, 160, 226n
Chamberlain, Austen, 26, 38
Chamberlain, John, 76, 96
Charbit, Fernand, 69

Chechnya, 178–9, 240n
chemical weapons, 126, 154, 178
  see also napalm
Cheney, Richard, 176
Chernobyl, 179
Chicago, 69
Chile, 167, 168
China, 15, 130, 150, 189
  and Russell Tribunal, 132
  and Tibet, 170, 178
  and Vietnam War, 105, 108, 144, 146
Chisholm, Shirley, 174
Chomsky, Noam, 163, 173
Chretien, Jean, 168, 171
Churchill, Winston, 26
Clark, Ramsey, 175–7
cluster bombs, 154, 156, 176
Coates, Ken, 108, 128, 164, 188, 229n
Cobb, Charlie, Jr., 125, 130
Cold War, 4, 104, 106, 143, 179
Commission of Inquiry into the
    Origins of the Reichstag Fire
  see Reichstag fire countertrial
Committee for Cultural Freedom,220n
Communist International (Comintern),
    11, 13, 15, 16, 17, 19–22, 29, 35,
    42, 45, 46, 47, 48, 50, 52, 54, 63,
    65, 66, 68, 76, 86, 99, 199n
Communist Party of the Soviet Union,
    46, 51, 52, 54
Communist Youth International, 19
Confederation Trabajadores de Mexico
    (CTM), 66, 76
Congo, Democratic Republic of, 187
Copenhagen, 15, 83, 96, 122, 152,
    153, 154, 155, 158
Cowley, Malcolm, 70, 93–4, 101
Cox, Courtland, 124, 130–1
Cox, Harvey, 5, 170
Coyoacan, 63, 81, 82, 88, 89, 91, 92,
    96, 97, 99, 100, 101
Cravath, Paul, 28
crimes against humanity, 1, 2, 4, 106,
    109, 135, 167, 169, 171, 177, 189

Cripps, Stafford, 23, 26, 27, 45, 49
Cuba, 104, 119, 126, 149, 155, 176,
    177
Czechoslovakia, 44, 60, 68, 72, 110,
    132, 133, 144, 160, 161, 176

Daly, Lawrence, 124, 125, 126
Darrow, Clarence, 28, 49
Davis, Angela, 184
de Beauvoir, Simone, 7, 109, 112,
    117, 124, 127, 154, 155, 156,
    157, 165, 166
Debray, Regis, 149
Debs, Eugene, 90
Dedijer, Vladimir, 112, 118, 119, 121,
    124, 126, 127, 128, 129, 132,
    136–7, 141, 152, 154, 156, 160,
    163, 164, 169, 178
de Gaulle, Charles, 120–1, 122, 139,
    140
Dellinger, Dave, 120, 128, 133, 150,
    153, 155, 163, 173, 224n,
    224–5n, 230n, 233n
Dellums, Ron, 173–4
Denmark, 23, 54, 122, 143, 152–60,
    165, 200n, 236n
  see also Russell Tribunal
Denver, 168
Detchev, Stepan, 28, 40
Deutscher, Isaac, 108, 112, 113, 114,
    118, 119, 121, 123, 124, 128,
    129, 131, 137, 154
Dewey, John, 7, 73, 75, 103, 118, 185
  and Carleton Beals, 84–8
  and Leon Trotsky, 67, 73, 79, 80,
    83, 84, 94–5, 97, 215n
  after Mexico hearings, 91–100
  and Mexico hearings, 76, 77,
    79–89
  philosophy, 9, 73, 80–1, 93, 98, 99,
    100, 165
  and Trotsky defense committee, 67,
    70, 72, 73
  see also Dewey Commission

Dewey Commission, 72–7, 79–101,
    103, 105, 106, 113, 115, 122,
    163, 187, 188, 190, 191, 192,
    193, 194
  documents, 83, 88, 91, 95, 210n
  formation of, 72–3
  French role, 92, 96
  in Mexico, 2, 5, 8, 9, 10, 82–9
  publications, 88, 89, 96, 97
  staff, 73, 79, 81, 82, 85
  testimony, 82–7, 91, 92, 99
Dimitrov, Georgi, 13, 22, 24, 28, 45,
    50, 53, 56, 64, 69, 71, 72, 83,
    202n
  and Comintern, 13, 16, 35, 41
  and Reichstag fire trial, 17, 27–8,
    33, 34, 36, 37, 40, 41, 42, 43,
    203n
  after Reichstag fire trial, 44–6, 206n
Dimitrova, Elena, 24, 38
Dirksen, Herbert von, 42
Dodd, Martha, 34
Dodd, William, 28
Dolci, Danilo, 118, 119
Dominican Republic, 169
Douglas, William O., 109
Dreiser, Theodore, 70
Dresden, 190
Dreyfus, Alfred, 56, 68, 136
Dubcek, Alexander, 133, 161
DuBois, David, 182, 183
DuBois, W. E. B., 182
Duranty, Walter, 218n

East Timor, 5, 170, 171, 180
Egypt, 162
Einstein, Albert, 7, 15, 20–1, 24, 73–4
El Salvador, 167, 169, 170, 171
Ensign, Tod, 173
environmental damage, 179, 181, 189,
    240n
Eritrea, 170
Erlander, Tage, 127, 128, 139–47, 152,
    160

Ethiopia, 116
European Economic Community
    (EEC), 143, 158
European Union parliament, 173,
    184

Falk, Richard, 5–6, 134, 165, 170,
    172, 174, 175, 180, 195n, 235n
Fanon, Franz, 131
Farley, Chris, 104, 128, 137
Farrell, James, 67, 79, 84, 93, 100
fascism, 11, 16, 20, 22, 45, 56, 60, 65,
    66, 69, 70, 92, 97, 100, 130
  see also Nazis
Faulkner, Daniel, 182
Fifth International, 149
Finerty, John, 75, 76, 82, 83, 85–6, 88,
    89, 96
Finland, 11, 144
Fischer, Louis, 70
Fourth International, 54, 65, 85, 99
fragmentation bombs, 126, 132, 160,
    176, 177
France, 6, 17, 20, 22, 23, 40, 44, 92,
    96, 112, 131, 142, 155, 172, 173,
    189
  and Russell Tribunal, 120–1, 122,
    129, 132
  and Leon Trotsky, 54, 55, 59, 60,
    68, 72, 98
Frank, Waldo, 93, 214n, 218n
Frankel, Jan, 81, 82
Frankfurter, Felix, 28
Fromm, Erich, 104

G-7, 10, 168, 179–80
Gallagher, Leo, 40, 44
Garcia Marquez, Gabriel, 169
Geneva, 122, 167, 170
Geneva accords (1954), 117, 131
genocide, 1, 4, 7, 111, 126, 132, 135,
    154, 155, 156, 167, 168, 169,
    171, 172, 173, 174, 176, 178,
    189, 195n, 235n

Genocide Convention (1948), 4, 155, 156, 172, 197n, 224n
Germany, 2, 11–50, 53, 55, 56, 67, 76, 114, 115, 127, 134, 143, 157, 158, 164, 172
and elections, 12, 14, 15
German Communist Party, 12–17, 19, 26, 27, 32, 35, 44, 45, 47, 48, 197n, 200n, 201n
and Great Britain, 2, 14, 26–7, 38, 44–5
judiciary, 22, 25, 28–45, 53, 201n, 203n, 213n
and Nazi laws, 3, 14, 16, 35–6
people's courts, 3, 47, 49, 50, 207n
and Soviet Union, 13, 15–17, 35, 41–2, 45–7, 54, 63, 69, 85, 92, 95, 198n, 199n, 206n
Supreme Court, 16, 25, 27–9, 31–2, 35, 202n
see also Reichstag fire trial
Gide, Andre, 20, 44, 76, 205n
"global capitalism," 5, 10, 163, 179–81, 189, 193
Glotzer, Albert, 82, 84, 85, 95
Gobel, Paul, 179
Goebbels, Joseph, 21, 34, 202n, 205n
Goering, Hermann, 12, 21, 23, 24, 25, 33, 34, 35, 36, 37, 38, 42, 43, 44, 45–6, 53, 72, 107, 197n, 199n, 202n
Goldberg, Arthur, 115
Goldman, Albert, 73, 81, 82, 83, 84, 85, 86, 96
Goldmann, Nahum, 209n
Goode, Wilson, 182
Grachev, Pavel, 179
Grant, Roberta Lowitz, 92, 216n
Great Britain, 23, 24, 39, 43, 48, 64, 68, 72, 92, 112, 132, 160, 171, 181, 189
Conservative Party, 26
and Germany, 2, 14, 26–7, 38, 44–5
House of Commons, 26, 38

Labour Party, 20, 21, 23, 26, 45, 105, 108, 121
Liberal Party, 26, 27
and Vietnam War, 105, 120–1
see also Reichstag fire countertrial
Greece, 11, 162, 169
Greene, Graham, 175
Greenland, 158, 160
Grigorev, Petr, 28, 40
Grigoryants, Sergei, 179
Grzesinski, Albert, 23
Guatemala, 167, 169, 170
Guernica, 130
Guevara, Ernesto (Che), 112, 116, 149, 233n
Gulf War, 176–7
Gumberg, Alex, 94
Guney, Yilmaz, 172

Haakon VII, King, 59
Hague Conventions, 5
Hague System, 3
Haiti, 169, 177
Halimi, Gisele, 124
Hallgren, Mauritz, 70–1, 213n
Hammarskjold, Dag, 144
Hanoi, 107, 146
Harriman, Averell, 115
Havana, 109
Hawaii, 6, 168, 174, 190
Hay, Eduardo, 60
Hayden, Tom, 116
Hays, Arthur Garfield, 49–50, 208n
and Dewey Commission, 74–6, 82, 88
and Reichstag fire countertrial, 10, 19, 22, 23, 25, 29, 38, 100, 189
and Reichstag fire trial, 28–9, 39–41, 49, 203n
Hays, Paul, 75
Heath, William, 146
Helldorf, Wolf von, 34, 203n
Hellman, Lillian, 70
Helsinki, 108, 154

Hernandez, Amado, 124
Hernandez, Melba, 113, 124, 136
Herz, Paul, 23
Hess, Rudolf, 26
Heydrich, Reinhard, 107
Hindenburg, Paul von, 12, 14
Hirohito, Emperor, 167
Hiroshima, 190
Hitler, Adolf, 3, 11, 12, 14, 15, 16, 21,
    22, 26, 31, 33, 35, 40, 42, 45, 46,
    48, 49, 51, 52, 106, 107, 125,
    135, 156, 157, 172, 197n, 198n
Hoare, Quentin, 128
Ho Chi Minh, 107, 110, 126
Hofer, Walther, 33
Holocaust, 114, 130, 156, 157, 172
Honduras, 169, 239n
Hook, Sidney, 66, 67, 68, 72, 73–4,
    77, 80, 88, 99
Horowitz, David, 106, 108, 119, 134,
    149
Huber, Johannes, 200n
Humphrey, Hubert, 141, 144
Hungary, 19, 132, 158
Hurum, 59, 60
Hvidt, Valdemar, 23, 200n

India, 181
indigenous peoples, 6, 165, 167–8, 169
Indochina, 112, 142
Indonesia, 171
International Association of
    Democratic Lawyers, 229n
International Committee for Political
    Prisoners, 80
International Control Commission, 131
International Court of Justice, 175
International Covenant on Civil and
    Political Rights, 4
International Covenant on Economic
    and Social Rights, 4
International Criminal Court, 4, 188
International Criminal Tribunals, 4,
    179, 187, 188

international law, 3, 5, 6, 9, 124, 125,
    126, 129, 131, 134, 164, 167,
    168, 171, 174, 175, 179, 228n
    see also Genocide Convention
International Military Tribunals
    at Nuremberg, 4, 6, 9, 103, 105,
        106, 109, 110, 112, 113, 114,
        115, 124, 132, 135, 136, 156,
        165, 175, 190, 195n
    at Tokyo, 4, 6, 150, 156
International Monetary Fund (IMF),
    170, 180
International War Crimes Tribunal (on
    Gulf War)
    see Gulf War
International War Crimes Tribunal (on
    Vietnam)
    see Russell Tribunal
International Workers' Aid, 19, 20
Iran, 176
Iraq, 162, 176–7
Israel, 133, 156, 162, 173, 237n
Istanbul, 54
Italy, 3, 5, 10, 11, 76, 96, 132

Jackson, Robert, 114, 224n
James, Edwin, 92
Japan, 15, 45, 55, 63, 155, 187
    and comfort women, 166–7
    Japanese Communist Party, 150
    Liberal Democratic Party, 150, 152
    and Russell Tribunal, 124, 132,
        149–51, 152, 192, 235n
    and Vietnam War, 132, 149–52, 154
Jenkins, Roy, 121
Jews, 15, 21, 26, 28, 29, 42, 49, 54,
    55, 56, 63, 68, 80, 106, 112, 114,
    116, 135, 136, 156, 157, 160,
    209n, 211n
John Paul II, Pope, 169
Johnson, Lyndon, 1, 103, 104, 105,
    107, 109, 112, 114, 115, 120,
    124, 125, 126, 129, 133, 135,
    140, 141, 146

Kahlo, Frida, 63, 85, 99
Kamenev, Lev, 52, 53, 55, 71, 80
Kasuri, Mahmud Ali, 118, 119, 124, 125
Katz, Otto, 20–2, 201n
Kaunda, Kenneth, 116
Kazakhstan, 54
Kerrl, Hans, 35, 37
Khinchuk, Lev, 16
Khrushchev, Nikita, 52
Kim Dae Jung, 181, 240n
Kirchway, Frieda, 70
Kirov, Sergei, 51, 53, 58, 60
Kluckhohn, Frank, 92
Kluger, Pearl, 73, 79, 82, 95
Knudsen, Konrad, 55
Koelble, Alphonse, 49, 207n
Koenen, Wilhelm, 13, 23
Koenigsberg, 46
Koht, Halvdan, 57
Kollontai, Alexandra, 54
Kosygin, Aleksei, 108, 160
Kozol, Jonathan, 184
Krag, Jens Otto, 153, 158–9, 160
Kronstadt, 96
Kuehne, Otto, 23
Kun, Bela, 20
Kurds, 162, 172, 177
Kuwait, 176, 177

Laborde, Hernan, 65
La Follette, Robert, 70
La Follette, Suzanne, 91, 213n
  and Carleton Beals, 84–6, 88
  and Dewey Commission, 76, 79, 82, 91, 95, 96, 97
  and Trotsky defense committee, 66, 71, 73
Lamont, Corliss, 70, 97
Lane, Mark, 109, 222–3n
Lanzmann, Claude, 119, 154, 183
Laos, 154, 156, 163
Larsen, Aksel, 158
Latin America, 164, 169, 176

Laughlin, Fred, 174
League Against War and Fascism, 20
League of American Writers, 93
League of Nations, 1, 3, 57, 209n
Leiden, 47
Leipzig, 17, 22, 23, 25, 28, 29, 30, 31–48, 53, 64, 192, 193
Lelio Basso International Foundation, 10, 164–5
Lenin, Vladimir, 52, 53, 56, 66, 69
Leningrad, 51, 52
Lerner, Max, 70
Lester, Julius, 125, 129–30, 131, 133, 134, 173
Levin, Bernard, 119
Levinson, David, 28, 39
Levy, Howard, 135–6
Libya, 177
Lidman, Sara, 124
Lie, Trygve, 54, 58–61, 144, 210n
Li Peng, 189
Lippmann, Walter, 2, 4
Lisbon, 170
Lithuania, 10, 189
Litvinov, Maxim, 15, 42
Livingston, Gordon, 174
Lodge, Henry Cabot, 107
Logevall, Fredrik, 143
London, 21, 22, 23, 26, 29, 38, 39, 48, 50, 76, 96, 105, 117, 118, 119, 120, 121, 136, 139, 141, 151, 167, 181
Luther, Hans, 39, 49
Lynd, Staughton, 115–16, 190, 225n

Macdonald, Dwight, 67
MacDonald, Ramsay, 26
Madrid, 169
Malcolm X, 130
Malraux, Andre, 20, 44, 100, 205n
Maly, Oswald, 36
Marable, Manning, 184
Marcos, Ferdinand, 170
Marcuse, Herbert, 113

Marley, Dudley, 20, 44, 207n
Martens clause, 5
Marti, Jose, 119
Martinson, Peter, 235n
Marxism, 34, 53, 55, 70, 73, 80, 94, 124
Marxism-Leninism, 50, 80
Matarasso, Leo, 124, 126, 155
McCarthy, Mary, 212n
McLendon, Gordon, 228n
McNamara, Robert, 107, 115
Meeropol, Michael, 183
Mejia, Olga, 176
Mercader, Ramon, 99
Merry, Sally Engle, 6
Metro-Vickers case, 27, 68
Mexico, 99
    and Dewey Commission, 75, 76,
        79–89, 91
    internal politics, 64–6
    and Leon Trotsky, 60, 61, 63–6, 68,
        69, 70, 72, 79–89
    and Soviet Union, 61, 64, 65, 84
Mexico City, 63, 72, 76, 77, 79, 81,
    84, 92, 170, 192
Meyer, Agnes, 94
Milan, 170
Miliband, Ralph, 106
Miller, Arthur, 112
Mink, Patsy, 174
Mitchell, David, 109–10, 135, 192,
    222–3n
Mitchell, Parren, 174
Mnacko, Ladislaw, 132, 133
Molotov, Vyacheslav, 42, 112
moral equivalence, 8, 116, 161, 170,
    190
Morgan, Charles, Jr., 135, 136
Morikawa, Kinju, 124, 163
Moro-Giafferi, Vincent de, 22, 23, 24,
    28, 38, 49, 189
Morrison, Toni, 184
Morrow, Felix, 66, 74
Moscow, 15, 19, 20, 42, 46, 48, 52,
    57, 73, 98, 179

Moscow show trials, 50, 53, 61, 63,
    66, 68, 70, 73, 74, 75, 76, 79, 80,
    82, 83, 84, 87, 89, 91, 93, 95, 96,
    97, 100
    of 1936, 55–7, 60, 67, 68, 71, 192
    of 1937, 63–4, 71, 85, 192
    of 1938, 98, 100
MOVE, 182, 184
Muenzenberg, Willi, 19–22, 44, 50,
    66, 73, 118, 199n, 208n
Mugica, Francisco, 66, 212n
Mumford, Lewis, 112, 113, 114
Munich, 24, 44
Murmansk, 51
Mussolini, Benito, 11

Nadolny, Rudolf, 42
Nagasaki, 190
napalm, 132, 134, 150, 151, 154, 177
National Liberation Front (NLF or
    Vietcong), 105, 106, 107, 108,
    116, 123, 125, 126, 133, 140,
    142, 144, 145, 146, 154, 157, 161
Nazis, 3, 12, 13, 14, 15, 17, 19–26,
    31–42, 44, 45, 46, 47, 50, 53, 56,
    68, 106, 107, 110, 114, 116, 132,
    134, 135, 156, 201n
Nazi-Soviet Pact, 99
Neilands, John, 125
Netherlands, 16, 22, 40, 47, 167
    see also Marinus van der Lubbe
Neurath, Konstantin von, 15
New Jersey, 184
New Left, 3, 113, 142, 147
New York, 39, 49, 50, 64, 65, 66, 68,
    69, 72, 76, 79, 91, 94, 96, 97,
    107, 120, 175, 176, 181, 184
New Zealand, 126, 132, 142
Nguyen Cao Ky, 152
Nguyen Duy Trinh, 146
Nguyen Huu Tho, 107
Nguyen Tho Chanh, 146, 233n
Nguyen Van Sao, 107
Nguyen Van Thieu, 152

Nicaragua, 175
Niebuhr, Reinhold, 97
Nikolaev, Leonid, 51–2
Nilsson, Torsten, 141–2, 144, 145, 146, 233n
Nitti, Francesco, 200n
Nixon, Richard, 174
Nkrumah, Gamal, 182, 183
Nkrumah, Kwame, 182, 225n
non-governmental organizations (NGOs), 165, 166, 180, 189
North Atlantic Treaty Organization (NATO), 139, 142, 143, 157, 158, 159, 160, 188
North Korea, 166, 167, 177
North Vietnam, 105, 107, 110, 112, 115, 116, 120, 121, 123, 125, 126, 132, 133, 140, 142, 144, 145, 146, 147, 149, 150, 152, 154, 155, 157, 159, 174
Norway, 63, 84, 143, 144
    Labor Party, 55, 209n
    Ministry of Justice, 55, 57, 58, 59, 60
    and Soviet Union, 55, 57–8, 210n
    and Leon Trotsky, 54–61, 64, 67, 101
Novack, George, 63, 66, 71, 73, 74, 79, 80, 82, 98
nuclear weapons, 104, 108, 144
Nuremberg
    see International Military Tribunal
Nyerere, Julius, 116–17
Nygaardsvold, Johan, 59, 60, 61

"Oberfohren memorandum," 14, 20, 25
Oberg, Jean-Christophe, 145
Ogasawara Islands, 152
Oglesby, Carl, 124, 128, 129, 130, 134, 156, 225n
Okinawa, 151, 152
Olof Palme International Center, 179
Oslo, 54, 55, 96, 155, 174
Ottoman Empire, 171, 172

Pakistan, 118, 131, 177
Palme, Olof, 141–2, 144, 146, 153
Panama, 175–7
Pankin, Boris, 179
Panter, Noel, 39
Papandreou, Andreas, 169
Paraguay, 169
Paris, 14, 15, 20, 22, 24, 28, 38, 56, 59, 64, 83, 99, 111, 112, 120, 121, 122, 127, 139, 152, 155, 168, 170, 172, 178
Parsons, J. Graham, 142
Pastrana, Andres, 171
Pennsylvania Supreme Court, 182, 184
Permanent People's Tribunal, 10, 164, 165, 189, 191
    and Afghanistan, 178
    and Armenians, 172–3
    and Chernobyl, 179
    and Guatemala, 169, 170
    and Latin America, 169, 170
    and Nicaragua, 175
    and the Philippines, 170
    and Tibet, 178
Peru, 169, 170
Petri, Lennart, 144, 146
Petrograd, 96
Pham Van Dong, 107
Philadelphia, 28, 181–4, 201n
Philippines, 151, 154, 156, 167, 170
Piatakov, Grigory, 63
Piatnitsky, Ossip, 19, 20, 45
Pieck, Wilhelm, 45
Piven, Frances Fox, 184
Poland, 42, 146
Popov, Blagoj, 13, 33, 45, 46
Popular Fronts, 20, 65, 66, 69, 100
Prague, 110, 121, 179
Prinkipo, 54, 69
Pritt, Denis Nowell (D.N.), 23, 24, 26, 34, 38, 43, 49, 56, 64, 74, 75–6, 189, 200n, 201n

Provisional American Committee for
the Defense of Leon Trotsky,
66–74, 79, 82, 95, 98, 99, 106,
189, 191
Pruett, Lorine, 218n
Prussia, 14, 35, 40, 46
Puerto Rico, 170

Quisling, Vidkun, 55, 59

Rabinovich, Gregor, 68
Radek, Karl, 42, 63–4
Ramos Horta, Jose, 5, 180
Reagan, Ronald, 239n
"Red Book," 59, 210n
Red Brigades, 3
Redgrave, Vanessa, 108
Reich, Ebbe, 154, 156, 158, 159
Reichstag fire, 12–16, 19, 20, 23, 26,
32, 34, 36, 37, 38, 41, 46, 50, 51,
52, 53, 202n
Reichstag fire countertrial, 2, 5, 8, 9,
10, 19, 21–7, 29, 31, 38–40, 45,
49, 50, 56, 67, 76, 83, 88, 100,
103, 118, 163, 187, 189, 191,
192, 193, 194, 205n
Reichstag fire trial, 22, 31–42, 48, 66,
70, 74
defense, 32, 34–7, 40, 41, 71
legal representation, 27–9
prosecution, 34, 36–7, 41
verdict, 41–3, 45
see also Georgi Dimitrov, Arthur
Garfield Hays and Ernst Torgler
Rendell, Ed, 182, 183
Reno, Janet, 183
Rhodesia, 168
Ribbentrop, Joachim von, 107
Ridge, Tom, 183
Rifkin, Jeremy, 173
Rios Montt, Ephrain, 169
Rivera, Diego, 63, 65, 87, 99
Roehm, Ernst, 24, 41
Rolland, Romain, 17, 22, 29, 69, 199n

Rome, 164, 168, 171
Rosenberg, Alfred, 26–7
Rosenberg, Ethel, 183
Rosenberg, Julius, 183
Rosenfeld, Kurt, 27, 28
Rosmer, Alfred, 68, 76, 96, 99
Rosmer, Marguerite, 99
Ross, Edward, 76
Rostow, Walt, 133, 140–1
Rotterdam, 167, 168, 170
Ruehle, Otto, 76, 79, 82, 83, 85
Rusk, Dean, 107, 115, 127, 133, 146,
158
Russell, Bertrand, 68, 112, 113, 114,
115, 116–17, 118, 119, 120, 121,
129, 133, 136–7, 154, 164, 185,
188
as philosopher, 103–4
as political activist, 1, 4, 76, 103–10,
134, 160–1
and Ralph Schoenman, 105, 107,
111, 118, 119, 128, 134, 161, 221n
and Roskilde tribunal, 152
and Stockholm tribunal, 123, 125,
126, 127, 132, 133, 139, 140, 141
see also Bertrand Russell Peace
Foundation and Russell Tribunal
Russell, Edith, 164
Russell Tribunal, 2, 4, 5, 7, 8, 9,
106–62, 163, 170, 173, 187, 188,
190, 191, 192, 193
evidence, 125–7, 130, 154–5, 160,
161
preparations, 111–22, 152–3
at Roskilde, 149, 152–7, 163
at Stockholm, 123–34, 139–41, 143,
144, 145, 146, 147, 149, 152,
157, 163
at Tokyo, 149–51, 153
verdicts, 131–2, 157, 160
witnesses, 9, 115, 123, 126, 127,
139, 140, 154–5, 160, 235n
Russell II tribunals, 10, 164, 167, 168,
237n

Russia
  see Soviet Union
Rwanda, 4, 179, 187
Rykov, Aleksei, 98

Sabo, Albert, 182, 183, 184
Sacco, Nicola, 75, 236n
Sack, Alfons, 29, 32, 34, 36, 39–40, 41
Safer, Morley, 133, 134
St. Louis, 77, 91
Sakata, Shoichi, 124
Salazar, Antonio, 162, 200n
Salisbury, Harrison, 112
Sartre, Jean-Paul, 7, 9, 110, 112, 113,
  118, 121, 122, 136
  and Paris group, 119, 129, 136–7, 154
  at Roskilde, 154, 156
  at Stockholm, 124, 126, 127, 128,
  129, 130, 131, 132
Sato, Eisaku, 150–2
Scheer, John, 44
Scheer, Robert, 128
Scheflo, Olav, 54
Schoenman, Ralph, 164
  and Bertrand Russell, 105, 107, 118,
  119, 128, 134, 161, 221n
  and Bertrand Russell Peace
  Foundation, 106, 111, 136, 161
  as political activist, 108, 109, 110,
  121, 130, 139, 149, 152, 222n,
  233n
  and Russell Tribunal, 106, 112, 113,
  114, 116, 118, 120, 122, 123,
  125, 126, 127–30, 132, 141, 153,
  154
Schwartz, Laurent, 112, 118, 127, 128,
  136, 137, 154, 163, 169, 178
Schwarzkopf, Norman, 176
Seattle, 179
Sedov, Lev, 54, 59, 63, 83, 96, 97, 98,
  210n
Selassie, Haile, 116
self-determination, 5, 114, 164, 168,
  178

Senegal, 116
Senghor, Leopold, 116
Serbia, 188
Serge, Victor, 69, 210n, 211n
Seuffert, Philip, 32, 36, 201n
Sevareid, Eric, 133
Shachtman, Max, 63, 72, 96
Shaw, George Bernard, 38, 68, 205n
Shiina, Etsusaburo, 151
Sierra Leone, 187
Simon, John, 26, 39
Siqueiros, David Alfaro, 65
Smerkonish, Michael, 241n
Solow, Herb, 66, 73, 82, 96
South Africa, 183
South Korea, 126, 132, 151, 166, 167,
  181, 240–1n
South Vietnam, 105, 106, 108, 120,
  125, 132, 142, 144, 149, 150,
  151, 152, 160
Soviet Union, 2, 3, 11, 23, 44, 56, 68,
  69, 71, 73, 76, 80, 84, 87, 88, 91,
  94, 95, 96, 97, 100, 105, 121,132,
  142, 143, 144, 146, 160, 161,
  164, 171, 173, 205n
  and Afghanistan, 178
  and Chechnya, 178–9
  and Germany, 13, 15–17, 35, 41–2,
  45–7, 63, 69, 85, 92, 95, 198n,
  199n, 206n
  and Mexico, 61, 64, 65, 84
  and Norway, 55, 57–8
  and United States, 28, 104, 107,
  108, 133, 161
  and Vietnam War, 108, 133
Spain, 56, 65, 70, 95, 99
Spock, Benjamin, 169, 173
Stalin, Joseph (including Stalinism and
  Stalinists), 11, 12, 13, 16, 41, 45,
  51–7, 60, 61, 63, 64, 65, 66, 67,
  68, 69, 70, 71, 72, 74, 75, 76, 80,
  81, 83, 87, 92, 93, 94, 96, 97, 98,
  99, 100, 101, 104
Steinem, Gloria, 165

Stenelo, Lars-Goran, 144
Stetler, Russell, 107, 120, 128, 155
Stockholm, 54, 61, 122, 139, 145, 146,
    154, 155, 170, 178, 179
    see also Russell Tribunal
Stolberg, Ben, 66, 67, 68, 73, 74, 76,
    79, 82, 84, 91, 96, 97
Stone, I. F., 113
Strasbourg, 170, 178, 184
structural adjustment programs (SAPs),
    180
Student Nonviolent Coordinating
    Committee (SNCC), 109, 112,
    125, 129, 130, 133, 155
    see also Stokely Carmichael
Students for a Democratic Society
    (SDS), 116, 124
Suekawa, Hiroshi, 150
Suharto, 171
Sweden, 22, 54, 139–47, 155, 179,
    181, 189
    Communist Party, 143, 145, 146
    Conservative Party, 145
    foreign policy, 141, 142, 143–6, 157
    internal politics, 139, 141–3, 146,
        147
    Liberal People's Party, 145
    media, 141, 145
    and Russell Tribunal, 106, 122,
        123–34, 139, 153
    Social Democratic Party, 123, 140,
        141, 142, 143, 145, 146
    support committee (for Russell
        Tribunal), 123, 124, 125, 127,
        139
Switzerland, 33, 60, 64, 122

Tampico, 61, 63
Tanev, Vassily, 13, 33, 44, 45, 46
Tanzania, 116
Teichert, Paul, 27, 28, 29, 33, 39,
    203n
Thaelmann, Ernst, 12, 14, 16, 17,
    47–8, 49, 50, 197n, 207n

Thailand, 132, 144, 151, 152, 154, 156
Thomas, Norman, 65, 67, 69, 74
Thomas, Wendelin, 76, 96
Tibet, 170, 178
Tobias, Fritz, 33, 200n
Tokyo, 120, 150, 166, 180, 181
Toledano, Vicente Lombardo, 66, 72,
    87
Torgler, Ernst, 12, 23, 24, 27, 28, 29,
    38, 49, 201n
    and Reichstag fire, 13, 16
    at Reichstag fire trial, 17, 32, 34, 36,
        37, 40, 41, 203n
    after Reichstag fire trial, 46, 47,
        207n
Torgler, Kurt, 23
Toronto, 173
totalitarianism, 3, 4, 11, 14
Toynbee, Arnold, 103
Tresca, Carlo, 76, 96
Trevor-Roper, H. R., 33
Tricontinental Conference, 109
Trotsky, Leon, 52, 108, 149
    and Dewey Commission, 72–7,
        79–89, 91–101, 187
    and extradition, 57, 64, 84
    and France, 54, 55, 59, 60, 68, 72
    and John Dewey, 67, 73, 79, 80, 83,
        84, 94–5, 97, 215n
    in Mexico, 63–66, 68, 71, 72, 77,
        79–89
    and Moscow show trials, 53, 55–7,
        61, 71, 92, 97
    in Norway, 54–61, 67, 101
    Trotskyism, 66, 67, 73, 74, 75, 76,
        77, 79, 80, 82, 93, 98, 99, 101,
        103, 108, 161, 222n
    in Turkey, 54
    and United States, 60, 64, 65,
        67–77, 94, 96, 99, 210n, 211n
Trotsky, Natalya, 61, 63, 99
Trotsky defense committee
    see Provisional American Committee
        for the Defense of Leon Trotsky

Troyanovsky, Alexander, 76, 80, 83, 92
truth commissions, 6, 196n
Tuck, David, 155, 235n
Tukhachevsky, Mikhail, 92
Turkey, 2, 54, 118, 156, 171–2
Tynan, Kenneth, 112

Ukraine, 179
Ulrikh, Vassily, 52
Unden, Bo Osten, 233n
Union of Soviet Socialist Republics
  see Soviet Union
United Nations (U.N.), 142, 144, 164, 165, 183
  Chapter VII, 4, 177
  Charter, 4, 5, 176, 177, 187
  Commission on Human Rights, 4, 172, 173, 178, 183
  General Assembly, 5, 177, 187, 188
  secretaries-general, 144, 161
  Security Council, 4, 176, 177, 179, 187
United States, 39, 48, 49, 50, 70, 76, 80, 87, 104, 121, 143, 145, 146, 149, 167, 168, 172, 188, 189, 191
  Central Intelligence Agency (CIA), 107, 169, 176
  Communist Party, 69, 76, 92, 93, 116
  Congress, 134, 173–4, 207n
  Department of Defense, 107, 126, 173
  and Guatemala, 169, 239n
  and Gulf War, 176–7
  Indians, 7, 164, 167
  and Leon Trotsky, 60, 64, 65, 67–77, 92, 96, 99, 210n, 211n
  National Security Council, 133, 140–1, 174
  and Nicaragua, 175
  and Panama, 169, 175–7
  Socialist Party, 65, 67, 69, 70, 93, 95

  and Soviet Union, 28, 107, 108, 133, 161
  State Department, 72, 145, 179
  and Stockholm tribunal, 126, 127
  Supreme Court, 109, 114, 135, 182, 184
  and Vietnam War, 1, 4, 103–10, 112–17, 120, 124, 126, 129, 130, 131, 132, 134, 139, 140, 141, 142, 144, 150–1, 154–9, 161, 163, 165, 173–4, 187
  see also Hawaii
Universal Declaration of the Rights of Peoples, 6, 164, 165
Uruguay, 168, 169
Urvansky, Jacob, 73
U Thant, 144, 161

Vancouver, 168, 171, 180
van der Lubbe, Marinus, 21, 24, 51
  execution of, 16, 47, 198n
  and Reichstag fire, 12–14, 17, 25
  and Reichstag fire trial, 28, 32–3, 36, 37, 38, 40, 47, 203n
van Heijenoort, Jean, 59, 81
Vansittart, Robert, 26
Vanzetti, Bartolomeo, 75, 236n
Vermeylen, Pierre, 22
Versailles conference, 2
Versailles, Treaty of, 15, 26
Vietcong
  see National Liberation Front
Vietnam War, 1, 4, 68, 103, 104–62
  diplomacy, 140, 144–46
  and Japan, 149–52, 154, 234n
  racial aspects, 109, 125, 130–1, 154–5, 174, 234n
  strategic aspects, 107, 108, 142
  and U.S. antiwar movement, 109–10, 115–16, 120, 125, 130, 133, 134–6, 146, 153, 159, 161, 173–4
  see also North Vietnam, Russell Tribunal and South Vietnam

Villard, Marcel, 40
Vogt, Paul, 16, 35
Vyshinsky, Andrei, 56, 98, 209n

Wald, George, 169, 170, 172, 175
Walker, Charlie, 82
Wallin, Frank Hallis, 127
Walsh, Frank, 75
war crimes, 1, 4, 8, 103, 106, 107,
    109, 110, 114, 119, 120, 125,
    127, 130, 132, 135, 140, 149,
    161, 169, 171, 174, 187, 230n
Warsaw, 146
Washington, D.C., 144, 151, 153, 173,
    179
Weden, Sven, 142
Weimar Republic, 11, 13
    see also Germany
Weiss, Peter, 106, 112, 118, 124, 125,
    139
Werner, Karl, 25, 29, 34, 36, 37, 38,
    40, 47, 203n
West Germany
    see Germany
West, Cornel, 184
Western Sahara, 170
Westmoreland, William, 107
Wexhall, 55
Wicken, Joan, 116–17
Wicker, Tom, 112
Wiesel, Elie, 179
Wilhelm II, Kaiser, 2, 12

Wilson, Edmund, 67, 93, 219n
Wilson, Harold, 105, 121, 227n
Wilson, Woodrow, 1
Wise, Stephen, 68, 212n
Wolfe, Bertram, 81
Wolff, Erwin, 59
women's rights, 165–7, 193
workers' rights, 180–1
World Bank, 170, 180
World Committee for the Victims of
    German Fascism, 20
World Peace Council, 104
World War I, 1, 3, 80, 171
World War II, 3, 4, 144, 149, 150,
    166
Wright, Julia, 182, 183
Wright, Richard, 182

Yagoda, Genrikh, 98
Yakubovich, I. S., 57, 59
Yeltsin, Boris, 179
Yemen, 162
Yenukidze, Abel, 52
Yugoslavia, 4, 112, 171, 179, 187, 188

Zaire, 170,
Zambia, 116
Zamora, Francisco, 76
Zborowsky, Mark, 56, 59, 99
Zhou Enlai, 222n
Zinn, Howard, 155, 184
Zinoviev, Grigory, 51–3, 55, 71, 80